VOICES OF INDIGENUITY

Intersections in Environmental Justice

The Nature of Hope: Grassroots Organizing, Environmental Justice, and Political Change
CHAR MILLER AND JEFF CRANE, EDITORS

Voices of Indigenuity
MICHELLE R. MONTGOMERY, EDITOR

VOICES *of* INDIGENUITY

Edited by
MICHELLE R. MONTGOMERY

UNIVERSITY PRESS OF COLORADO
Denver

Published by University Press of Colorado
1580 North Logan Street, Suite 660
PMB 39883
Denver, Colorado 80203-1942

The University Press of Colorado is a proud member of the Association of University Presses.

The University Press of Colorado is a cooperative publishing enterprise supported, in part, by Adams State University, Colorado State University, Fort Lewis College, Metropolitan State University of Denver, University of Alaska Fairbanks, University of Colorado, University of Denver, University of Northern Colorado, University of Wyoming, Utah State University, and Western Colorado University.

∞ This paper meets the requirements of the ANSI/NISO Z39.48-1992 (Permanence of Paper).

ISBN: 978-1-64642-508-2 (hardcover)
ISBN: 978-1-64642-509-9 (paperback)
ISBN: 978-1-64642-510-5 (ebook)
https://doi.org/10.5876/9781646425105

Library of Congress Cataloging-in-Publication Data

Names: Montgomery, Michelle R., editor.
Title: Voices of indigenuity / edited by Michelle R. Montgomery.
Description: Denver : University Press of Colorado, [2023] | Includes bibliographical references and index. | Includes Hawaiian, Maori, Lakota and Salish (Muckleshoot) with parallel English translations.
Identifiers: LCCN 2023020188 (print) | LCCN 2023020189 (ebook) | ISBN 9781646425082 (hardcover) | ISBN 9781646425099 (paperback) | ISBN 9781646425105 (ebook)
Subjects: LCSH: Ethnoscience—Web-based instruction. | Traditional ecological knowledge—Web-based instruction. | Indigenous peoples—Communication. | Indigenous peoples—Effect of technological innovations on.
Classification: LCC GN476 .V65 2023 (print) | LCC GN476 (ebook) | DDC 500.89—dc23/eng/20230525
LC record available at https://lccn.loc.gov/2023020188
LC ebook record available at https://lccn.loc.gov/2023020189

This book will be made open access within three years of publication thanks to Path to Open, a program developed in partnership between JSTOR, the American Council of Learned Societies (ACLS), University of Michigan Press, and The University of North Carolina Press to bring about equitable access and impact for the entire scholarly community, including authors, researchers, libraries, and university presses around the world. Learn more at https://about.jstor.org/path-to-open/.

Cover illustration: © Elina Li/Shutterstock

Contents

Illustrations

Figures

Table

VOICES OF INDIGENUITY

1

Indigenuity of Indigenous Knowledges and Community Conversations

MICHELLE MONTGOMERY

Beginning in 2015, Indigenous Knowledges and Community Conversations, a virtual platform, has held a constant, nurturing environment at the heart of sociopolitical challenges and change, the University of Washington Tacoma (UWT), and the American Indian Studies (AIS) minor, and it continues to develop an increased awareness of Indigenous people's cultures, experiences, and histories. The AIS minor identifies and articulates critical questions and approaches that respect and utilize Indigenous paradigms throughout the Pacific Northwest region and beyond. In collaboration with community partnerships, the focus of the platform has been to uplift and empower the voices of Indigenous peoples' sovereignty, exemplify decolonization, and promote Indigenous Knowledges (IK). The contributions of a webinar platform continue to develop a safe space for IK and communities to dialogue about Indigenous peoples' cultural and traditional lived experiences (i.e., climate justice, traditional food sovereignty, cultural and traditional practices, education, language retention and revitalization, and human health), while utilizing IK as a means to ask the question—What does justice demand

https://doi.org/10.5876/9781646425105.c001

(Montgomery and Blanchard 2021; Montgomery 2022)? Utilizing a traditional leadership approach, the platform has hosted multiple community conversations with multigenerational, diverse Indigenous Nations. The vision is to embolden an interdisciplinary platform for critical Indigenized ideologies that upholds a deep respect for the relationship, respect, and reciprocity of IK and its traditions as well as a thorough understanding of the current political realities of Indigenous communities.

For this reason, it is important to sustain a welcoming virtual, safe space for articulating critical questions through dialogue and personal stories to unveil superficial, institutionalized approaches that do not demonstrate decolonized settler-colonial narratives for "who" decides for "whom" the meaning of open spaces for Indigenous peoples' perspectives and knowledges. Indigenous Knowledges and Community Conversations created a culturally distinctive sociopolitical platform to bring together multi-interdisciplinary insights from sovereign Nations, IK, and Indigenous languages that through authentic representations uplifts the more-than-often-erased, marginalized bodies and voices of Indigenous peoples. Participants engage with the following concepts and content: (1) cultural and traditional ethical interrelationships between humans, more than humans, and the ecosystems within place-based environments; (2) Indigenous identities to place; (3) Indigenous theories and methods utilized to conduct inquiry-based research and evaluation that respond to the needs of Indigenous peoples to promote self-determination; (4) valuable communication between Indigenous and non-Indigenous multi-interdisciplinary audiences; and (5) fostering of approaches to cross-cultural understandings.

Throughout history, the legacy of colonial and epistemological forms of racism has erased IK and frequently addressed Indigenous issues in the past tense. The oppressive historical relationships with Indigenous people are intentional acts of cultural extermination (Child 1998; Minthorn, Montgomery, and Bill 2021). From a lens of reciprocity of place-based IK, Gregory Cajete (1994) explains that within Indigenous epistemologies, land/water often provides our learning curriculum; it becomes the central reference point for how we relate to the earth, to each other, and to the very act of creation. Likewise, maybe more than anything else, the land/water is what connects Indigenous peoples to our ancestors and what connects our responsibilities to land/water and our ancestors are our voices—the stories

(Menzies 2006; Kimmerer 2012; Shilling and Nelson 2018). As Indigenous peoples, we are constantly reminded of Indigenous ways of knowing: respect, deep listening, reciprocity, and mutual gratitude.

As a result of a deep cultural and spiritual connection to the land/water, Indigenous people are the first to experience climate change and are the people who intensely feel the unspoken destruction, given our close relationships with the natural world. These challenges have drastically affected Indigenous peoples' culture and traditional lived experiences, including spiritual wellness. A promising solution is to expand place-based Indigenized education that infuses Indigenous epistemologies for student success in science, technology, engineering, and mathematics (STEM) curricula. To decolonize harmful STEM pedagogical research training about the natural world, an Indigenous-guided approach is an essential first step to rebuilding a healthy relationship while acknowledging all relationships come with an ethical responsibility. One such approach is Tribal Participatory Research (TPR) and how it places emphasis on sociopolitical change and empowerment, which in turn are grounded in underlying principles that guide the relationship between Indigenous Nations and other entities, including governments, governmental agencies, researchers, tribal self-governance, tribal self-determination, and tribal consultation (Fisher and Ball 2003; Thomas et al. 2011). Tribal Participatory Research approaches require additional steps that acknowledge and respect the unique sovereign status and self-determining authority of Indigenous peoples and the cultural context of their communities. Therefore, the Indigenous Knowledges and Community Conversations virtual platform is synergistically similar to TPR as an Indigenous-community-guided method for sharing IK for long-term solutions.

Informed by climate justice, environmental health inequalities, and IK, as well as Traditional Ecological Knowledges, the webinars have drawn from the principles of respect and reciprocity of IK as living research through engaged, place-based conversations. The platform prioritizes building on strengths, resources, and relationships of Indigenous communities while acknowledging tribal sovereignty and land-water–based interconnectedness to identities. In this way, the voices and stories become an increased political and social power that uplifts rather than co-opts narratives from Indigenous peoples.

In January 2020, in collaboration with the Native Environmental Science Faculty at the Northwest Indian College, Nez Perce Campus, Ciarra Greene

(Sapóoq'is Wíit'as Consulting), the webinars have continued to expand with Indigenous communities. We (including community partnerships) expanded the platform to become acknowledged as the Indigenous Speaker Series (Series). Multiple community partnership collaborations beyond the UWT have provided a platform for speakers locally, nationally, and internationally with varying backgrounds to share their cultural, traditional, and academic lived experiences in modern society, while honoring their long-standing relationship and responsibility to their homelands, communities, and ancestors. From a decolonized and Indigenized lens, the platform uplifts living research and stories that are developing through the conversations among the presenters and participants. The Series has drawn in over 1,900 participants from across the world to engage in discussion with speakers about cultural and traditional practices with foundations in sustainability, resilience, and dedication to future generations.

The expanded initiatives from Indigenous Knowledges and Community Conversations cultivate a long-term goal to continue building collaborative partnerships with Indigenous communities, academic institutions, centers, and foundations to respond to the question—What does justice demand? Alongside community partnerships with Rising Voices (RV) and the Salish Sea Research Center (SSRC), a living research approach and IK will continue to build the support for Tribal College and University (TCU) students as well as Indigenous students attending non-TCUs to participate in the annual RV workshops. The purpose is to provide inclusive mentoring opportunities, cultural and traditional appropriate peer-to-peer learning, and STEM educational training and place-based ways of knowing. The Series has also included Indigenous discussions about living (working, studying, and educating) in a modern society. It infuses the moral nature of how IK, when put into practice, creates a safe space for virtual conversations among the presenters, participants, and facilitators. Set in motion in early 2022, the Series continues as a monthly webinar, which includes a collaborative partnership with the SSRC (https://www.salishsearesearchcenter.com), Clean Up the River Environment (https://www.cureriver.org), and RV (https://risingvoices.ucar.edu). The Series has featured over thirty-six webinars since January 2020. Most of the webinars were recorded with permission of the speakers and can be found on our current website, https://www.indigenousspeakerseries.com.

As the virtual platform evolved, we developed our evaluation through Zoom polls and Continuing Education Units (CEUs). Responses have been overwhelmingly positive:

- 94 percent "Strongly Agree / Agree" the Series fostered Indigenous wellness, political sovereignty and self-determination, cultural revitalization, and cross-cultural understanding;
- 86 percent "Strongly Agree / Agree" the Series provided effective communication between multiple audiences, including Indigenous communities, policy makers, scientific communities, and the general public;
- 93 percent "Strongly Agree / Agree" the Series provided concepts and applications of the value the interrelationships between people and the environment;
- 85 percent "Strongly Agree / Agree" the Series provided grounding and applications of concepts and methodologies to place;
- 86 percent "Strongly Agree / Agree" the Series included Indigenous theories and methods utilized to conduct inquiry-based research and evaluation that respond to the needs of Indigenous communities and serve to promote Indigenous self-determination;
- 83 percent "Strongly Agree / Agree" they can apply what they have learned during the Series.

Quotes from CEU evaluations when participants were asked, "How has your engagement in the webinar advanced your understanding and vision for reflection, action, and perpetuation of the concepts previously mentioned?":

> "The presentation given during this webinar really grounded me in thinking about ways to collaborate and network within my own work. Just hearing the work being done by the speakers was inspiring in itself. It really got me brainstorming ideas to implement actions of decolonization within the work that I do."

> "[The webinar] gave me information that I can use when interacting with the tribal communities I serve."

> "This webinar has helped me as I continue to better understand my role as a student and an educator in the environmental field. I have been inspired to read Dr. Wildcat's book [Wildcat 2009] and I can't wait to read the second one.

I will also continue to learn about the Indigenous Peoples Climate Change Working Group."

"This webinar showed sovereignty in action and how to utilize traditional knowledge systems in everyday practices. The implementation of IAK in existing Indigenous spaces to progress toward indigenizing practices and holistic healing is a necessary step toward furthering resiliency efforts and sovereignty."

"Environmental data and its representation have become a vital contribution to preserving tribal lands and sovereignty. The many hoops and obstacles laid upon this path may seem incredulous but are actually more time laden. There is an array of methodologies and data analysis applications available to improve representation of data, i.e., mapping flood waters/plumes, models, drought monitoring, and other forms."

"Learning about the Sustainability model is a powerful way to consider relationships in decision making."

"I am more aware of the connection between the environment and our culture. More action is needed in Indigenous communities to protect the environment."

"This webinar has been incredibly helpful for me as an educator to rethink how I teach these topics."

The platform has been grounded and influenced by the voices of its presenters to preserve a commitment to Indigenize and decolonize narratives to uplift through two common and related aims: (1) make known the equity and inclusion barriers of the political, social, and environmental inequalities of Indigenous peoples as land-water–based interconnectedness to identity; and (2) include efforts to ensure that Indigenous peoples and knowledges from diverse backgrounds, experiences, and perspectives are empowered. Since 2015, these aims were immersed into all levels of the expanding platform, and collaborative partnerships call attention to the importance of acknowledging the responsibility of knowledge and, in turn, unlearning and relearning the spiritual and emotional connections to acquire knowledge.

Acknowledgments

Indigenous Knowledges and Community Conversations and its expanded virtual platform Indigenous Speaker Series are supported and co-sponsored by the Bay and Paul Foundations, Rising Voices, Clean Up the River Environment, UW EarthLab, UWT Office of Community Partnerships, UWT School of Interdisciplinary Arts and Sciences, UW Center for Global Studies, UW Center for American Indian and Indigenous Studies, and UW Office of Minority Affairs and Diversity. I would like to thank my colleagues—Dr. Paulette Blanchard (Kickapoo / Absentee Shawnee), Ciarra Greene (Sapóoq'is Wíit'as Consulting, Nez Perce), Hannah Smith (White Earth), Jasmine Neosh (Menominee), Pah-tu Pitt (Warm Springs / Wasco), Joshua Denis (Navajo/Diné), and Hokulani Rivera (Kanaka Maloui from Pauoa Valley)—who provided insight and expertise that assisted the virtual success, and its expanded version, the Series. I would also like to show my gratitude to Ciarra Greene (Nez Perce, Sapóoq'is Wíit'as Consulting) for providing technical support and contributing data. I am also immensely grateful to our presenters and participants as a humble, forever student.

References

Cajete, G. 1994. *Look to the Mountain: An Ecology of Indigenous Education*. Rio Rancho, NM: Kivakí Press.

Child, B. 1998. *Boarding School Seasons: American Indian Families, 1900–1940*. Lincoln: University of Nebraska Press.

Fisher, P. A., and T. J. Ball. 2003. "Tribal Participatory Research: Mechanisms of a Collaborative Model." *American Journal of Community Psychology* 32 (3–4): 207–216.

Kimmerer, R. W. 2012. "Searching for Synergy: Integrating Traditional and Scientific Ecological Knowledge in Environmental Science Education." *Journal of Environmental Studies and Sciences* 2 (4): 317–323.

Menzies, C. R. 2006. *Traditional Ecological Knowledge and Natural Resource Management*. Lincoln: University of Nebraska Press.

Minthorn, R., M. Montgomery, and D. Bill. 2021. "Indigenous Centered Pedagogies through a Tribal-University Partnership." Special Issue: Possibilities and Complexities of Decolonising Higher Education: Critical Perspectives on Praxis. *Genealogy* 5 (1): 24.

Montgomery, M. 2022. "An Indigenous Feminist Lens: Dismantling the Settler-Colonial Narratives of Place-Based Knowledges in a Climate Change World." In *The Routledge Handbook of Sustainable Cities and Landscapes in the Pacific Rim Planning and Engagement*, edited by Taufen and Yang, 862–868. Routledge International Handbooks. Abingdon, UK: Routledge.

Montgomery, M., and P. Blanchard. 2021. "Testing Justice: New Ways to Address Environmental Inequalities." *Solutions Journal*. https://www.resilience.org/stories/2022-02-17/testing-justice-new-ways-to-address-environmental-inequalities/.

Shilling, D., and M. K. Nelson. 2018. *Traditional Ecological Knowledge: Learning from Indigenous Practices for Environmental Sustainability*. Cambridge: Cambridge University Press.

Thomas, L. R., C. Rosa, A. Forcehimes, and D. M. Donovan. 2011. "Research Partnerships between Academic Institutions and American Indian and Alaska Native Tribes and Organizations: Effective Strategies and Lessons Learned in a Multisite CTN Study." *American Journal of Drug and Alcohol Abuse* 37 (5): 333–338.

Wildcat, D. R. 2009. *Red Alert! Saving the Planet with Indigenous Knowledge*. Golden, CO: Fulcrum.

2

Indigenous Relationality

Advancing Theory and Praxis in Educational Research

EMMA ELLIOTT AND TIMOTHY SAN PEDRO

Although fraught with challenges, our current moment of overlapping pandemics—COVID-19, racism, and looming environmental catastrophe—offers a necessary opening and opportunity for educators and researchers to reimagine, redesign, and co-construct approaches to education that promote the thriving livelihoods of not just all learners but all living beings (McCoy et al. 2020). The magnitude of the cumulative threat faced by humankind necessitates consequential, creative, deliberate, and diverse approaches to educational practices and research (Bang and Vossoughi 2016; Barab et al. 2007; McCoy et al. 2020; Philip, Bang, and Jackson 2018; Rosebery 2010). The perpetuation of or, worse, the return to the prepandemic status quo is neither acceptable nor sustainable.

We are collectively faced with the simultaneous task of reimagining future societies while reenvisioning contemporary learning environments, perpetually shaped by the relational dynamics and consequential agendas to which we aspire.

https://doi.org/10.5876/9781646425105.c002

Scholars have called for "the revitalization of Indigenous educational practices that prioritize preparing young people to tend to the land, community, and one another" (McCoy et al. 2020). Indigenous knowledge systems, practices, and ethical frameworks are informed by an understanding of self in respectful and sustainable relations with all living beings (Cajete 1994; Cajete 2000; Simpson 2017). Indigenous existence, and more broadly human existence, is predicated on this relational understanding of the world. Similarly, scholars across disciplines acknowledge the relational nature of human learning and development and in many corners of education are calling for sustainable and consequential approaches to educational research. To that end, we offer *Indigenous relationality* (Indigenous intellectual traditions) as a framework for understanding human learning and development. We present here *Indigenous storying* (story, storytelling, and story listening) as a methodological and pedagogical approach that is, at once, relational, sustainable, and transformative. We also identify explicit parallels between Indigenous theory and practice and fundamental knowledge about human learning and development.

Indigenous Relationality

Indigenous peoples have sustained themselves (and 85% of the world's biodiversity) across time by engaging in "relationships of reciprocity, humility, honesty, and respect with all elements of creation, including plants and animals" (Simpson 2017). Indigenous relationality is grounded in the notion that human existence is predicated on living in reciprocal, consensual, and sustainable relations with other humans, plant and animal nations, natural world elements (e.g., land and water), and ancestral or spiritual entities (Cajete 1994, Cajete 2000; Simpson 2017). Each relationship, and therefore each social interaction, is imbued with and shaped by ethical commitments, including "respect, reverence, responsibility, reciprocity, holism, interrelatedness, and synergy" (Archibald 2008). Indigenous intellectual traditions, including perspectives on the nature of being, are rooted in deep relationship with land and shaped by a deep sense of relational reciprocity and, as such, cannot be successfully compartmentalized and transmitted. As a way of realizing and living such intellectual traditions, Indigenous storying is a methodological approach that is inherently relational, integrated, dialogic, and co-constitutive. Concurrently, it is a pedagogical approach that allows for cultural constructs to learning, which centers thriving pathways for youth to develop relational and axiological connections and responsibilities to families, communities, lands, and beyond-human connections.

Indigenous Storying as Methodology

Indigenous storywork, as theorized and shared by J. A. Archibald (2008), breaks down storying into three deeply interrelated elements—story, storytelling, and story listening—a description that aids in a clearer understanding of the methodological contribution. Those telling a story are the storytellers, while those listening to a story are story listeners. In a dialogic interaction, these roles move back and forth as ideas are connecting and constructing and weaving into a shared story (Kinloch and San Pedro 2014). Story, then, is that dialogic space between people transmitted through words (orally and written but also through other means such as art and music) to expand one's understanding of self in relation to one's surroundings; it provides opportunities to critically examine the interactions between one's own history, culture, and life experiences when they come into contact with another's realities, which we believe should be at the heart of any educational setting for all learners.

Storying involves active participation: "The story doesn't work without a participant," suggesting that those listening cannot be passive but instead active in the process (Vizenor 1987). Active listening involves grafting one's own story—lived experiences, histories, cultural truths—onto the stories offered by another. Stories serve a variety of functions, including knowledge transmission, identity development, and healing from traumatic experiences. For example, storying is the process through which knowledge is transmitted across generations; it is a pedagogical practice. The social space is cultivated so that participants can re-narrate their sense of identity based on the meanings exchanged through the storying process. In some cases, re-narrating a story in the presence of a caring other person (e.g., a mental health practitioner or a loved one) can help develop the safety and trust needed to heal from trauma. The active, alive, and emerging exchange of ideas and knowledge through stories becomes the process of storying—the action of "ing" in story*ing*. As such, storying is an active and mutually constitutive learning process through which knowledge is shared.

Discussion

Inherently relational in nature, Indigenous intellectual traditions have been collaboratively and dialogically constructed, transmitted, and co-created in relationship to the land and all living beings. Indigenous relationality and Indigenous storying offer theoretical constructs in alignment with what we know about human learning and development. Indigenous intellectual traditions acknowledge the dynamic and co-constitutive nature of learning and human development. Learning and human development occur within everyday social interaction, highlighting the importance of relationships in either supporting or undermining human learning and development (Osher et al. 2020). Similarly, Indigenous relationships are the cornerstones of Indigenous existence (Cajete 2015). All learning and human development are predicated on and informed by cultural and social knowledge (Gutiérrez and Rogoff 2003; Lee 2002; Nasir and Hand 2006). This interdisciplinary approach can inform locally specific and/or culturally sustaining approaches to educational research and practice (Paris 2012). Indigenous intellectual traditions offer a counternarrative to settler-colonial systems and processes. The inherent relational nature of Indigenous intellectual tradition pushes against the assumption that knowledge lies solely in the individual. Within a western research and teaching paradigm, the researcher/teacher subsumes the role of storytaker, narrator, and storyteller—roles that perpetuate existing inequitable power and privilege structures. Instead, by relying on the strengths of relationships, researchers and educators can deconstruct unequal power dynamics and disrupt practices that perpetuate cultural superiority, thereby offering theoretical, pedagogical, and practical approaches to decolonizing methods.

Conclusion

Indigenous intellectual traditions, including interdependent systems of relationality, and their underlying axiological precepts, are designed to generate life; not only Indigenous lives but all lives (Simpson 2017). Embedded within Indigenous intellectual traditions are frameworks that can strengthen collective social resilience for all living beings. By centering Indigenous intellectual traditions, researchers can disrupt extractive research practices and inform the ways in which local knowledge is co-constructed and transmitted. M. Bang and colleagues (2016) urge researchers to deliberately cultivate transformative agency and to deeply engage local ethical commitments throughout the research process. Indigenous intellectual traditions are frameworks through which to consider innovative research methods that not only contribute to knowledge co-creation broadly but more so offer concrete strategies (e.g., storying) that promote sustainable local and cultural practices. In this context, the goal of transformative educational approaches (and the ways we participate and observe those approaches) becomes about knowledge co-construction for the purposes of self-determination, adaptation, and, ultimately, survival. We cannot return to what was; we must envision anew while relying on intellectual traditions that have allowed peoples, communities, and environments to survive and thrive even in the midst of continued destruction from settler colonial systems.

References

Archibald, J. A. 2008. *Indigenous Storywork: Educating the Heart, Mind, Body, and Spirit.* Vancouver, BC: UBC Press.

Bang, M., L. Faber, J. Gurneau, A. Marin, and C. Soto. 2016. "Community-Based Design Research: Learning across Generations and Strategic Transformations of Institutional Relations toward Axiological Innovations." *Mind, Culture, and Activity* 23 (1): 28–41.

Bang, M., and S. Vossoughi. 2016. "Participatory Design Research and Educational Justice: Studying Learning and Relations within Social Change Making." *Cognition and Instruction* 34 (3): 173–193.

Barab, S., T. Dodge, M. K. Thomas, C. Jackson, and H. Tuzun. 2007. "Our Designs and the Social Agendas They Carry." *Journal of the Learning Sciences* 16 (2): 263–305.

Cajete, G. 1994. *Look to the Mountain: An Ecology of Indigenous Education.* Durango, CO: Kivaki Press.

Cajete, G. 2015. *Indigenous Community: Rekindling the Teachings of the Seventh Fire.* St. Paul, MN: Living Justice Press.

Cajete, G. 2000. *Native Science: Natural Laws of Interdependence.* Santa Fe, NM: Clear Light Publishers.

Gutiérrez, K. D., and B. Rogoff. 2003. "Cultural Ways of Learning: Individual Traits or Repertoires of Practice." *Educational Researcher* 32 (5): 19–25.

Kinloch, V., and T. Pedro. 2014. "The Space between Listening and Storying: Foundations for Projects in Humanization." In *Humanizing Research: Decolonizing*

Qualitative Inquiry with Youth and Communities, 21–42. Thousand Oaks, CA: SAGE Publications.

Lee, C. D. 2002. "Interrogating Race and Ethnicity as Constructs in the Examination of Cultural Processes in Developmental Research." *Human Development* 45 (4): 282–290.

McCoy, M., E. Elliott-Groves, L. Sabzalian, and M. Bang. 2020. "Restoring Indigenous Systems of Relationality." Center for Humans and Nature. https://humansandnature.org/restoring-indigenous-systems-of-relationality/.

Nasir, N. I. S., and V. M. Hand. 2006. "Exploring Sociocultural Perspectives on Race, Culture, and Learning." *Review of Educational Research* 76 (4): 449–475.

Osher, D., P. Cantor, J. Berg, L. Steyer, and T. Rose. 2020. "Drivers of Human Development: How Relationships and Context Shape Learning and Development 1." *Applied Developmental Science* 24 (1): 6–36.

Paris, D. 2012. "Culturally Sustaining Pedagogy: A Needed Change in Stance, Terminology, and Practice." *Educational Researcher* 41 (3): 93–97.

Philip, T. M., M. Bang, and K. Jackson. 2018. "Articulating the 'How,' the 'For What,' the 'For Whom,' and the 'With Whom' in Concert: A Call to Broaden the Benchmarks of Our Scholarship." *Cognition and Instruction* 36 (2): 83–88.

Rosebery, A. S., M. Ogonowski, M. DiSchino, and B. Warren. 2010. " 'The Coat Traps All Your Body Heat': Heterogeneity as Fundamental to Learning." *Journal of the Learning Sciences* 19 (3): 322–357.

Simpson, L. B. 2017. *As We Have Always Done: Indigenous Freedom through Radical Resistance*. Minneapolis: University of Minnesota Press.

Vizenor, G. 1987. "Follow the Trickroutes: An Interview with Gerald Vizenor." In *Survival This Way: Interviews with American Indian Poets*, edited by J. Bruchac, 287–310. Tucson: University of Arizona Press.

3

Walking the Land in Silence

Experiential Learning around Us

DAWN HARDISON-STEVENS

The land is the real teacher. All we need as students is mindfulness.
—*Robin Wall Kimmerer*

This chapter presents walking and reading the land as an Indigenous pedagogy (teaching and learning strategy). Land-based or embodied learning practices, such as this, facilitate learning about the world, oneself, and one's responsibility to others. For generations, Indigenous people have been living in close observation with the land and the natural world. Walking in silence involves engaging senses, close observation, listening with heart and mind to build appreciation and respect with one's surroundings. This process allows students to learn in deeper ways. The walking in silence embraces an Indigenous teaching and learning strategy and discusses the experiential Native knowledge one can gain by engaging senses while doing so. To quietly experience the lands where learners call home, places of work, or points of exploration helps show our interconnectedness to all the life around us. Most of the content here is from my 2013 doctoral dissertation: "Knowing the Indigenous Leadership Journey: Indigenous People Need the Academic System as Much as the Academic System Needs Indigenous People." It pulls from my experiences as an educator with the University of Washington, which I am honored to share.

https://doi.org/10.5876/9781646425105.c003

Walking in Silence

Curricular Themes

In my courses, I encourage undergraduate and graduate students to walk the land in silence based on the course titles and themes. Students and teacher candidates in my classes engage with the teachings of the lands they walk. Students consider Indigenous customs, traditions, and learning processes with place. One cultivates their observations walking through, mapping any sensory experience. For example, in a course titled Leadership and Change, doctoral students have walked their lands in silence, writing and mapping areas, pointing out senses and perspectives of the land's teachings, and making observations of land teachings. They have also walked the land in silence, engaging the senses and noting what the land can teach them as part of the course Human Capacity Development and the land's teachings based on another course, Leadership and Healing.

Teacher candidates have walked the land in silence, viewing the teachings of understanding Indigenous perspectives. Education master's students focused on themes about learning; collaborative consultation with schools, families, and communities; Native American education narratives; and centering tribal sovereignty. Course themes help demonstrate areas of various perspectives the land can teach, whether walking in an old-growth forest, a second-growth forest, or a young forest. Even if walking in different locations and observing the variances based on location, whether north in Alaska, the Pacific Northwest, eastern Washington State and Oregon, western Washington and Oregon, or the Southwest and Rocky Mountain locales, the differences between the lands and their teachings are immense. I would like to acknowledge parts of my student experiences are adapted from mapping the land work of a colleague, Dr. Megan Bang, when we both were at the University of Washington.

Place

Students have walked in areas of their choice, such as around their homes, neighborhoods, places of work, a favorite trail or beach, urban and rural areas, islands—even cities. Each location provides teachings. In each instance, I hear how senses were opened, including gut feelings, engaging solitude, peace, happiness, or even fears. Students have commented on living in spaces and for the first time seeing the trees, Indigenous plants, and teachings of diversity with the lands.

The land is our teacher, providing experiences differently when we walk in silence and engage all the senses—visual, smelling, listening, tasting, touching, and feelings—from the gut. Students of all ages view their own individual perspectives in various ways by engaging their senses. When given a specific viewed theme, experiences change from one person to the next. The land around us shows diversity that brings a healthy balance when in its natural state and a determination to remain from strong root sources. V. Drywater-Whitekiller and J. Corntassel (2022) shared, "Indigenous land-based relationships are central to community knowledge systems, stories, governance, economies, languages, ceremonies, food sovereignty, and sacred living histories" (99). Native knowledge is around us when people are provided an opportunity to understand and engage senses. P. L. Chartrand (2007) quotes a grandmother's words: "When you look around in nature, in creation, you will see many different plants and flowers. All are different but have a role in making the land a healthy place. They do not say that one of them does not belong. They all make room for each other. They depend on each other and make creation beautiful for us" (18).

I stay close to Mother Earth, viewing and reflecting upon some of the most determined educators, the communities of diverse forests with leaders standing tall or arms branched out, collaborating on the growth of their surrounding community. At my home, I peer out windows and sit among the Indigenous second-growth Douglas Fir, Western Red Cedar, Big Leaf Maple, Western Hemlock, Golden Chinquapin, and Red Alder. These trees are the Elders, keepers of story and wisdom, as the neighboring logged areas grow young saplings. Deer graze as chipmunks, robins, ravens, owls, and an occasional cougar speak their voices. My Seattle home floats on Portage Bay, embracing the water community, while the surrounding Earth roots with the vast diversity of Indigenous Western Hemlock, Western Red Cedar amongst transplants of Honey Locust, European White Birch, Pin Oak, Zelkova Serrata "Village Green," Norway Maple, Summit Green Ash, Chinese Scholar Trees, Japanese Black Pine, White Pine, Rocky Mountain Juniper, Atlas Cedar, Sugar Maple, and Austrian Pine. There is so much to observe when walking the lands in silence wherever one travels.

People have long walked on Alaskan lands, but on my travels I reflect on the teachings in the environment with Indigenous Sitka Spruce, Western Hemlock, and Yellow Cedar among backdrops of glaciers and an expansive Lynn Canal in Juneau, with the Chilkat and Chilkoot Mountains rising in the far distance. Whales emerge, with eagles and ravens greeting each day with resonating voices. Walkers in Leavenworth east of the Cascade Mountain Range in Washington State could witness variances of Western Cedar, Ponderosa, Lodgepole, Western White Pine, Quaking Aspen, Water Birch, and Oregon White Oak standing tall along granite-walled rock cliffs with the roaring white water of Icicle Creek. These majestic teachers comfort Earth's life from where their ancestral roots dig deep, and understory life flourishes wherever I walk, standing tall with arms stretched up toward the ancestral Spirits against an ever-changing sky of clouds, sun, stars, and moon. I have been blessed my whole life with these big people, rich in diversity and feeding the mind. In customary Indigenous tradition, these are all our relatives, honoring all in our World with the Two-legged Ones, Four-legged Ones, Feathered Ones, Finned Ones, Ones That Crawl, Rooted Nations, Mineral People, and Sky Nations. This interconnectedness honors all creations with the understanding that we are all related and created equal—and that, in turn, affecting one affects all.

Identifying Self

Honoring my Cree (*N_hiyawak*) ancestry, I will share the philosophy that "the land gives you your culture" (*Miyo-W_hk_htowin*) and to "all my relations" (*Niw_hk_m_kanak*) (Chartrand 2007, 5). Like the plants, animals, soil, and environment that are "Native" or "Indigenous" to their location as developing "successfully," I consider these terms in thought with us "human people" living on a land they are accustomed to based on their Ancestors. To be "successful" in a chosen profession, one should consider their environment and consider their surrounding human and nonhuman relations, knowing a uniqueness and being placed in a space for a reason. Time will be needed to walk the lands in silence and find the connections with places wherever you are located. Like the lands we walk, an effective mentor guides toward their own individual success, knowing each person should be aware of their own cultural selves (Pewewardy 2003). The conceptual framework of interconnectedness relates to Native communities today through "mutuality and equality" (C. Pewewardy, personal communication, November 7, 2013).

For generations, Indigenous people were educated forcibly, submissively, and oppressively in a system oriented toward limiting their education to fulfill servitude roles. Native philosophy traditionally focuses on balance and interconnectedness "grounded in experience and representing specific contexts, particular tribes, diverse lands, inherent values and beliefs, varieties of protocols, a plethora of languages, and a tremendous variety of circumstances" (Kenny and Fraser 2012, 13). Everyone brings his or her own history and perspectives with the land. C. Kenny and T. N. Fraser (2012) shared, "The road to leadership is paved with land, ancestors, elders, and story—concepts that are rarely mentioned in the standard leadership literature. These are embodied concepts unique to Native Leadership" (16). Here, I like to replace the term "leadership" with terms such as "Life" and acknowledge that we are all determined leaders and educators from birth to death, as is our land.

Some Native-born people have had the honor of growing up in two worlds: On the one hand, there is the world of the Indigenous learning, of listening to the elders' stories with their experiential wisdom, in addition to observation within the environment of the land, forests, and animals (Lemoine 2003). On the other hand, some people become educated in a conventional Euro-Western style with college and university books and professors. Each one brings its own unique spirituality as traditional Native people honor the wise ones who speak to guide through destined life paths or journeys. Many Native people honor the fact of building a lifeworld through experiences that come along a path (Lemoine 2003).

Relationships

Native people have historically had a relationship with the land based on respect. The land was the source of determining relationships and leadership. Mother Earth modeled a natural transformative leadership style as one element affects the other. Kenny and Fraser (2012) shared: "In order to maintain this sense of coherence, we can accept the Earth as our first embodied concept of leadership. We follow the Earth. We respond to the guidance of the processes expressed in our home place. Many say we listen and respond to our Mother. Everything begins here. We mirror the patterns, textures, colors, sounds, and processes of the Earth as embodied beings" (15). Earth nurtures, knowing the land provides food, home, and all of life's symbiotic relationships. M. Jennings (2004) wrote: "Views of the land represent entire worldviews that encompass the relationship between the environment and all other aspects of social life. Land has been and continues to rest at the core of Indigenous worldviews; at the heart of Native American values is the belief that we come from the earth and that we are bound to the cosmos by spiritual links to all things" (2). This view speaks to establishing a constant balance, not placing one being over another but living in collaboration. Life in a balance is not hierarchical but rather placed within a circle, the circle Mother Earth beholds as she has no beginning or no end. "The culture of Native students refers to the worldviews that encompass complete ways of being in the world like bundles of relationships" (13).

Native people view life differently. Non-Native people who have worked and lived in the forest have built within them this common understanding. For many who live with the land, inspiration is found in the considerate and respectful use of the land. To live as one in balance with the land is to perceive and honor the lifeworld as the plant and animal people give to the human people. The counterbalance would be the human people honoring the plants and animals by giving back to their communities. M. Wheatley (2007) compared human life with the natural world, observing: "Social insects, bird flocks, schools of fish, human traffic jams, all exhibit well synchronized, highly ordered behaviors. Yet any leader does not direct these sophisticated movements. Instead, a few rules focused at the local level lead to coordinated responses. Computer simulations mimic flocking, swarming, or schooling behaviors but program in only two or three rules for individuals to follow. There is seldom a rule about a leader or direction. The rules focus only on an individual's behavior in relation to that of its neighbors. Synchronized behavior emerges without orchestrated planning" (35). Education comes from all beings, whether human, plant, or animal within their own lifeworld. Education builds perspectives that are developed.

Communities

Telling conventional educators who are unfamiliar with such a concept is an education. Jennings (2004) shares: "The Euro-American conception of land is also central to Western worldviews. Both Christianity and scientific materialism distinguish humans from nature and set them above it, contrasting the intellectual or spiritual capacities of humans with the resources that exist for their manipulation and exploitation" (2). The bridging of a community's individual knowledge areas and belief systems may establish understanding as they enmesh thoughtfulness and respect of notable differences.

M. Wheatley (2007) noted how community is all around us, wherever we are living life or experiencing life. The communities "know how to connect to others through their diversity, communities that succeed in creating sustainable relationships over long periods of time; these communities are the webs of relationships called *ecosystems*" (45). Life systems live in a diversity of sustainable relationships that builds on self-determination to succeed. Each species establishes and partakes in its own talent as part of an interconnected web system (Wheatley 2007). Raquel Gutierrez stated in Kenny and Fraser (2012): "We are moving towards a doing that grows more deliberately out of being; an understanding that freedom from external systems of oppression is dynamically related to liberation from our internal mechanisms of suffering. It provides us with a way to release the construct of 'us versus them' and live into the web of relationships that links all" (142).

All things enmeshed in life seek survival—as some say, survival of the fittest—as one matures. J. Heider (1985) addressed an Indigenous perspective, comparing a wise leader to water: "Consider water: water cleanses and refreshes all creatures without distinction and without judgment; water freely and fearlessly goes deep beneath the surface of things; water is fluid and responsive; water follows the law freely" (15). Heider goes on to compare a leader of behaving like water in benefiting all that is served. Water, through its yielding characteristics, can soften what is rigid and solid. "Water will wear away rock, which is rigid and cannot yield. As a rule, whatever is fluid, soft, and yielding will overcome whatever is rigid and hard" (155).

Reciprocity

Most Indigenous cultures see everything as deeply interrelated, whether it is human relationships to the land and other living beings, belief, or spirituality, or social life. Native peoples learned to adapt in a harmonious manner to the land on which they lived. T. Stagich (2001) identified that people have lived in respectful and reciprocal relations with animals and other natural world relations from which seasonal sustenance is provided. Indigenous cultures only hunted and farmed respectfully and as needed, identifying that taking life gives life to another. There is an honoring of the plant or animal that gave itself to the Native people. The land offered respect based on the life it provided with an understanding that the territory supplied plentiful resources to survive. The land's bountiful wealth provided life in the form of food, shelter, and clothing from the vast array of resources. Native circles honored the balance (Jennings 2004; Stagich 2001). As Stagich (2001) stated: "These practices were successful in maintaining the rich abundance of North America for many thousands of years. They were the experts on ecology demonstrating an interrelation worldview or Indigenous understandings of relationally thus providing local and culturally based strategies for ethical and sustainable relations with all living beings" (200).

Spiritual beliefs of Native and other Indigenous people who are one with the Earth encompass every living being. In this belief system, living things—whether human, plant, or animal—behold a natural spirituality that includes ancestors from the past and people who have not come to the Earth yet. "Human beings are but one of the many intrinsic parts of a much larger, interrelated universe. When Native people speak of kinship with nonhuman beings, they are being quite literal because of their belief system" (Jennings 2004, 27). Many rituals honor the plant or animal, such as the Coastal Salish peoples' First Salmon Ceremonies. The practice of honoring existed among many cultures within North America. Stagich (2001) explained anthropological studies of cultures "uncovered a deeper appreciation of the power and influence of nature," sharing: "By living, working and adapting in harmony with nature, the Native Americans have given the world an example of how all cultures and civilizations can live in oneness with nature and preserve the environment for all future generations. Such a synergistic understanding and appreciation of nature must become a standard for all future civilizations if they are to be considered highly developed" (200–201).

Stagich (2001) shares that if leaders viewed their position, considering the plant and animal kingdoms, they would provide the models to reflect and learn from as the change we need as a people.

> Collaboration in organizations and group cultures is changing the way we think about leadership as well as individual, social, and global transformation. Change is inevitable and the transformations, which occur through collaboration and group synergy, are reshaping the world in which we live in every area of community life. We are becoming a more collaborative society. Leaders who understand how to facilitate collaboration are better able to improve performance and motivate people to learn, develop, share, and adapt to changes at home, at work, and throughout the global community. The transformations, which occur through this process, help each individual and group to reach their highest potential and in the process generate benefits for society and the environment. (8)

Envision being in a forest and looking around. There are plants of many shapes and sizes like there are people. Look at the vast array of colors, like the diverse tones and hues with the human people. Each plant works collaboratively with another by protecting, shielding, or providing nourishment to it. The tall tree canopy provides shade and shelter to the understory, which in turn provides nutrients and feeds root systems that sustain the life of the broader plant kingdom. Stagich (2001) affirmed: "Clearly, as we think more collaboratively, we are producing changes which are more collaborative in nature. And, as our worldview becomes more in line with nature and the synergy principle, greater global accomplishments will be possible with benefits for all" (8).

A. Marin and M. Bang (2018) share that "relationships with land and walking are important to knowledge-making processes, especially when it comes to knowing ecosystems" (91) and to knowing an interconnectedness in which we as humans come in balance with the Land.

Students are guided to walk in thematic ways based on course title and theme. The candidate's task is to walk the land in silence and observe the teachings from class themes. What does the land teach regarding Leadership and Change? Human Capacity Development? And Leadership for Healing? Candidates wrote reflective responses with maps identifying the senses seen, heard, smelled, tasted, touched, and deeply sensed. Typically students complete the task alone for their first time. Another method was taking doctoral candidates on a field trip to Muckleshoot Tribal Lands through Tomanamus Forest. As a cohort, together we walked the trail in silence as candidates sketched notes without words. The path led us to old-growth forest species, waterfalls, ponds, and other spaces alive with diversity.

Interconnectedness

I see we as human people; then there are the tree people, finned people, and feathered people. And I am aware of how we are all connected to our world. We are all one with Earth, where one interconnects with another; affect one, and you affect the other. R. Pierotti and D. Wildcat (2000) mentioned disconnects when contemporary Western approaches derived from a Western European philosophy regard natural resources as to be controlled: "[Westerners] they assume that humans are autonomous from, and in control of, the natural world," but there is a natural phenomenon "combined with a concept of community membership that differs from that of Western political and social thought" (1333). Community includes the animals, plants, and landforms within an environmental locality: "As a consequence, native worldviews can be considered to be spatially oriented, in contrast to the temporal orientation of Western political and historical thought. Connectedness and relatedness are involved in the clan systems of many Indigenous peoples, where nonhuman organisms are recognized as relatives whom the humans are obliged to treat with respect and honor" (1334).

This sums up knowledge of Indigenous thought processes related to interconnectedness through leadership and educational development.

Listening to Ancestors on many occasions, while visiting various locations, mysteriously, I felt at home, overwhelmed by a loosening peace embodying my soul, as if the land had been traversed previously in another life before my present one, spaces Ancestors walked. There are areas around western and eastern Washington, British Columbia, Thunder Bay, Winnipeg, Selkirk, Lake Nipigon, and others where my spirit just wants to "drive" the vehicle because there's a story ahead. I've wandered around "getting lost" in places to find familial histories. An example is when I stepped off a twin prop plane and checked in at a motel where a hotel staff member asked, "What brings you here," only to quickly learn that we were related. Shortly after, he introduced me to his uncle, who bore a strong resemblance to my father.

Globally, Indigenous cultures have survived physical and epistemic violence by maintaining their customs, land, language, and the essence of a

TABLE 3.1. Description of senses and experiences

Sensory	*Experience*
Touch	Hands-on experiential learning as one can touch and not break teaching; we as human people can heal; perseverance in all things we do as human people.
Smell	Breathing the fresh air as trees extract pure carbon dioxide; organic fragrances from natural sources.
Hear	Storytelling as a lesson teaching life's education; listening to the whispers the wind brings traveling through the branches and leaves, telling us of change.
Taste	Generosity in all that we can give from knowledge to possessions; culture that gives us our understanding and foundation as to who we are as a collective people.
See	Observation of the diversity and differences each species possesses in a healthy environment like that of us as a human people; witnessing life that comes on the life path for observation and reflective purpose.
Sense	Instruction and the transmission of knowledge as the knowing is passed down from generation to generation; patience and persistence in practicing new skills as they stay with us forever; heritage honoring our ancestors who walked before us.

belief that reaches deep in honor of the past, present, and future of peoples. Today, Indigenous cultural practices continue to be threatened by the impact of colonial encroachment on Indigenous lives and lifeways. With change and awareness, young people can learn in schools to seek interconnectedness of the traditional lands and realize they are our future to carry on the legacies. Traditions once feared lost come forward through education and traditions. G. Cajete (2000) stated: "The Indigenous 'physicist' not only observes nature, but also participates in it with all his or her sensual being. Humans and all other entities of nature experience at their own levels of sensate reality. The Indigenous experience is evidenced not only through collective cultural expressions of art, story, ritual, and technology, but also through the more subtle and intimate expressions of individual acts of respect, care, words, and feelings that are continually extended to the land and its many beings" (20). All things possess their own energy and something to teach humans if they listen. When walking in a forest or on any land, like many Indigenous people, embrace the teachings experienced using all the senses as described in table 3.1.

I watch, listen, breathe, taste, touch, and sense many things around me and learn. L. Hogan (1995) reminds us to include all life, wherever you are; in the presence of a human, forest, animal, desert, one can find peace in just silently engaging the innate sensory awarenesses.

Conclusion

I encourage everyone to walk in silence on the land where they are located and embrace the energies engaging our senses with an understanding I share often: "We Are Our Ancestors' Future." The land does not just cycle and feed us as human but teaches. As we walk the lands in silence, consider the wisdom from a Skokomish Tribal elder and relative, Bruce Subiyay Miller: "The plants are our greatest teachers—that all the wisdom we need for living on earth is contained in the plants themselves," noting experiential learning is all around.

References

Cajete, G. 2000. *Native Science: Natural Laws of Interdependence*. Santa Fe, NM: Clear Light Books.

Chartrand, P. L. 2007. "Niw_Hk_M_Kanak ("All My Relations"): Metis-First Nations Relations." https://fngovernance.org/wp-content/uploads/2020/09/paul_chartrand.pdf.

Drywater-Whitekiller, V., and J. Corntassel. 2022. "Learning on and from the Land." In *Unsettling Settler-Colonial Education: The Transformational Indigenous Praxis Model*, edited by C. Pewewardy and A. Lees, 99–111. New York: Teachers College Press.

Hardison-Stevens, Dawn. 2013. "Knowing the Indigenous Leadership Journey: Indigenous People Need the Academic System as Much as the Academic System Needs Indigenous People." PhD diss. Antioch University, Seattle.

Heider, J. 1985. *The Tao of Leadership: Leadership Strategies for a New Age*. Atlanta: Humanics New Age.

Hogan, L. 1995. *Dwellings: A Spiritual History of Living*. New York: Simon and Schuster.

Jennings, M. 2004. *Alaska Native Political Leadership and Higher Education: One University, Two Universes*. Walnut Creek, CA: Altamira Press.

Kenny, C., and T. N. Fraser. 2012. *Living Indigenous Leadership: Native Narratives on Building Strong Communities*. Vancouver, CA: UBC Press.

Lemoine, T. 2003. *Giving Back to Community: A Factor in College Persistence. The American Indian Graduate*. Tempe, AZ: American Indian Graduate Center.

Marin, A., and M. Bang. 2018. "'Look It, This Is How You Know': Family Forest Walks as a Context for Knowledge-Building about the Natural World." *Cognition and Instruction* 36 (2): 89–118.

Miller, B. 2006. "Teachings of the Tree People." IslandWood. https://www.youtube.com/watch?v=u2SaRE8Sy6g.

Pewewardy, C. 2003. "To Be or Not to Be Indigenous: Identity, Race, and Representation in Education." *Indigenous Nations Studies Journal* 4 (2): 69–91.

Pierotti, R., and D. Wildcat. 2000. "Traditional Ecological Knowledge: The Third Alternative." *Ecological Applications* 10 (5): 1333–1340.

Stagich, T. 2001. *Collaborative Leadership and Global Transformation*. Global Leadership Resources. United States: 1st Books.com.

Wheatley, M. 2007. *Finding Our Way: Leadership for Uncertain Times*. San Francisco: Berrett-Koehler.

4

Sacred Circle x̌ax̌aʔ qaləkʷ

DENISE BILL AND ELISE BILL-GERRISH

In honor of "Breaking the Sacred Circle" by Willard Bill Sr.

The Sacred Circle represents the holistic health of Native people. Using this as a self-assessment tool, people can reflect on their whole being and identify areas that are out of balance. Many areas have been impacted by trauma over the past 500 years and need healing. The Sacred Circle provides a framework for reflection and moving forward with proactive engagement in the healing process.

This version of the Sacred Circle was created by Dr. Willard Bill Sr., late Muckleshoot elder and historian, in his 1987 curriculum, "Breaking the Sacred Circle." This is one Muckleshoot perspective on the medicine wheel, which is recognized throughout Indian Country. Dr. Willard Bill Sr.'s work discusses the historical impacts Native Americans have endured and how they have impacted our collective well-being. His daughter, Dr. Denise Bill, and granddaughter, Elise Bill-Gerrish, carry on this important work by honoring his call to action, for the people of the twenty-first century to repair the Sacred Circle.

https://doi.org/10.5876/9781646425105.c004

Introduction

"Breaking the Sacred Circle" (Bill 1987) is a curriculum used by the Office of Superintendent of Public Instruction, from the late 1980s to present, designed for secondary teachers to implement. It was to serve as a "springboard for student discussion of American Indian issues" (Bill 1987). This article/curriculum covers "The Sacred Circle," "Intrusion," "Spiritual Confusion," "Acquisition," "Justification," "Dissolution," "Exclusion," "Lack of Harmony," "Cultural Disintegration," and a call for Natives to heal the Sacred Circle. W. Bill (1987) says, "to have lived for thousands of years on the North American Continent is a testimony to the Indian's ability to maintain a balance between the physical, mental, spiritual, and cultural aspects of life" (1). Bill (1987) goes on to say, "the goal of the traditional Indian was to strike a harmonious balance with nature and not to attempt to control it" (1).

The Sacred Circle represents four components: Mental, Cultural, Spiritual, and Physical. This article goes on to say, "American Indian-Alaskan Native cultures were cooperative societies that depended on each facet of their environment for sustenance" (Bill 1987, 4). Further, "there was a need to interrelate for survival, and this need was passed on through the centuries" (4). Bill (1987) lays out how the US government wrote, promoted, and enforced policies to disrupt the Native American way of life. One example of disruption of the Sacred Circle was creating the reservation system, taking people from their traditional lands where Natives hunted, fished, gathered berries, roots, plants, and moving Natives to undesirable pieces of land called reservations. Bill (1987) goes into greater depth about the significance of the land being sacred and outlines many facts of how the Sacred Circle was broken.

The conclusion in this article states that Natives have survived. Native children are being taught respect for the land. Native Tribes are reclaiming the reservations that were once meant for harm. Bill (1987, 49) concludes with using A. P. Elkin's term "contra-acculturation," stating it "takes place when the culture physically survives contact with alien cultures and revives its culture in a modified form," which provides hope for the survivors of the breaking of the Sacred Circle. He goes on to provide an example from the Seneca's and Alaskan Native's villages of repairing the Sacred Circle through teachings of the ancestors, reestablishment of culture, health, and spirituality.

The principles of the Sacred Circle were used in our interpretation and analysis of our storying and the overarching approach to the conceptualization of reclaiming emotions (Minthorn et al.).

Physical

Overview

The ability to maintain the physical health of our bodies is integral to people's physical well-being. Native people have a strong connection to the natural world. Our physical health was built up by using the plant medicine, traditional foods, and natural elements of our environment. The visual healing of leading a life outside in nature, amongst the tree people, plant people, animal people, and the water is an important part of Native life.

Impacts

Prior to contact, Native people were strong, healthy, and thriving. Colonization devastated the physical health of our people with exposure to diseases, sugar, alcohol, and warfare. The United States government strategically removed Native people from their ancestral lands (Dawes Act of 1877) and placed them onto reservations. This was an intentional strategy to disconnect Natives from their life source and their usual and accustomed gathering areas, and therefore weaken populations. The US government went on to forcibly remove Native children from their families and place them in (1819 Indian Civilization Act, and Peace Policy of 1869) boarding and residential schools. Here they began their egregious offenses by cutting the hair off of Native children, regardless of its cultural significance or respecting basic human dignity. This was one of many approaches used to break the child's spirit, and connection to their culture, and ultimately erase their Native identity at any cost.

Healing

Native communities are able to find physical healing through reconnection to the natural world, feeding our bodies with whole foods and traditional foods, leading a healthy lifestyle, working out, learning how to gather plants, hunting and fishing, navigating the land, earthing, activating all of our senses in the natural world (elements), and so on. There has been much movement in the twenty-first century to reclaim food sovereignty and the practicing treaty rights in the area of healthcare for Native people.

Plant Ally—Cottonwood Tree, qʷədiʔq’ʷac

The buds of this tree are harvested from fallen branches during Winter. They are infused into oils to make powerful pain salves. When the wind blows through cottonwood trees, it has a distinct calming fragrance.

Intellectual

Overview

Native American populations have held sophisticated knowledge systems since time immemorial. The inherent wisdom of the natural world guided how we conducted our lives. Ancestral knowledge such as weaving, gathering, hunting, fishing, teaching, languages, ability to read the land, technology all demonstrate how intelligent Native people are. We now utilize contemporary adaptations of these same skills. Native people also documented their personal histories through traditional storytelling. In Denise Bill's dissertation, "Pacific Northwest Native Educational Leaders," Cecelia Svinth-Carpenter says, "Our people are very oral. They're still oral. They still can tell, you can sit down with any of our elders and they'll tell you the history of their family or about when something happened."

Impacts

Europeans had difficulty accepting that the Sacred Circle existed for Native people. They thought they were more culturally advanced than those who inhabited the North American continent for thousands of years. When attempts were made to establish relationships, the outsiders chose not to make an offer that would strengthen the Native culture. History didn't have to play out the way it did. Europeans could have made a different offer to work together but instead chose warfare and policies against Native people. These policies included relocation, loss of land, control, assimilation, boarding schools, loss of family relationships, and the negligent food diet imposed upon us. E. Duran and B. Duran state in Native American Postcolonial Psychology, "A few generations before the effects of the Jewish Holocaust, Native American people were suddenly separated not only from loved family members, but also from the Earth, another close relative" (1995, 4).

Healing

We are entering a new age in which Indigenous knowledge is validated in many arenas. Many Natives are engaged in educational systems on their terms, whether they attend tribal schools, tribal colleges, or private and public universities. Pursuing higher education is a powerful healing tool Native people use to pursue what they are passionate about. Duran and Duran cite, "Native Activism resulting in the 1975 Native American Self Determination and Educational Assistance Act has ushered in a new era of Native Scholarship and Tribal control on research and in program planning" (1995, 24). Over the last twenty years, there has been a surge of Native people publishing their stories, histories, in books and academic journals. Bridging the gap between traditional and contemporary knowledge creates a more balanced world for Native populations.

Plant Ally—Nettles, sc'əd^{z}x̌

This early Springtime plant nourishes the whole body. It is grounding and fortifying, and it helps our bodies transition from Winter to Spring. This strong plant helps reduce symptoms of brain fog, anxiety, and stress.

Spiritual

Overview

The spiritual part of a person can represent the religion they choose to practice or other ways of connection to the creator or higher power. For some people, the creator is nature itself. Like the rest of the world, spiritual practices can vary from community to community. Traditionally, Native people found spiritual connection in the form of dancing, singing, drumming, and gathering together.

> One of the traditional ways I was reminded of by one of our elders is that before you worship, take time to be by yourself. I have tried to practice taking time for myself, being quiet, and, to be alone. I don't think people know how to do that. The place where I live still allows me the opportunity to practice that. The sage brush is all around me, the mountains are right there, and, I can take time to be by myself and listen to the birds sing and coyotes howl, and, to be just quiet. (Patsy Whitefoot, qtd. in Bill 2012)

Impacts

The US government banned Natives from gathering for spiritual practices up until 1978, when the American Indian Religious Freedom Act was passed. This included traditional food ceremonies, making plant medicine, singing, dancing, and more. Natives had to live in fear and hold spiritual ceremonies in hiding. This spiritual part of the Sacred Circle was also damaged by representatives of churches (priests, nuns, etc.), who had a big hand in boarding schools—many of whom were heavy handed with our Native children and people.

Healing

It is important to respect the freedom to choose what spiritual practice a person wants to participate in. Whether that's going to the Shaker Church, Pentecostal Church, Smokehouse, any denomination. Canoe journey can be a spiritual practice. Going into the mountains can be a spiritual experience, as well as smudging, prayer, and so forth. Ceremonies play a significant role in most Natives' lives, such as naming ceremonies, the first salmon ceremony, food burning for the ancestors, waking up the canoes, and putting them to rest.

Plant Ally—Cedar Tree, x̌əpay'ac

The cedar tree is well known throughout Indian Country. This is a sacred tree to our people due to its ability to lift people up. Every part of the tree can be used and is still used to sustain our lives.

Cultural

Overview

The cultural quadrant represents the well-being of a Native person. This includes personal basic needs being met like food security, shelter, clothing, and family connections. Traditionally, families were very close. Our people lived in Longhouses together with multiple families. Women typically kept their children with them while going about their daily routines. The Native family units were the first teachers to children—parents, uncles, aunties, grandparents all raised the children together to teach them various skills. Such as hunting, fishing, weaving, cooking, gathering, sewing, speaking the language, learning other dialects, and creating tools to use for daily life, as well as art creations.

"You need to keep encouraging children and making them know what they do is important. Just living their life is important. You don't need to accomplish anything—just living and doing what you're doing is enough. Don't let people hurt your confidence by telling you that you should do this or that, or, you can't do this or that. Take it with a grain of salt and keep pushing yourself, doing what you want to do" (Dr. Willard Bill Sr. qtd. in D. Bill 2012).

Impacts

Cultural well-being was dismantled by taking away land, housing, access to traditional foods, religious practices, and overall safety. The underlying theme was creating a sense of isolation.

Healing

Traditional ways to take care of this part is by being with other people, developing healthy friendships, maintaining familial ties, and attending tribal gatherings, participating in community events. Learning how to speak your Native language, how to weave baskets, create art, gather, and make plant medicine, hunt and fish, make a drum, all of these things can be done at any age—it is never too late. It is just as valuable for adults to receive these types of opportunities as it is for our children. These cultural activities can increase someone's sense of cultural belonging and self-esteem.

Plant Ally—Hawthorn Tree, čibadac

Hawthorn flowers and berries are powerful heart medicine capable of supporting us through times when we are experiencing grief. It helps mend heartbreak and helps us to move forward. Taking care of our hearts is integral to maintaining our cultural health. This helps us ensure we are conducting our lives in a good way—with a good heart.

The Sacred Circle Team

Dr. Willard Bill Sr., Muckleshoot

Dr. Willard E. Bill Sr. began his teaching career began in the Auburn School District, where he taught middle school, coached football and track, and served as a home visitor to the children of the Muckleshoot Tribe. From Auburn, Willard moved to Skagit Valley Junior College, then on to the University of Washington, where he earned his doctorate degree, continued working at Indian Heritage High School in Seattle Public Schools, became Director of Indian Education and Equity Education for the Office of Superintendent of Public Instruction, and then became a Dean at North Seattle Community College. Willard chose to spend the last portion of his professional career back with his people, the Muckleshoots. Willard served as an administrator and educator for several years, and then became a historian for the Muckleshoot Indian Tribe. Willard was instrumental in founding several organizations in Washington State: the United Indians of All Tribes, the Washington State Indian Education Association, and the Native American Higher Education Consortium. He served on many local and national boards, including the Advisory Board for the President of the University of Washington. He published many articles and contributed to the writing of several books.

Dr. Denise Bill, Muckleshoot

Denise Bill, Ed.D, is a Muckleshoot tribal citizen. She currently serves as the Executive Director of Adult and Higher Education for the Muckleshoot Tribal College. She received her doctoral degree from the University of Washington Seattle. Dr. Bill has been an educator in Washington state for over twenty years and has experience in K–12 teaching and administration,

Adult and Higher Education, and adjunct faculty at college/university levels. Her research and publications are centered in areas around Native American Educational Leaders in the Pacific Northwest and Working in Tribal Communities. Dr. Bill is a fierce advocate in education for Muckleshoot community members and has created various pathways in education for her tribal community.

Elise Bill-Gerrish, Muckleshoot

Elise Bill-Gerrish (Davis) is a Muckleshoot woman currently working as a Muckleshoot Language Teacher to help revitalize the Southern Lushootseed Language, the language of her ancestors. Her proudest achievement is being a mother to her daughter, Lily Hope, who is often by her side while speaking their Native language and working with traditional plants. Elise graduated from Antioch University Seattle in 2014 with a BA in Leadership and Organizational Studies. Her research during that time inspired a lifelong passion for social justice by advocating for holistic healing in all of its forms. She believes that it is essential to address historical trauma in Native communities in order to move forward in a "good way."

References

Bill, D. 2012. "Native American Educational Leaders in the Pacific Northwest." PhD diss., University of Washington, Seattle. Washington University Libraries.

Bill, W. 1987. "Breaking the Sacred Circle." Olympia, WA: publisher unknown.

Duran, E., and B. Duran. 1995. *Native American Postcolonial Psychology*. State University of New York Press, Albany.

Minthorn, Robin Zape-tah-hol-ah, Michelle Montgomery, and Denise Bill. 2021. "Reclaiming Emotions: Re-Unlearning and Re-Learning Discourses of Healing in a Tribally Placed Doctoral Cohort." *Genealogy* (Basel) 5 (1). Basel: MDPI AG: 24. https://doi.org/10.3390/genealogy5010024.

5

Art, Science, and K–12 Outreach / Education

THAYNE YAZZIE

Introduction

My name is Thayne Yazzie, and I am the Science, Technology, Engineering, and Math (STEM) Education Outreach Coordinator for the Salish Sea Research Center (SSRC) at Northwest Indian College (NWIC). Over the course of four years, I have developed, implemented, and facilitated science education materials for PreK–12 students throughout Washington State. These educational materials include topics such as ecological food webs, ocean acidification, harmful algal blooms, place-based science, and Indigenous knowledge. For this chapter, I would like to share with you the artwork I have created to teach K–12 students about environmental science through an Indigenous perspective.

Art and Design

One of the first projects I created was a logo for the SSRC. With influences from local Indigenous art and design, I was determined to create a logo that represented the values, cultural influences, and diversity found at NWIC

https://doi.org/10.5876/9781646425105.c005

FIGURE 5.1. *Salish Sea Research Center logo first draft*. By T. Yazzie, 2018, pencil on paper.

FIGURE 5.2. *Design elements for Salish Sea Research Center logo*. By T. Yazzie, 2018, pen on paper.

and the SSRC. Because research projects are always changing and evolving, I believed the logo should represent a diverse collection of animal species through the Salish Sea ecosystem. Thus, various revisions and new drawings were created to reflect on the animals and species found specific to the Salish Sea region.

Figure 5.1 is an initial first draft of the design for the SSRC logo. This design includes an orca, various plankton, and some shellfish. Within the orca design there are fish, camas, and various symbols found throughout Coast Salish artworks. My goal for this logo was to include artwork that was not particular to a single tribe. Instead, I wanted the design to be ambiguous with hints of various Coast Salish art styles. With over 125 Indigenous Tribes represented through NWIC's academic programs, I felt this was important to be inclusive of all Indigenous people.

Figure 5.2 is a rough sketch of additional design elements to be included in the final logo. Portrayed in this sketch are a variety of animals such as a jellyfish, phytoplankton, zooplankton, a porpoise, salmon, krill, a Dungeness crab, a whale, an eagle, and shellfish. An anchor was included to represent the technological uses and impacts within our scientific environmental endeavors.

In the final logo design (figure 5.3), I streamlined the illustration of the orca whale and combined it with various elements of the previous sketches. The final design comprises a complete food web along with an intertidal zone to represent the research facilitated at the SSRC. This design is now embedded and represents the SSRC and is recognized as an inclusive symbol for the work that the SSRC completes.

FIGURE 5.3. *Salish Sea Research Center Logo.* By T. Yazzie, 2019, digital media.

Food Webs and Harmful Algae

In developing STEM education activities and materials for students, I wanted to include species that were from the Pacific Northwest. While there are many K–12 educational materials available in regard to marine ecology, there are rarely materials dedicated to specific places or ecosystems. For instance, generic K–12 ecology materials include animals species that are usually most recognizable throughout the world (sharks, sea turtles, etc.). However, I felt that it was important to include animals from our student's own backyards.

The food web map in figure 5.4 depicts a place-based foodweb and how energy transfers throughout various trophic levels of animals species in the Salish Sea. Additionally, this piece includes animal species that are central to the research at the SSRC. These research topics include longfin smelt population dynamics, toxins in shellfish, and harmful algal blooms. Additionally, this diagram demonstrates how algal bloom species (*Pseudo-nitzschia, Alexandrium*) are introduced into the local foodweb.

COVID-19 Internship and Outreach

In March 2020, Northwest Indian College and the Salish Sea Research Center had to adopt to a new environment of online learning. While this presented

FIGURE 5.4. *Salish Sea Food Web Map*. By T. Yazzie, Digital Interactive Media.

many challenges, long-distance learning also presented a variety of opportunities, such as increasing capacity for students who could not have been physically present on campus. Students who participated in the 2020 Internships were able to do so in the comfort of their own home, and the SSRC was able to provide opportunities to students who had obligations in places other than Bellingham, Washington. Over the course of this long-distance-learning process, I created a variety of educational materials and artworks that I have used as resources for K–12 students to learn about important environmental science topics. Throughout the SSRC Summer Internship Program, I helped students design, develop, and implement their own interdisciplinary STEAM (inclusion) projects on place-based science topics. For example, students produced comic books on medicinal plants, video narrations of the local river system, STEM drawing activities for young students, and final presentations shared at the end of the summer internship.

For the next part of chapter, I will share some activities and the artwork I created both for the Summer 2020/21 internships and for K–12 Outreach.

An online activity that I felt was a great success was video tutorial *How to Draw a Salmon*. This activity (figure 5.5) was designed for college internships

FIGURE 5.5. *How to Draw a Salmon.* By T. Yazzie, Video Animation.

and tailored for K–12 students, with anticipation that the undergraduates could lead this tutorial for younger students. This video tutorial showed participates how to draw the anatomy of an adult salmon including details such as the gills, the lateral line, and fins (caudal fin, dorsal fins, pectoral fins). For this specific drawing I included the adipose fin to help students identify wild salmon, as the adipose fin is usually cut off when raised in a hatchery.

After the salmon anatomy is drawn, salmon habitat components are added (figure 5.6). This includes everything from oxygen (bubbles); to carbon in the form of rocks, which is necessary for salmon egg nests known as Redds; to other important habitat species such as eelgrass and food sources such as plankton. In our K–12 outreach, we focus on teaching the "C's" for healthy salmon water habitat (i.e., cold water, clear water, clean water, connected waters such as deltas and river systems, and complex water systems that include various plant life and other important animal species).

After drawing all of these habitat components, students finish their artwork by drawing the life cycle of the salmon below the adult salmon. The life-cycle drawing portion included salmon eggs, alevin, fry, and smolt (figure 5.7).

FIGURE 5.6. *Salmon Habitat Drawing*. By T. Yazzie, Video Animation.

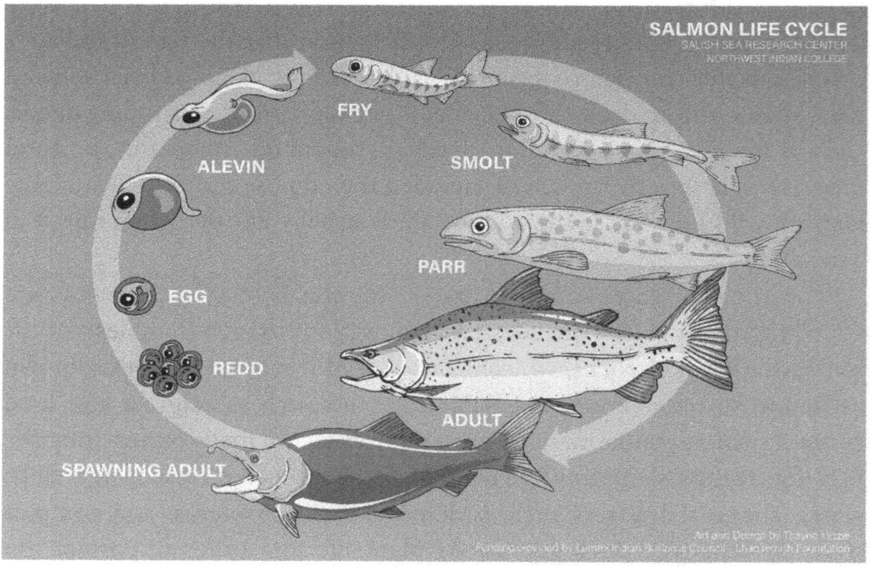

FIGURE 5.7. *Salmon Life Cycle*. By T. Yazzie, Digital Media Illustration.

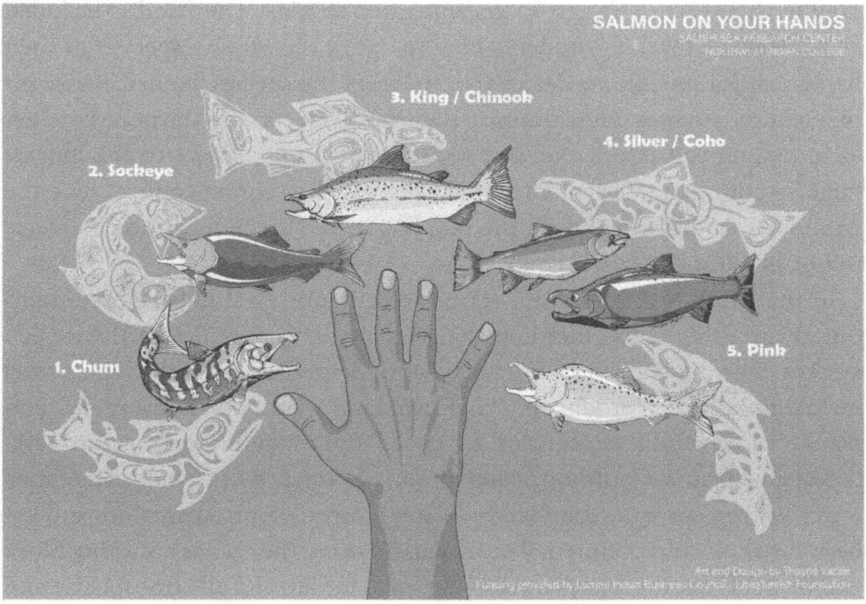

FIGURE 5.8. *Salmon On Your Hands*. By T. Yazzie, Digital Media Illustration.

In summary, the Salmon Drawing activity demonstrates the SSRC's commitment to providing place-based and culturally responsive outreach and education through a hands-on and STEAM (art)–inspired project.

In partnership with the Lummi Indian Business Council's Lhaq'temish Foundation, I developed multimedia projects for K–12 students. These multimedia projects included artwork to support an online Salmon-In-The-Classroom livestream. Before the COVID-19 pandemic, Lummi Natural Resources and the SSRC collaborated on raising salmon in the classroom at Lummi Nation School. Aquariums were set up in second- and fourth-grade classrooms, and students were able to observe salmon grow from eggs into alevins and eventually be released as young fry. When COVID-19 stopped in-class activities, I began raising salmon at the SSRC lab and placed a camera on the aquarium to document the process and livestream it over YouTube and Facebook over the course of several months.

The artwork in figure 5.8 was created to go along with the virtual Salmon-In-the-Classroom project. All five salmon species are represented (Chum, Sockeye, King/Chinook, Silver/Coho, and Pink) along with a unique Coast Salish design to go with each species. The hand is included as a means of teaching students how to count the salmon species on their hands using a mnemonic device to remember the species' names. For example, "chum" rhymes with "thumb"; sockeye connects with the pointer finger as in poking someone's eye; chinook/king salmon connect to the longest finger on our hand, the middle finger; silver/coho salmon connect with the common wedding ring finger, the ring finger; and the pink salmon connects to our smallest finger, the pinky.

In the Salish Sea Food Web art piece in figure 5.9, I illustrate the salmon's relationship with other important species in the Pacific Northwest ecosystem. Starting with the Sun, the artwork demonstrates each trophic level including primary producers (phytoplankton), primary consumers (zooplankton), second-level consumers (small fish / longfin smelt), third-level tertiary consumers (salmon), apex predators (orca whale), and decomposers. This concept is the foundation of my K–12 outreach curriculum and is a basis for all my environmental outreach. By using the Sun as a starting block and the fact that the Sun is the driving force for life and all atmospheric and oceanic processes on earth, I am able to connect simple scientific topics (i.e., foodwebs) to more challenging scientific topics such as ocean acidification, climate change, and human impacts on the environment.

Hozho Nahasdlii and The Energy Pyramid (figure 5.10) is a painting I created that is intended to further explore my understanding of complex ecosystems and incorporate my own Indigenous perspective. The term *Hozho Nahasdlii* is a closing prayer and philosophy for the Diné people. It means to *live in balance; spiritually, mentally, and emotionally*, and some have even stated it to mean *walk in beauty*. This artwork represents the beauty and balance found in nature, particularly, the beauty of the marine ecosystem. Included in this artwork are an orca, an eagle, salmon, an octopus, jellyfish, shellfish, bull kelp, eelgrass, and various plankton. At the center of the painting, a red salmon egg represents the beginning of the cycle of life. Throughout the painting, salmon eggs are dispersed through the crashing waves. In the middle-top right of the painting, young salmon fry hide between the leaves of eelgrass. The overall shape of the triangle represents the connection between mind, body, and spirit. Additionally, the triangle shape represents a trophic pyramid and is used to represent the flow of energy within a food web. Surrounding the "energy pyramid," black negative space represents mystery, uncertainty,

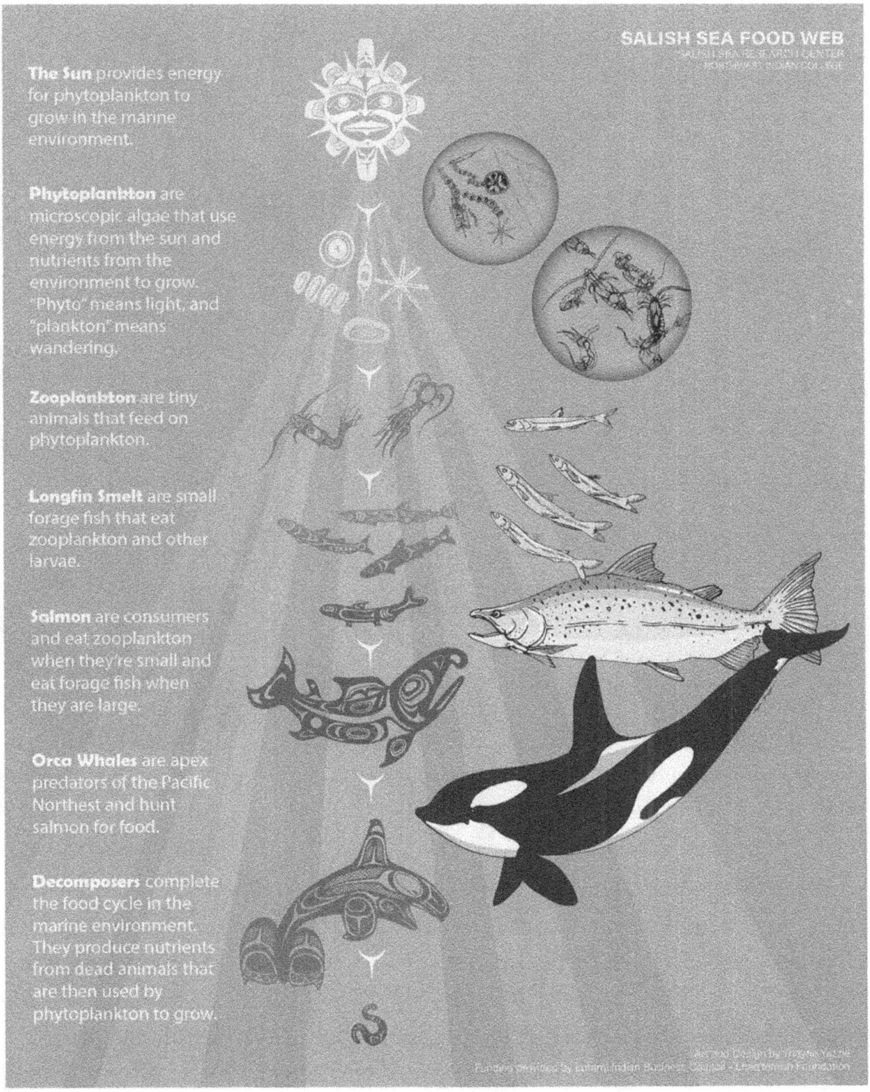

FIGURE 5.9. *Salish Sea Food Web*. By T. Yazzie, Digital Media Illustration.

and the unknown. In regard to science, this black space represents all of the questions yet to uncover, discover, and answer and the knowledge still left unknown. In Diné philosophy, understanding the interconnectedness of all

FIGURE 5.10. *Hozho Nahasdlii and The Energy Pyramid.* By T. Yazzie, painting, acrylic on canvas.

of these things helps Diné people live a life through *Hozho* (i.e., actions and thoughts based in love, compassion, faith, and well-being).

As an artist and a STEM educator, it is my hope that in an ever-growing vast and expanding universe of unknowable and limitless possibilities, science and art become a tool for future generations. As an Indigenous scientist, it is my hope that we may utilize the sacred teachings found in nature so that we may further learn to coexist with our natural sounds and better understand what it means to be human. With that said, I would like to conclude my chapter with a poem I wrote after a ceremony with my family.

Shine Bright

by Thayne Yazzie

Looking up into the stars, my sister said,
"Isn't it weird that people make wishes on stars
when so many stars are actually burnt out and dead?"
and I said, "oh Kelly, that's dreadful. I never thought of it that way."
But as the drumbeat echoed throughout the night,
I thought more about what she said.

The ceremony continued reverent and sincere
with family members and friends
sharing one fire and a song beneath the tipi's skin.
And as I stood outside that morning
I observed an electric blue world above, and
it occurred to me—we should all be like stars.
Shine bright and be bold
with all the kindness we can give, so that
when we meet our final resting bed
our souls will shine bright,
enough to inspire wishes, far beyond our death.

6

Climate Justice in Undergraduate Medical Curriculum

A First Step

GEORGINA CAMPELIA AND MICHELLE MONTGOMERY

The responsibility to counteract compounding environmental inequities and work toward environmental justice is an increasingly pressing issue. Once absent or marginalized in medical education, competencies now include understanding connections between environmental factors and health equity, as well as building skills to counteract these inequities in clinical practice (Association 2022). Medical students, faculty, and connected communities continue to press for greater inclusion of climate justice and planetary health in medical education. In the University of Washington School of Medicine (UWSOM), medical students initiated the Planetary Health Report Card project in 2020 (https://phreportcard.org/). Their work motivated space in an early clinical block, "Infections and Immunity," for a deeper dive into climate justice. Once learning about this space, conversations began between Georgina Campelia (director of the ethics curriculum at UWSOM), Michelle Montgomery (expert in climate justice), and Sarah Murphy (family physician and site lead in Anchorage, Alaska). Together, we developed a two-hour in-person session for medical students that is grounded in Indigenous

https://doi.org/10.5876/9781646425105.c006

knowledges and values, introduces key concepts of climate justice and environmental inequalities relating to infectious disease, and creates opportunity for students to practice connecting with each other emotionally on these challenging issues.

Session Development: Asynchronous Pre-session Content

With no predefined map for how to incorporate either Euro-Christian or Indigenous Knowledges and practices related to climate justice, there is opportunity for creativity and collaboration to build better practices in healthcare. While there is some discussion internationally about including climate change, climate justice, and planetary health in core medical curriculum, most scholars or curriculum developers do not incorporate Indigenous Knowledges (Gómez 2013; Walpole, Mortimer et al. 2015; Walpole, Barna et al. 2019). For our group, this meant centering the voices of communities who are most impacted by environmental injustices but categorically excluded from conversations about change. While lessons from climate science were incorporated, it was Indigenous voices and values that were centered through pre-session videos and texts, as well as in-person discussion. Materials were both created by Indigenous leaders on climate justice and centered the knowledges and values of Indigenous communities. As teachers we hoped to open a dialogue with first-year medical students about the meaning of taking responsibility as future physicians in the context of environmental or place-based relationships.

One of the early foundational blocks for medical students at UWSOM is "Infections & Immunity," which created an opportunity to introduce climate change curriculum partly through the lens of this block.

Session Title: "Justice, Climate Change and Infectious Disease"
Session Pre-class Time: Two Hours
Session In-person Time: Two Hours
Session Learning Objectives:

1. Identify key connections between climate change, environmental inequalities, and vector-borne, food-borne, and water-borne diseases.
2. Discuss key values and principles of justice for responding to environmental inequalities.

The title and objectives connect the Infections & Immunity block with environmental inequalities, climate science, and Indigenous perspectives on relationship to place and community. Pre-session content and in-session discussion question the dichotomy between healing and curing. Overall, the session emphasizes how the responsibility to heal through the promotion of justice in healthcare depends on understanding different relationships to place.

Pre-session Materials

In preparation for in-person discussion, students engage with an introduction to climate science as well as multiple videos and texts that embed Indigenous Knowledges in relationship to specific lands, cultures, and communities to counteract the Euro-Christian fabrication of a static pan-Indigenous framework (Montgomery and Blanchard 2021). Students begin with an introductory video created by Dr. Sarah Murphy on how climate change and environmental inequalities relate to vector-borne, food-borne, and water-borne diseases and directly impact health and well-being. Students then read Howard Frumkin's "Hope, Health and the Climate Crisis" (2022) to center the emotional content of the topic and offer reason for hope in the context of the severity of the crisis. This is followed by a TEDx Talk by Sheila Watt-Cloutier (2016), who speaks to the intimate connection between the trauma of Aboriginal peoples and the deterioration of the global climate, connecting historical and contemporary realities. The students then read the essay "Testing Justice: New Ways to Address Environmental Inequalities" by Michelle Montgomery and Paulette Blanchard (2021), which identifies a framework of key values of justice to guide addressing, counteracting, and preventing environmental inequalities. Finally, students engage with a recorded talk by Dr. Daniel Wildcat (2021), "Climate of Community: Dan Wildcat, Author and Activist," which focuses on the hope and beauty of centering climate in community and relationships to place.

In-person Session Experience

With this work to build foundational knowledge on environmental inequalities and climate science through the expertise of Indigenous voices and communities, students are prepared to come together in conversation. The in-person session purposefully begins with emotional connection and critical thinking by asking students to join small groups with the following discussion prompts:

1. Introduce yourselves by sharing your emotional/spiritual connection to place or disconnection to place (e.g., connection to land, connection to childhood or family place, displacement in the pandemic, displacement in fires, etc.).
2. What does acknowledging the land or land acknowledgment mean to you?
3. From what you learned in the pre-class material or from your personal experience, how is climate change or are environmental inequalities disruptive of your connection to place?
4. What does it mean to be a healer in connection to place?
5. How do you imagine or practice staying true to yourself and to place as you embark on this journey as a healer?

After sharing their discussions in the larger group, the facilitator asks how the pre-session material impacted the students and then reinforces some key concepts:

a. Climate Change
b. Environmental Inequality/Inequity
c. Climate Justice
d. Curing vs. Healing (play min 47:11–50:08 https://www.youtube.com/watch?v=WVn2SW8_Jf8)

Following these definitions and discussion, students return to small groups to consider case-based representations of situations they may encounter in clinical practice as physicians. With each case, they are asked:

1. What climate justice issues are present in this case?
2. As a healthcare professional, how do you understand the difference between curing and healing in this case? How are they different or how do they overlap?
3. What does climate justice look like in this context for this patient? Consider:
   a. Equity responds to . . .

   b. Inclusion asks . . .
   c. Justice responds . . .
   d. Diversity asks . . .
4. How can healthcare professionals address healing, or learn to address healing with our patients?

These questions are meant to support mindfulness, humility, and grace, encouraging students to recognize the rich understanding of Indigenous people as the first to experience climate change and who feel it the deepest given their close relationships with the land/water and other parts of the natural world. Finally, students return to the large group and consider what they have learned in the session through an Indigenous lens:

1. How are climate change or environmental inequalities disruptive of your connection to place?
2. Has your understanding of your relationship with place changed in the course of this session?
3. What does it mean to be a healer in connection to place?
4. How do you imagine or practice staying true to yourself and to place as you embark on this journey as a healer?
5. What questions remain for you at this point that we could answer here or come back to in future sessions?

These questions center connection to place, relationships, and healing, thus decolonizing, expanding, and reimagining the responsibilities of future physician-healers. For Indigenous medical students, this practice may reinforce values and knowledge with which they are already familiar, offering recognition of knowledges and values that they are often pressured to abandon in medical education. For other students, this session offers expanded ways of thinking, new skills to build in connection with colleagues, patients, and families.

Sessions at UWSOM are typically facilitated differently across the Washington, Wyoming, Alaska, Montana, Idaho (WWAMI) region. Dr. Montgomery facilitated the session for students in Seattle. In this session, she focused on defining place-based knowledges and the difference between curing and healing, and directed students toward justice as eco-mindfulness.

Grounding Eco-mindfulness in Climate Justice Curricula

As we continue to witness the realities of climate justice, students were reminded to always ask themselves—How do they bring their whole selves while simultaneously acknowledging the emotional journey of knowledge? How do we invite each other into a conversation with humility and grace? Mindfulness is shaped by our identities as forever students and guided by our actions. We should engage in ways that hold deep commitments to serving underserved and underrepresented communities through decolonizing the act of curing versus healing. Aspire to be an equity-minded bidirectional student and empowering decolonizer to redefine best practices for human health. Knowledge should be a form of healing through a lens to enact accountability and responsibility for difficult, complex problems. Regardless of discipline, curricula must find ways to support the learning and sharing of knowledges, particularly in adaptation to the changing climate.

When we acknowledge the reciprocity of relationships, there is a gentle reminder: *we* are all authors responsible for writing the narratives of memories for future generations. We must ask ourselves, Who will remain a part of the story? Community conversations create an environment where traditional knowledge is viewed as having a moral value, experienced, and integrated into the lives of participants. Stories connected to place and identity illustrate the importance of cultural traditions and knowledge of Indigenous communities; yet, as we move forward, there are thousands of stories that remain untold. Regardless of discipline, universities and faculty must find ways to support the learning and sharing of traditional knowledge, particularly how the connection between changes in the climate and impacts on people's physical, mental, and community health. Dr. Wildcat reminds us, "In North America many Indigenous traditions tell us that reality is more than just facts and figures collected so that humankind might wisely use resources. Rather, to know 'it'—really—requires respect for the relationships and relatives that constitute the complex web of life" (Wildcat 2009, 9). Although people's understanding and knowledge of climate change can increase by experiencing the effects directly, we must practice calling each other into safe conversations with grace and humility to build resilience that is essential to address the physical and emotional health impacts of climate change.

While no one is safe from the risks of the unfolding climate crisis, it is important to provide an opportunity to engage in emotional conversations about justice. From this lens, justice is a freedom to practice love by acknowledging how our emotions play a key role in recognizing patterns to decolonize our minds. As bell hooks (2008) poetically states, "The moment we choose to love, we begin to move against domination, against oppression. The moment we choose to love we begin to move towards freedom, to act in ways that liberate ourselves and others. That action is the testimony of love as the practice of freedom" (297). By engaging and thinking critically through emotional conversations, we begin to create a transformation to move beyond who defines for whom the meaning of justice or caring. bell hooks continues to guide us by sharing that "care is a dimension of love, but simply giving care does not mean we are loving" (2000, 39). With the quest of agency and identity, it is important to assist personal relationships and the ways in which people interact in communities and with each being affected by a changing climate.

Conclusion

Ultimately, the session opens a dialogue that is new to standard undergraduate medical school curriculum in two ways. First, it decolonizes core curriculum by centering Indigenous voices and knowledges. Second, it expands core curriculum on health equity and healthcare justice by addressing environmental inequalities and planetary health. Beyond this, we found that the session was healing for students, transforming a competitive medical school environment into a space for emotional connection and reflection on connection to place. In this way, the session structurally modeled the material content, demonstrating the power of healing through eco-mindfulness.

Acknowledgments. We are grateful to the student advocacy at the University of Washington School of Medicine, including Sonja France, Summer Lawson, Megan Meyer, Jordan Nichols, and Marley Realing for their critical advocacy.

References

Association of American Medical Colleges. 2022. "Diversity, Equity, and Inclusion Competencies across the Learning Continuum." In *AAMC New and Emerging Areas in Medicine Series*. Washington, DC: Association of American Medical Colleges.

Frumkin, H. 2022. "Hope, Health, and the Climate Crisis." *Journal of Climate Change and Health* 5 (February): 100115.

Gómez, A., S. Balsari, J. Nusbaum, A. Heerboth, and J. Lemery. 2013. "Perspective: Environment, Biodiversity, and the Education of the Physician of the Future." *Academic Medicine* 88 (2): 168–172.

hooks, bell. 2008. *Outlaw Culture: Resisting Representations*. New York: Routledge Classics.

hooks, bell. 2000. *All About Love*. New York: William Marrow and Company.

Montgomery, M., and P. Blanchard. 2021. "Testing Justice: New Ways to Address Environmental Inequalities." *Solutions: Perspectives*. https://www.resilience.org/stories/2022-02-17/testing-justice-new-ways-to-address-environmental-inequalities/.

Walpole, S. C., S. Barna, J. Richardson, and H. A. Rother. 2019. "Sustainable Healthcare Education: Integrating Planetary Health into Clinical Education." *Lancet Planet Health* 3 (January): e6–7.

Walpole, S. C., F. Mortimer, A. Inman, I. Braithwaite, and T. Thompson. 2015. "Exploring Emerging Learning Needs: A UK-wide Consultation on Environmental Sustainability Learning Objectives for Medical Education." *International Journal of Medical Education* 6 (December 24): 191–200.

Watt-Cloutier, S. 2016. *Human Trauma and Climate Trauma as One*. YouTube video, 15:43. September. TEDxYYC. https://www.youtube.com/watch?v=5nn-awZbMVo.

Wildcat, D. R. *Climate of Community: Dan Wildcat, Author and Activist*. YouTube video, 47:00. March 1. https://www.youtube.com/watch?v=R2kES5Up7Qw.

Wildcat, Daniel R. 2009. *Red Alert! Saving the Planet with Indigenous Knowledge*. Golden, CO: Fulcrum.

7

The Journey of a Muckleshoot Language Teacher

dxʷsgʷalčšid ti bəqəlšułucid kʷi šəgʷł

ELISE BILL-GERRISH

sləx̌il, Elise Bill Gerrish tsi dsdaʔ. bəqəlšułabš čəd. dxʷsgʷalčšid čəd ʔə tə bəqəlšułucid. Brent Davis ti dsč̓istxʷ. Lily tsi dbədəʔčəł. bədəʔ čəd ʔə tsi Denise Bill yəxʷ ti Dennis Gerrish. ʔibac čəd ʔə ti tuWillard Bill Sr. yəxʷ tsi tuMary Ann Bill. sč̓abiqʷ čəd ʔə tsi tuIola Bill Lobehan yəxʷ ti tuLyman Willard Bill. ʔəkʷyiqʷ čəd ʔə ti tuAugust Bill yəxʷ tsi tuClara Siddle, yəxʷ ti tuGeorge Lobehan yəxʷ tsi tuAnnie Jack.

Good day, my name is Elise Bill-Gerrish. I am a Muckleshoot Tribal Member and a Muckleshoot Language Teacher. My husband is Brent Davis, and we have a daughter, Lily Hope Davis. I am the child of Denise Bill and Dennis Gerrish. I am the grandchild of the late Willard Bill Sr. and the late Mary Ann Bill. I am the great-grandchild of the late Iola Bill Lobehan and the late Lyman Willard Bill. I am the great-great-grandchild of the late August Bill and the late Clara Siddle, the late George Lobehan, and the late Annie Jack (figure 7.1).

My family and I primarily come from the villages of Stuck, Burns Creek, Little Herring House Crossing Over Place, and Katilbc at the south end of

https://doi.org/10.5876/9781646425105.c007

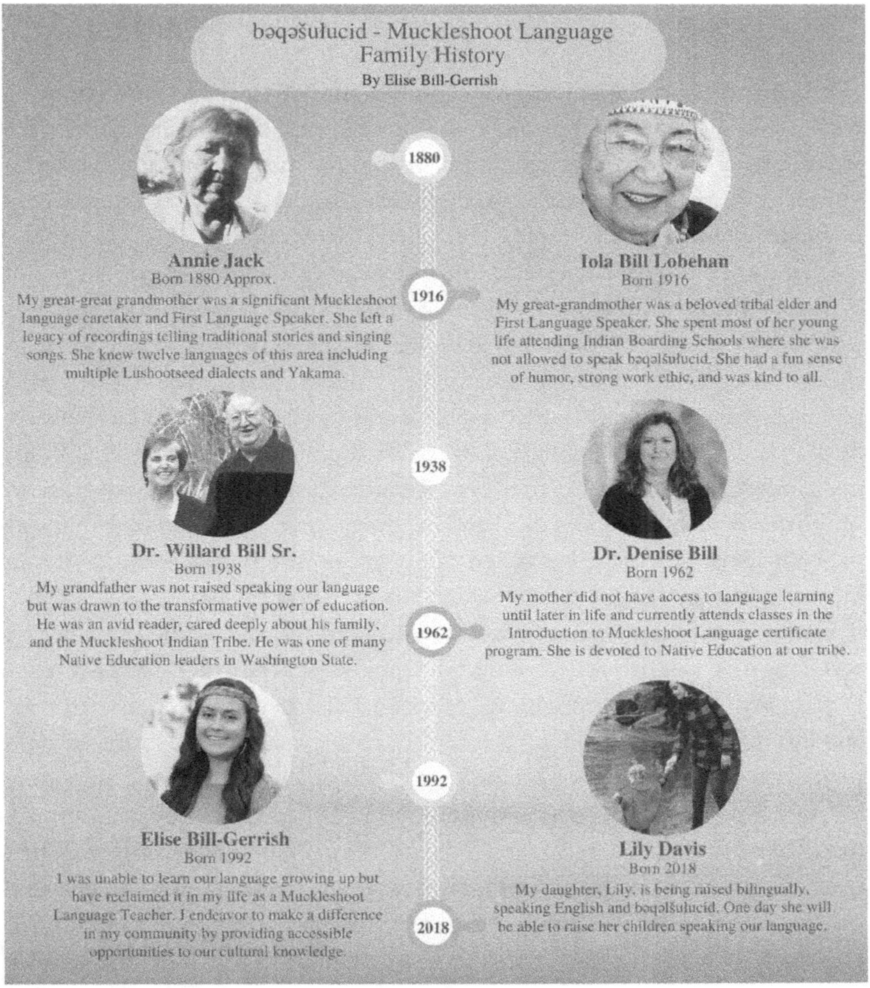

FIGURE 7.1. Muckleshoot language family history timeline

Lake Washington. While my ancestors came from a wide array of villages, they settled at Muckleshoot because of prominent familial ties. All these villages are high class, as is typical of Muckleshoot families. High class has nothing to do with money but with how one conducts oneself. Attributes of high class would be qualities like people who are generous, people who are kind, cultural knowledge keepers and teachers, people who encourage others, people who show leadership, and people who pay attention to those in need.

It is protocol in my culture to introduce myself to those I am speaking with, especially in formal settings. In this chapter, I plan to share about my journey as a language teacher, and how that journey has influenced me to approach Native/Indigenous language learning, and how to document a new part of Indigenous peoples' collective history taking place.

There is a shared Native teaching that ancestral languages are alive and always with us; they have a way of finding people. I have witnessed this teaching come to fruition in my own life and become part of my story. In the spring of 2017, I was twenty-four years old when I applied for an open language apprentice position at my tribe and received the job. I have always been interested in our language, but I felt hesitant to apply at first. Thankfully, my mother encouraged me to move forward by reminding me how great an opportunity this was. Looking back on everything, I can see that this was no coincidence how the language found me at the perfect time. I was in between jobs, no longer in school, and ready to find my path.

I studied our language as an apprentice for three and a half years before receiving the title of Muckleshoot Language Teacher in December 2020. During my time as an apprentice, I received a number of direct instructional lessons, I was introduced to basic resources, pushed into studying independently, and ultimately becoming my own teacher. It was a challenging journey, but I found support from the ladies I worked with; they were apprentices too who had started eight months before me and became certified teachers. Because this study was intensely self-driven, I developed a genuine love for our language, *bəqəlšułucid* the Muckleshoot Language. bəqəlšułucid is an incredibly sophisticated oral language that holds much of our peoples' history. Our language, like other Indigenous languages, has a unique ability to connect us with our ancestors, to connect us with the natural world, and it gives us a glimpse into what life was like for our people long ago and how they viewed the world around them.

Three years into my language apprenticeship, the Covid-19 pandemic began. In the middle of March 2020, our entire tribe suddenly closed for what we thought might only be a few weeks. Little did we know the amount of change the next few years would hold for us all. In the beginning, employees at our tribe were furloughed for several months and had to file for unemployment. At the end of summer, some of us received news that we would keep our jobs and we would work from home for the time being. We ended up working from home until June 2021. This pandemic affected the globe in a substantial number of ways. It ripped us out of our comfort zones and forced us to adapt to new living conditions. I respectfully acknowledge the layers of loss we collectively experienced during this time. Most of us are aware of the negative effects of this pandemic, but it is important to shed light on the good that arose from this time as well.

Despite the challenges, I loved working from home! I no longer had to worry about two hours of daily commute, and I could efficiently focus my energy into my work. I was able to study for teacher testing, take my tests, and complete everything necessary to complete the teacher certification process. The Covid-19 pandemic provided me many opportunities: (1) I was honored to collaborate with the Muckleshoot Language Department, the Muckleshoot Culture Department, and Highline School District on a language grant. Through this project I wrote and published a bilingual children's book, *Nature Adventures with Lily*, based on taking my daughter to the beach; one of our favorite nature adventures. (2) I took a Cinematography certificate program at the Muckleshoot Tribal College in the fall of 2020 which led to being able to personally create twelve films for our community. (3) I was a member of Native Action Network's Legacy of Leadership program. My team and I created a traditional foods educational program that provided thirty traditional meal kits to Native families living in Washington State. We also led three classes discussing the importance of traditional plants and foods in our lives. (4) Most important, I was able to spend precious time with my daughter. Overall, I had noticeably less stress while working from home. I was one of countless people across the world who thrived while working from home during the pandemic. A recent Pew Research Center study collected data about changing work conditions; "For those who have made the switch to telework, their work lives have changed in some significant ways. On the plus side, most (64%) of those who are now working from home at least some of the time but rarely or never did before the pandemic say it's easier now for them to balance work with their personal life" (Parker, Horowitz, and Minkin 2022).

Eventually tribal employees were informed that we would be returning to work in person at the end of June 2021 and that working from home was no longer an option. I started brainstorming . . . as I make this transition back to working in person, what can I focus my efforts on to make the most difference? After much consideration, I developed a plan with my supervisor's support to launch a higher education certificate program. A program specifically for adult Muckleshoot Tribal and community members to learn/continue learning the Muckleshoot Language. I relied on my leadership and organizational skills to design and manage this program, create the necessary curriculum, and teach all classes as effectively as possible.

As of October 2022, Muckleshoot has over approximately 3,000 enrolled tribal members. For many years, the adult population of our tribe has not had as much access to language learning opportunities as we would wish. Like so many other tribes, language learning is something we are continually trying to increase opportunities for across the board. When I was first hired, I voiced that I am most passionate about teaching adults in higher education and echoed this passion regularly throughout my years in service to our Muckleshoot Language. My grandfather, the late Willard Bill Sr., was a prominent Native educator in Washington State and he used to say, "There are no throw away Muckleshoots." He meant that all our Muckleshoot people are of value and deserve a chance. This philosophy is something I stand by and is part of why I advocate for language services be accessible to our adult and elders population. Tribal adults and elders want to connect to their language and culture now more than ever.

The certificate program, Introduction to Muckleshoot Language, launched in the summer of 2021. We began by offering nine classes per week, and the program ran for two months. Thirty-one tribal and community members signed up and received fifty-eight total hours of Muckleshoot Language learning. In our classes, we practiced the alphabet, conversational language, traditional plant names, seasons, days of the week, months of the year, canoe journey protocol, lyrics to community songs in our language, Lushootseed history, and so much more. Students had to complete twenty class hours to receive a certificate, but most students attended many more hours because they enjoyed it so much. All classes were available on Zoom, a popular distance-learning platform made popular during the pandemic, but we welcomed anyone who wished to attend in person. Due to safety concerns around rising Covid cases in our community, we did not have many students attending in person, so we eventually made the decision to offer only Zoom classes until things improved.

The summer program received such a positive response that leadership gave their blessing for me to run the program again for Fall Quarter. This time, 71 students signed up to receive 66 total hours of Muckleshoot Language learning, and 15 students graduated. The program was a hit once again! After Fall Quarter's success, I was given approval to lead the program again for Winter Quarter 2022. We had 54 classes, 66 total students, and 20 graduates. In Spring Quarter 2022, we had 59 students in class, 54 classes, and 21 graduates. With each season, the program continued to positively impact and engage our community. This certificate program has run successfully for over a year now and provided our community with a total of 222 hours of Muckleshoot Language learning as of June 2022.

Something I found telling in the data was the number of returning students each quarter: 6 returning students in the fall, 29 in the winter, and 35 in the spring. The amount of returning students grew each quarter. Even though the content resembled previous quarters, these students returned to language classes because of how impactful the courses were for them. I share this story not to boast but to humbly invite our Indigenous relatives and allies to be witnesses to this incredible journey. This is not only a victory for me and my tribe but a victory for all Indigenous people. Our resilience to adapt with ever-changing living conditions demonstrates the strength of our people time and time again.

This is a contemporary approach to Native language learning and is the first of its kind at our tribe to utilize a distance-learning format. I found inspiration from online classes I attended with the Puyallup Language Department during my work from home time. Their team found a way to reach their tribal and community members from wherever they were to focus on speaking Southern Lushootseed. Our tribes are both part of the Southern Lushootseed Language, and our dialects are closely related. Being a part of the Zoom classes with Puyallup helped to show me a new, innovative path that could be taken with language learning, and I am thankful to them for this.

There is a common belief that language learning needs to be done in person to be successful. While that concept has merit, I respectfully offer the results from this past year—how this virtual learning program has demonstrated otherwise. My students' ages range from eighteen all the way into their eighties. Tribal members of all ages have expressed their appreciation and love for this program. A handful of students had never used Zoom prior to these classes but quickly got the hang of it. Now they are pros! Students consistently have their cameras on and turn their microphones on to participate in class and be present, just as if we were together in person. "The COVID-19 pandemic has engendered a newfound proliferation in resources for online education at all levels. If programs are designed specifically around decolonizing learning methodologies and prioritizing Indigenous perspectives, traditional Indigenous beliefs can be integrated into curriculums to preserve valuable cultural and historical views" (Toth 2022). Adults and elders have seemed to be searching during the pandemic for positive ways to connect to our language and culture. These are the generations who did not always have access to language due to historical traumas. They soak up every second of class time because it is precious to them. It brings us joy to speak our language and hear others speaking it. While in these classes we are in a safe, positive learning environment where we can fine-tune our speaking, learn new words and phrases, have a sense of community, share our stories, and not feel like we're under any pressure.

While the pandemic brought challenges, it also opened the door for a program like this to take place. It would have been difficult for a program like this to be approved if the circumstances were different, primarily because of the deep-rooted belief that language learning can only be taught face to face, in person. The data from this new method confirm that in our Muckleshoot community, having language classes available via Zoom has profoundly increased accessibility to language learning! Tribal members can attend class from wherever they live; as many students do not live or work on the reservation, they can join class while they are driving, attend while they are at work, wherever they happen to be. Students are carving time out of their busy lives to engage with our language because it brings them happiness, fulfillment, and intellectual stimulation and promotes a sense of cultural belonging. It is heartwarming to see how much my students love our language, bəqəlšuɬucid. "Reciprocity in language revitalization work means we cannot keep our languages alive alone. We know that our work must respect the legacy of traditions left to us by our ancestors and that it must be relevant to the communities in question and acknowledge their interconnectedness with the land" (Gardner 2012, 133–134).

As each quarter nears the halfway mark, I begin planning how to get the next quarter approved. How can I ensure our community continues to have access to these classes, and how do I demonstrate to leadership that this is a worthwhile cause? Knowing how fast things can change in tribal communities, I worry that something might happen, and our people could lose this program and this level of access to language learning. This motivates me to make each quarter better than the one before it by constantly refining my curriculum and approaches to increase engagement in classes. I am determined to make the time I have as a Muckleshoot Language Teacher count and stay grounded in the fact that no matter where life takes us, I will always be a dedicated caretaker of our language and culture.

Often people associate Native / Indigenous languages with the term "dying languages." "While they differ in setting, culture, and phonetics, one aspect that most dead Indigenous languages share is that they perished as a result of colonization and the subsequent rise of international languages. As Indigenous languages go extinct, so too do the culture and history that they carry with them" (Toth 2022). Language caretakers try to shift that mindset by sharing our narrative; our language has simply been sleeping, and it is waking up. After everything ancestral languages have been through, they have been in fragile condition for quite some time. One especially harmful impact on our languages was the introduction of Indian Boarding Schools. In these facilities, Native children were intentionally stripped of their cultural identities to assimilate into the new world by force. When they were caught speaking their Native languages, they were punished severely. When these children—survivors of Indian Boarding Schools—eventually grew up, they often chose not to teach their own children and grandchildren their ancestral language—in hopes that they would have a better life with less hardship and trauma. Lest we forget, innumerable children did not survive these institutions.

When reminded of this country's painful history, it is common to think of those children as being from a long time ago. That automatic disconnection can be dangerous. These stories and children are real and are not from long ago at all. This is the story of my family, like so many others. My great-grandmother Iola Bill Lobehan spent most of her young life in Indian Boarding Schools. When she entered the first school as a young child in approximately 1924, she did not speak any English and the adults in charge punished her for it by means of starvation. She relied on her cultural knowledge of traditional plants to survive. "She had a kind heart and a strong will," said Willard Bill of Seattle, the oldest of Mrs. Bill's three children (Tuinstra 2005).

Because my Grandma Iola's experiences, she ended up not teaching her children our Muckleshoot Language. Then her child, my grandfather, the late Willard Bill Sr., could not teach what he did not know and was unable to teach my mother, Dr. Denise Bill, our language. All these years later, I have been fortunate to experience this time of prosperity by working for our tribe's language program and reclaiming our ancestral language in my family. I am the first Muckleshoot Language speaker in my family since my great-grandmother Iola. I am also raising my daughter, Lily, to speak our language regularly and because of this, she will never know the pain of being disconnected from such a huge part of our identity as Indigenous people. My mother is one of the students in my classes and is finally able to learn her ancestral language. These are all healing parts of my family's story. Though my family's trauma regarding Indian Boarding Schools happened before I was born, I am directly connected to my great-grandma and other ancestors' experiences. Effects of profound trauma ripples down through the generations, which we now identify as intergenerational trauma. This can be defined as "The cumulative emotional and psychological wounding over one's lifetime and from generation to generation following loss of lives, land and vital aspects of culture" (Dr. Maria Yellow Horse Brave Heart qtd. in Native Hope 2022).

Finally, we are in a time where it is safe to speak our languages openly with each other. The individuals and systems who sought to "Kill the Indian, save the Man" (R. H. Pratt [1892]; Carlisle n.d.) failed. *didiˀɬ čəɬ; həliˀ čəɬa wələx̌ʷ!*—we are still here; we are alive and strong! We are healing the effects of intergenerational trauma one step at a time. I do not take this privilege for granted, and I pay my respects to those who came before me who were denied this opportunity. I hold space for the suffering that our people and our language have experienced and do everything in my power to advocate for healing in our communities. Witnessing the suffering happening in our communities—like our loved ones who are in the grasps of addiction—I can see how intergenerational trauma has a significant role in their lives. Instead of ignoring these people, we should hold out hope that one day they might also find healing through connection to our culture, to our language, and to the ways of our ancestors. We can show compassion and give them as many chances as it takes. If we conduct ourselves in a good way, with a good heart, and be high-class people, I have faith that every little bit we do adds up and this embodies our traditional values.

Native languages are a gift not to be taken lightly. We have a responsibility to care for our language and share it with those who will listen. An essential lesson that I share in my classes is that the Lushootseed Language comes from the land—it was given to us by the land. When listening to the sounds that make up our language, we can hear how they are actually the sounds of the earth. In the film *Huchoosedah: Traditions of the Heart*, beloved Upper Skagit elder the late Vi Hilbert said, "The sounds of the language originally came from the sound of the earth. I feel it would be a very sad day if no one tried to keep the language alive because without the language there is no culture" (New Canoe Media 2022). When we look closer at translations of our language, they are in relation to the earth—a perspective rooted in our connection to the natural world.

Indigenous language revitalization must be considered holistically to be successful. There are many interwoven parts shaping how we conduct ourselves as tribal members, language learners, and language teachers. It is a natural part of the process to feel uncertain or overwhelmed at times when trying to figure out how to orchestrate it all. By staying grounded in our cultural teachings, our history, and our reasons why, we can make great strides to revitalize our languages, utilizing a combination of past and contemporary methodologies.

In conclusion, I raise my hands up to give thanks to everyone who has been a steward of our language. First, to my ancestors and elders who kept our language alive and left this gift for us. To the ladies I have worked with, fellow Muckleshoot Language Teachers, for putting their love for the language into all that they do for our community. To my mother, for encouraging me to apply for this job and mentoring me throughout this journey. To my four-year-old daughter, Lily, for being the person I can speak the language with most and for teaching me the new words she has created in the language. Last, to all my students who have been part of this program. Without them, this program would not have been possible. Sharing the time together in our classes has been incredibly special to me. *ʔuk'ʷədiidəxʷ čəd dxʷʔal gʷəlaapu*, I am thankful for you all.

References

Carlisle Indian School Digital Resource Center. n.d. "'Kill the Indian in him, and save the man': R. H. Pratt on the Education of Native Americans." https://carlisleindian.dickinson.edu/teach/kill-indian-him-and-save-man-r-h-pratt-education-native-americans.

Gardner, Stelomethet Ethel B. 2012. *The Four R's of Leadership in Indigenous Language Revitalization in Living Indigenous Leadership: Native Narratives on Building Strong Communities*. Edited by Kenny, Carolyn, and Tina Ngaroimata Fraser. Vancouver: UBC Press.

Native Hope. 2022. "How Trauma Gets Passed Down through Generations." Accessed October 15. https://pages.nativehope.org/how-trauma-gets-passed-down-through-generations.

New Canoe Media. 2022. *Huchoosedah: Traditions of the Heart*. Vimeo. Accessed October 12, 2022. https://vimeo.com/396538899.

Parker, K., J. M. Horowitz, and R. Minkin. 2022. "COVID-19 Pandemic Continues to Reshape Work in America." *Pew Research Center's Social and Demographic Trends Project*, February 16. https://www.pewresearch.org/social-trends/2022/02/16/covid-19-pandemic-continues-to-reshape-work-in-america/.

Toth, K. 2022. "The Death and Revival of Indigenous Languages." *Harvard International Review*. Accessed October 12. https://hir.harvard.edu/the-death-and-revival-of-indigenous-languages/.

Tuinstra, R. 2005. "Muckleshoot 'Grandma Iola' Loved Life, Tribe." *Seattle Times*. October 6. Accessed October 12, 2022. https://www.seattletimes.com/seattle-news/eastside/muckleshoot-grandma-iola-loved-life-tribe/.

8

Journey Rediscovered

JESSICA DENNIS

I grew up on the homelands of the Diné, the Navajo People. I did not appreciate growing up on the Navajo Reservation until I was much older and had left to pursue my ambitions. However, I had always respected and understood how I was raised. I was taught to follow the path of kindness and share with those I encounter the lessons I had learned and, in turn, learn from them.

There were various challenges that I faced growing up as a biracial female. I was not immediately accepted by my people. Yet, as cis female, I was conditioned to fill the caretaker/provider role in our matriarchal culture. I learned to be quiet and reserved, and often found that I was minimizing myself to disappear into the periphery of my community. I was obedient, did what I was told, but more often than not, found myself being a mother figure to my older brother and being the problem solver in our family. Not having much of a childhood, I had no choice but to quickly mature mentally and emotionally.

During my middle school years, I began to question our education system. We had outdated textbooks that were handed down to us from other public

https://doi.org/10.5876/9781646425105.c008

schools in the county; teachers were coming and going long before the seasons had a chance to change. We were condescended to and made to feel small & insignificant. By the time I reached high school, I was tired of the horrific treatment. I felt that the curriculum and those teaching us, were not adequately prepared to foster our success. I became a member of my student body government my first year of high school; changes needed to be made, and we needed to be heard. It was then I began to build a foundation for my life's journey. I wanted to make changes happen for our people, but I was not sure how to begin to close the gaps in our massive health, economic, and educational disparities. These were the effects of intergenerational traumas from settler-colonialism genocide, which has been affecting Indigenous people. Growing up, I was told that graduating high school and going to college were the only choice I had. I had this hidden fear about being stuck on the reservation, being swallowed, and never being able to escape to eventually return to help my family, the Diné.

My reality became all too real when I found out I was expecting a child, in my senior year of high school. My grandiose dreams of leaving the reservation and attending Stanford to be a doctor became an image in the rearview mirror of my life the day I decided to become a mother. I applied to the University of New Mexico during my senior year and was accepted into the fall semester after my high school graduation. I graduated from high school in the top five of my class with a three-month-old baby boy. After high school, my son and I remained living with my mom while I worked and began my college career. There were a lot of unknowns while attending college, but one thing I was sure of was that I had to work even harder to ensure my son wanted for nothing. By eighteen, I had married my son's father and found myself leaving college to be a mother and a wife. We moved to California to be a family while my then-husband was fulfilling his military obligations. In less than six months, I found myself taking my son and me back to New Mexico to escape domestic violence. Eventually, I had saved enough money to move us to Washington so that I could continue my education and be in a healthier environment.

Moving to Washington opened many doors on my journey. Still, I have faced so many hurdles that often make me want to give up. I was raising my son by myself, working full time, and attending school full time. I often questioned whether any of it was worth the exhaustion, mentally and physically. I attended Pierce College and received my Associate of Arts. Still not knowing what I wanted to major in, I applied and was accepted to the University of Washington in Tacoma. It was there that I rekindled my love for science and received my Bachelor's in Environmental Science with a focus in Biology. I wanted to do research and work in a lab for the rest of my life. However, I found the mostly autonomous work to be unfulfilling. Consequently, I began craving to be back in spaces where I was helping others. I wanted to help others realize their purpose, their worth. I wanted to get back to discovering what it was that I needed to do to help the folks back home on the reservation. Around this time, I decided to marry my passion for science with my passion for helping people by pursuing a Master's in Secondary Science Education. Here, not only would I be able to work in the science field, but I would also be able to help guide the youth. I received my teaching certification and Master of Education from the University of Washington Tacoma. I decided that I wanted to become an educator so that the youth of the future should be able to see faces that resembled theirs and backgrounds that weighted cultural similarities, and to show students that there is a place in society for us and that we do matter. I have chosen to take on the challenge of helping not only my tribe but also Indigenous peoples across the globe in realizing their academic, as well as life, goals. Education provides me the opportunity to incorporate my life and cultural experiences in order to be an uplifting, empowering, and adept educator. My ancestors carved a path of guidance for me to follow in order to fulfill my purpose, so now is the time for me to do the same for our youth, our future.

9

As We Journey, We Are Not Alone

JOSHUA DENNIS

When I was growing up, I went to a reservation school in the Navajo Nation. This meant low budgets, beat-up textbooks, dinosaur computers, and some educators who did not have the cultural sensitivity to teach rez kids. The teachers who cared or pushed us beyond curriculum expectations often burned out quickly. I believed that I didn't have any type of future. I internalized the feeling of being stuck; I never thought I would make it off the rez. I could not envision any semblance of the life that I have now. I am currently off the reservation and in a community with other Indigenous people from so many different nations while doing Climate Justice work. I found my joy in good work with like-minded people. More important, to me, is the hope for the future that I wish little Josh could have felt.

The media showed glimpses of how the ideal life is "supposed" to look like. My life was nothing like the movies or the shows. Those ways of thinking and being are not intuitive and demand the currency of exploitation. Our People were discussing access, health, and education disparities with the government, oftentimes to people who see Indigenous as the cartoonish

https://doi.org/10.5876/9781646425105.c009

stereotypes that persist across the zeitgeist. As a young person, I did not have the language to describe how hopeless it was when everyone was telling me to go to college yet I didn't know anyone with a degree.

My Mom moved home after her service in the military. We had my Grandma, Aunts, Uncles. We had the community that stretched between Shiprock to Zuni and Flagstaff to Albuquerque and beyond. My Mom made sure that everyone knew that her children were going to college. When I visit with relatives, they always asked about school. Then they would tell me of their stories of their days in school. Although they often tell me how it didn't work for them, every person believed that I needed to go to college so that I would do well in life. When I met the President of the Navajo Nation, I was surprised he knew how much my Mom was pushing me to go to college. While I didn't do as well as I could have, I graduated high school with the help of my community. Some of the teachers and staff were Diné, so there was always a relative who made sure I was on track.

Fall semester at the University of New Mexico (UNM) in Albuquerque was going to be my first semester at college. In preparation, I packed up all my belongings into my little car. The orientation began the next day and I had to make the drive from Gallup to Albuquerque, to my Aunt's house. She was going to let me stay with her while I started college. So many people had words of wisdom and well wishes for me as I was leaving. Leaving the next day was a hard thing to do. I had to fight the urge to cry because of how scary it was out there, and I had to leave the comfort of my Land, my People.

It is a two-hour drive from my mother's house. I left for the freshman orientation, on the day of the event with not a minute to spare with all the belongings I had wanted to take with me. My little car was full. Naturally, halfway between Gallup & Albuquerque, my car broke down on the highway, outside of Laguna, New Mexico.

I was numb. I missed orientation for school. I was stuck a couple of hours from any of my family who could help me, and I didn't know if my car was totally dead. I was devastated & resigned myself to what was unfolding. I was so shaken, psychologically, that I couldn't even think of a tomorrow or a yesterday. I could only exist in that one moment of pain & shame. I was so worried about what they'd say back home if they found out: "There goes ol' Josh, the guy who couldn't even make it two hours before he had to come home." I felt the burden of how disappointed my family was going to be in me.

I took the keys out of the ignition and picked myself up out of the car. Staring into the vast plains and mesas of northern New Mexico, I took a deep breath, and started walking. I just put one foot in front of the other. I was terrified. The left foot in front of the right. The right foot in front of the left. I made it that way until I got to the nearest gas stop and used the pay phone to call my Uncle for help. Two and a half hours later, he finished repairing my vehicle and told me, "Don't do it again." I was back on the road to my Auntie's house in Albuquerque, although I missed the orientation. Fortunately, the following day, they let me register after I explained my situation. Then I was a college student in the big city.

Reflecting on my car fiasco, all those years back, that was one of the most impactful moments in my life. I was in so much despair, I threw up my hands and told the universe that I was lost. In those moments, I learned more than ever before. I have grown when I have been thrust out of my comfort zone. I have been to places I could not have imagined and met people who turned into family. I felt a sense of finality whenever I "failed," when I was younger. "Black Native People don't get many chances and I squandered mine" was my thought. Even though I made it into the UNM, I ended up dropping out during the first semester. I thought that was my one chance and I screwed it up. Yet, my world did not fall out from beneath me.

My community wouldn't allow it. They gave me the time and space to think about my next steps. Although I may have stumbled, I rise with the knowledge that I have gained before. I finished my degree and discovered a passion working with Indigenous people. In my darkest times, I put my left foot in front of my right foot because I know that my ancestors are looking after me. As we journey through life, we are not alone: we bring our community and our ancestors with us.

10

The Journey of Ses yehomia / tsi kuts bat soot

LAURAL BALLEW

Introduction

As I prepared this writing, I reflected on my own personal journey in academia throughout the years. A colleague of mine suggested I write my personal story to represent my passage that influenced years of work experiences with leadership and principles as it relates to being a traditional mother/grandmother. As a Native American woman, I understand the cultural beliefs and principals through oral traditions that were modeled by my elders. For me, the first recognition of leadership and ethics is how you care for people, which then becomes immersed in your everyday actions as a tribal member.

My Lummi name is Ses yehomia, which means "she cares for." I also carry the female version of my father's name, tsi kuts bat soot, and I recognize in our culture I am carrying on his legacy by keeping his name alive. My English name is Laural Wilbur-Ballew. I am a member of the Swinomish tribe located on Puget Sound, on the southeast side of Fidalgo Island in Skagit County, Washington. I currently live on the Lummi reservation with

https://doi.org/10.5876/9781646425105.c010

my husband, Timothy Ballew Sr., and we have two sons—Timothy II and Raymond and two grandsons—Hunter and Tandy.

As Native people, we are recognized by our family ties. In the honor of tradition, I will explain mine here. I have always considered myself an intertribal—Native woman as I descend from the Upper Skagit, Nooksack, Sauk-Suiattle, Suquamish, and Aleut people. My family settled on the Swinomish reservation, which is where I am a tribal member. I am the fourth of five children to Claude Wilbur Sr. and Marie Charles. My paternal grandparents are Tandy Wilbur Sr. and Laura Waun-Wilbur; my maternal grandparents are Raymond Charles and Agnes Smith-Charles.

I descend from a family of tribal leaders, my great-great grandfather Charles Wilbur was a signer of the Point Elliott Treaty of 1855. It is his leadership role that encouraged my grandparents to continue working in support of the Swinomish community. My grandparents were active leaders in tribal government by organizing the Swinomish tribe through the Indian Reorganization Act and the Termination Era. My grandfather Tandy Wilbur Sr. was a founder of the current Native Congress of American Indians. Both my grandparents Tandy and Laura represented Swinomish in regional, state, and national legislation for the sake of tribal development for the tribe. These were my role models of tribal leaders as I grew into adulthood.

My own personal beliefs in the concepts of leadership have led me to understanding the commitment of educating future tribal leaders. I was encouraged by my parents and grandparents to pursue education to best serve my tribal community. Tribal nations are pursuing educational opportunities for their members; therefore, it is important to prepare tribal members with academic and foundational knowledge to become the future leaders of their respective communities. These ideals have inspired me to support higher education in developing curriculum and supporting institutional policies to prepare Native students with skills and knowledge to grow into productive tribal leaders.

Practitioner Perspective

Early on, I realized that my academic and personal experiences allowed me to serve as an example of successful leadership for tribal communities within Pacific Northwest. To fulfill my desire to be a role model for Native American students, I returned to the institution that inspired my success—Northwest Indian College (NWIC). With over forty years of experience working in tribal administrative and financial management roles, I gained a unique perspective regarding the social, economic, and academic progression within tribal communities. My deep involvement with family and community combined with a background in leadership and management skills have inspired me to continue serving tribal communities within academia.

As Western Washington University's (WWU's) first Executive Director of American Indian / Alaska Native and First Nations Relations & Tribal Liaison to the President, I give testimony of my life experiences that has prepared me for an educational pathway as a Native woman scholar. My commitment to professional development has always been the inspiration of what I can give back to my tribal community.

The Office of Tribal Relations advises the President of WWU on legislative and policy matters of concern to tribes and First Nations. The office functions as support for fostering working relationships with the twenty-nine federally recognized tribes across the state of Washington. The office recognizes the partnership opportunities with tribal communities to enhance the support and success of Native students. The office works to encourage the development of programs, events, and activities designed to educate the campus community and increase capacity to serve American Indian, Alaska Native, and First Nation communities. The Tribal Relations Office functions as support for establishing working relationships with tribal communities to sustain the success of Native American / Alaska Native and First Nation students at WWU. The Tribal Liaison has formed an advisory committee that offers interdepartmental collaboration with students, faculty, staff, academics, and student services to ensure students' needs are met holistically and to ensure community-based collaboration occurs when developing programming for Native students at WWU.

The university's Native American Student Union (NASU) is a positive example of student leadership. On May 16, 2016, NASU sent a formal request advocating for action by the University President and Board of Trustees. The first request was to implement a Tribal Liaison position. The second request was for a traditional Coast Salish Longhouse. The final three requests have been met through the support of the Tribal Liaison: (1) to certify Native tribal enrollment or descendance at WWU to ascertain an accurate count of our Native student population, (2) funding for NASU's annual powwow, and (3) government-to-government training. By the power and actions of the NASU group leaders, along with support from Native faculty and staff at WWU, the inaugural first Tribal Relations Department and Tribal Liaison position were appointed by the WWU Board of Trustees in 2019.

To date, I am pleased to report all five of the NASU requests have been met by the administration of WWU. Most significant of these requests is the successful funding for a Coast Salish–style Longhouse to be built on WWU's campus. Most important is to recognize and commend the WWU Native American Student Union for their leadership and perseverance in fighting for a dedicated space for the Native students on WWU's campus. The Coast Salish Longhouse will provide a sense of belonging for current and future Native students attending WWU, where they can build community and support their academic achievements and activities. The Coast Salish–style Longhouse will also honor the historic importance of place within the Lummi territory, which WWU currently sits on, and give acknowledgment of the university's responsibility to promote educational opportunities for Native students.

During the Covid pandemic, one of the main concerns within the university is how we will be prepared to "welcome" back students to campus once classrooms and dormitories are occupied once again. We recognize students will not return to a "normal" way of education they once experienced. For Native students who returned home, their lives have been affected by the pandemic. Some have experienced loss in so many ways, as the pandemic has affected tribal communities in record numbers with high death rates. These losses have been compounded with lifestyle changes felt most drastically among Native communities. For Native students who are left financially and emotionally broke, retention and enrollment will be a high concern. Having the means to assist students with sensitive and fiscal resources may be a challenge, but it will be necessary to undertake these challenges in the best way possible.

There is an opportunity for Native students to learn from the benefit of educating faculty and staff as positive role models. By becoming positive change agents for Native nation building, Native students are empowered to share their stories. The Longhouse model is an opportunity to share generational cultural practices and ceremonies as well as western academic knowledge to navigate a contemporary world. The Longhouse is intended to serve as a "house of healing" to acknowledge the past trauma and distress affecting Native peoples, as well as the current grief and suffering caused by the global pandemic, long-standing racial injustices, and ensuing economic crisis. Coast Salish peoples have long understood the importance of collective healing in response to historical trauma, as well as holding the power of traditional and cultural practices to overcome hardship.

Although there is much to learn with regard to building Indigenous leadership, this is my contribution to academic knowledge for building successful leadership. As a Native mother and grandmother, I use my teachings and knowledge to share with my family, students, faculty, staff, and community to develop Native nation building. My hope is to recognize the desire from community members who wish to learn and share the knowledge to continue building a unified and healthy Native community of learners.

Be the change . . .

11

Protect Kaho'olawe 'Ohana and the Sacredness and Return of Kaho'olawe

LESLEY IAUKEA

Social movements play a big role in Hawai'i's modern history. The social movement to stop the bombing of Kaho'olawe became the catalyst for the second Hawaiian Renaissance, which included a reclaiming of religious practices, the *aloha 'āina* philosophy and practices, and a reconnection to traditions of navigation. In this chapter, I look at the movement to protect the island of Kaho'olawe and highlight the Protect Kaho'olawe 'Ohana (PKO) movement and its role in saving the island from US military bombing. I give a chronology of the 'Ohana's history and show how the collective effect of Hawaiians helped steer the movement through different pathways of agency in order to return the island to its people and reconnect Hawaiians back to the sacred island through the voices of indigenuity. The changes in organizing brought a new approach to responding with prayer, reverent resistance, and the *kapu aloha* philosophy with the *kūpuna* (elders) in the foreground making for a profound impact in a Native Hawaiian approach.

I focus on what has come from the fight to save the island and highlight several cultural affirmations from this movement. The first affirmation was the

https://doi.org/10.5876/9781646425105.c011

dedication of the sacred island to the god Kanaloa in reviving the aloha 'āina philosophy as the foundation to the Hawaiian belief of showing respect and love for the land through different pathways. The second cultural affirmation was in reviving religious practices and traditions for Laka, Kāne, and Kanaloa. The third affirmation was the revitalization of the annual Makahiki ceremony honoring Lono, the Hawaiian god of agriculture, rainfall, and peace.

In redefining ourselves through revitalization, a *kuleana*, or responsibility, takes precedence in expanding the space for Hawaiian people. I discuss aloha 'āina activities and show who employs this philosophy today and how Hawaiians are navigating an approach that encompasses ecological and cultural understanding through the ideas of aloha 'āina. Expanding participation in cultural activities is another pathway in reviving the island, and it is here that voyaging education and practices come into perspective. Bringing more resources to the island is another way to move Hawaiian agency from the periphery and back to the center. "The contemporary rediscovery of Kaho'olawe as a sacred island dedicated to Kanaloa led to a revival of the traditional Hawaiian value of aloha 'āina, or love and respect for the land. Ancestral memories of the kūpuna focused upon aloha 'āina as the Hawaiian value at the core of traditional spiritual belief and custom" (McGregor 2007, 264).

Growing up on Maui in the 1970s and feeling the land shake and tremble when the military dropped the many bombs on Kaho'olawe were a normal part of life in my memory. The village that surrounded me was mostly Native Hawaiians who were angry at the bombings. The emotions experienced as a child felt as though it was a deep, personal wound that could not be explained yet was felt to the depths of my bones when the bombs would detonate. It wouldn't be until years later that I could put my feelings to words though still not quite explaining exactly how it felt and being reminded that the *na'au*, the touch, the hearing sometimes has a stronger emotion connecting to it than words could ever explain.

I grew up around Charlie Maxwell and danced hula for his wife. Uncle Leslie Kuloloio's (Uncle Les) mom, Aunty Alice, babysat my sister and me at a young age, and as we grew up Uncle Les, together with Uncle Charlie Keau, would take us to contested sites that they monitored on the island. As an adult I am informed by my experiences from my childhood and in reflection, this connects to my own epistemology and agency and informs my own philosophy as demonstrated in my endeavors. Uncle Les would later accompany my mother and me to Kahoʻolawe in 2018 to *kilo*, or observe, from navigational platforms. It would end up being Uncle Les's last trip to Kahoʻolawe before his passing in 2020.

History

Kahoʻolawe is the smallest of the main Hawaiian islands, with just forty-seven kilometers of general coastline that wraps a single shield that formed 1.03 million years ago. The island is aligned with the southwest rift zone of Haleakalā Volcano on Maui less than ten kilometers to the northeast. The terrain is rugged, with cliffs, valleys, and hills, and is surrounded by ocean channels, shorelines, and reefs. "Archeological evidence suggest that Hawaiians came to Kahoʻolawe as early as AD 400, settling in small fishing villages along the island's coast. To date, nearly 3,000 archeological and historical sites and features—inventoried through 2004—paint a picture of Kahoʻolawe as a navigational center for voyaging, the site of an adze quarry, an agricultural center, and a site for religious and cultural ceremonies. Traditionally, the island has been revered as a wahi pana and a puʻuhonua" (KIRC n.d.b).

In the latter part of the eighteenth century goats were introduced to the island, and in 1858 the island was leased for sheep ranching (KIRC n.d.b). Due to allowing feral goats and sheep to overgraze, the natural flora was destroyed and the island became vulnerable to wind and rain. During the Hawaiian Monarchy in the nineteenth century, the island was used as a penal colony (Corbin 2014). However, in the early part of the twentieth century, cattle ranching worsened the island's ecosystem further.

Pearl Harbor was attacked on December 7, 1941, by the Japanese forces. Over 2,400 Americans died, and over 300 airplanes, 8 battleships, and 20 other naval vessels were destroyed (Gilbert 2009). The next day, President Franklin D. Roosevelt asked the US Congress to declare war on Japan. Also in response, the US declared martial law in Hawaiʻi (Green and Judge Advocate General's School 1943, 101), and the island of Kahoʻolawe became a bombing range (KICC 1993). On December 11, Japan's allies Germany and Italy declared war on the US. In return, the US declared war on the European powers and the US entered into World War II as one of thirty countries involved. Weapons testing started almost immediately with ship-to-shore bombardment of the island and, later, with American submarines testing torpedoes by firing them at the shoreline cliffs of Kaho'olawe. By September 1945, 150 navy pilots; the crews of 532 major ships; and 350 navy, marine, and army officers had trained on Kaho'olawe. Another 730 service members had trained in joint signal operations on the island. During World War II, "Kaho'olawe soon gained the reputation as the most shot-at island in the Pacific" (*Honolulu Star Bulletin*, August 16, 1946, 19). The war came to an end in 1945, and Nazi Germany and Japan were defeated.

Rather than returning the island to the jurisdiction of the Territory of Hawai'i on February 20, 1953, by use of an "Executive Order #10436, Dwight Eisenhower secured Kaho'olawe for the use of the US Navy as a bombing target and placed the island under the jurisdiction of the secretary of the Navy" (Graves and Kehaunani 1993, 12). Over the decades after World War II, the wars would change but the bombing would continue. During the Korean War (1950–1953), navy carrier planes used Kaho'olawe to practice airfield attacks and strafing runs on vehicle convoys as targets (McGregor and MacKenzie 2015). In 1965, during the Cold War (1947–1991), three 1-kiloton nuclear explosions were simulated on the island when the US Navy detonated 500 tons of TNT in three tests. During the Vietnam era (1955–1964, 1965–1973, 1974–1975), navy and marine corps jets practiced attacks on surface-to-air missile sites, airfields, and radar stations on the island. By the time of the Gulf War (1990–1991), live fire training on Kaho'olawe was reduced, and the navy shifted its focus to other target ranges.

Beginning of the Protect Kaho'olawe 'Ohana

In 1974, the Aboriginal Lands of Hawaiian Ancestry (A.L.O.H.A.) Association introduced a bill in the US Congress to provide reparations to the Native Hawaiian people for the illegal role of the US in the overthrow of the Native Hawaiian Constitutional Monarchy (Charlton 1974). As the bill was not making any progress in Congress, the president of A.L.O.H.A., Charles Maxwell, a policeman on Maui, decided that Native Hawaiians needed to demonstrate on federal land, in order to draw national attention to the desperate conditions of Native Hawaiians that led A.L.O.H.A. to seek reparations (McGregor and MacKenzie 2015). Maxwell consulted with Native Hawaiians through the islands, and the decision was made to put out a call to occupy Kaho'olawe to draw attention to the A.L.O.H.A. bill for US reparations.

At dawn on January 6, 1976, a flotilla of fishing boats with grassroots Native Hawaiians from various Hawaiian Islands made its way toward Kaho'olawe. Someone had contacted the news media, and the US Coast Guard that patrolled the waters between Maui and Kaho'olawe was alerted. The Coast Guard warned the fishing boat captains that their boats would be confiscated if they entered the nearshore waters around Kaho'olawe that were under the control of the US Navy. As the boats provided the fishermen with their livelihood, all but one boat, which carried some of the news reporters, turned around. Nine protesters boarded that boat and landed at Kūhe'eia on Kaho'olawe (oral history of Noa Emmett Aluli and Ian Lind, UHM Center for Oral History, Kaho'olawe Aloha 'Āina Movement project). One protester, George Helm, then departed from the island with the news reports, six were arrested, and two, Noa Emmett Aluli and Water Ritte, remained overnight on the island and were arrested on the second day.

When Aluli, Ritte, and Helm returned to their home island of Moloka'i, they sought out their kūpuna to explain what they had experienced. On one hand, they witnessed the destruction of the island. Exploded and unexploded bombs and ordnance littered the landscape. However, they also felt a strong spiritual force emanating from the land. The kūpuna explained that the island had been sacred to Hawaiian ancestors, that it had been named and dedicated to Kanaloa, the Hawaiian deity of the ocean, and had been a center for the training in navigation. Feeling the pull of the island, Aluli and Ritte returned to the Kaho'olawe with Ritte's wife, Loretta Ritte, and sister, Scarlett Ritte, on January 12, 1976, to further explore and experience the spiritual force of the island.

Aluli, Ritte, and Helm began to organize meetings on every island, to share their story and draw in more Native Hawaiians to identify with the island and get involved to protect the island from the abuse of the US Navy. More occupations of the island were organized with supporters coming from Hawai'i to Kaua'i. In all, nine landings to occupy the island in protest of the bombing and military use of the island were organized from January 6, 1976, through July 17, 1977 (KICC 1993, 97). All were carried out in a Hawaiian manner, with chants, prayers, and offerings, and with peaceful and nonviolent, caring actions. This same year, Civil Lawsuit no. 76-0380, *Aluli et al. v. Brown, Secretary of Defense et al.*, was filed (MacKenzie, Serrano, and Kaulukukui 2007). The outcome of this case brought about a significant change for not only the island but Native Hawaiians and the people of Hawai'i. In 1977, a partial summary judgement mandated that the navy must conduct an Environmental Impact Statement (EIS) on Kaho'olawe (*Aluli et al. v. Brown et al.*, 602 F.2d 876, 9th Circuit, 1979).

Surprisingly, the movement struck a chord among Native Hawaiians and local people across the islands. Thousands rallied and held educational concerts, signed petitions, and demonstrated against the bombing of Kaho'olawe. Breaking with protocol, George Helm was even invited to address a joint session of the Hawai'i State Legislature and also traveled to Washington, DC, to lobby Congress and to draw national attention to the island of Kaho'olawe.

In 1976, as the grassroots movement to stop the bombing of Kaho'olawe grew, the leaders were advised by Aunty Edith Kānaka'ole of Hawai'i island to organize themselves into an 'Ohana, or extended family for the island, rather than to function as a western-style association. They formed themselves into the Protect Kaho'olawe 'Ohana. In the same year, George Helm and Noa Emmett Aluli also incorporated a 501(c)3 nonprofit corporation, Kohemalamalama O Kanaloa / Protect Kaho'olawe Fund (PKF) to fundraise and conduct education about the spiritual significance of Kaho'olawe and about the beliefs and practices of aloha 'āina, and to engage in the protection of Hawaiian cultural sites on Kaho'olawe and throughout all of the islands (McGregor 2007).

On the eighth landing of George Helm, Kimo Mitchell, and Bill Mitchell on March 5, 1977, George Helm and Kimo Mitchell were lost at sea in mysterious and suspicious circumstances that led to the speculation of a politically motivated assassination (McLeod 2013). These two young Hawaiian heroes continue to be remembered for their courage, dedication, leadership, and '*ike* by the Protect Kaho'olawe 'Ohana. More broadly, they are also remembered for shaping the movement that eventually succeeded in stopping military use of Kaho'olawe in 1990 and sparking the revitalization and renaissance of Hawaiian culture, music, navigation, arts, agriculture, and aquaculture for the Hawaiian people and Hawai'i.

The tragic martyrdom of Helm and Mitchell was a major setback for the movement. Nevertheless, the Protect Kaho'olawe 'Ohana ('Ohana), led by Noa Emmett Aluli, persisted in organizing to stop the bombing of Kaho'olawe, so that the work of aloha 'āina, to heal the island, could begin. The occupations and arrests had taken a huge toll, playing out in lengthy court cases, imprisonments, and banishment from the island. The final illegal landing occurred on July 17, 1977. After that began the ʻOhana exercises wherein the participating foreign navies did ship-to-shore shelling of the island. The ʻOhana lobbied Congress, the legislature, and county councils to stop military use of the island.

In October 1980, because of a civil suit filed in 1976 by George Helm—*Aluli et al. v. Brown, Secretary of Defense et al. No. 76-0380*—the US Navy was ordered to enter into a Consent Decree and Order with the Protect Kahoʻolawe ʻOhana. This Decree recognized the Protect Kahoʻolawe ʻOhana as the steward of Kahoʻolawe and provided access to the island for Native Hawaiian religious practices for four days during ten months of every year. Therefore, "in practice and as a matter of law, a native Hawaiian political organization exercised shared governance responsibility with the US Navy over the island of Kahoʻolawe from 1980 until 2003, while the United States Navy retained control of access to Kahoʻolawe" (McGregor and MacKenzie 2019, 52). The navy was mandated to conform to the National Historic Preservation Act of 1966 (Duerksen, Bonderman, and Dennis 1983) and to survey and develop a plan to protect historic sites, complexes, and features on the island. In addition, "the Navy was mandated to stop bombing the island for ten days of each month, to limit their bombing and shelling to the central third of the island, to clear two-thirds of the island of surface ordnance, to eradicate the feral goats, and to begin soil conservation and revegetation programs" (McGregor 2007, 265). In compliance with the American Indian Religious Freedom Act of 1978, Protect Kahoʻolawe ʻOhana was acknowledged to be Ke Kahu O Ka ʻĀina, or stewards of the land, and allowed access to the island for religious, cultural, and educational activities for four days in ten months of each year (PBR Hawaiʻi 1995). These events served as a critical turning point in the struggle to restore Kanaloa to the people of Hawaiʻi, allowing the Protect Kahoʻolawe ʻOhana to reclaim and reassert Hawaiian agency on the island. The following were done as the stewards of Kahoʻolawe:

> (1) An average of sixty participants were taken to the island each month to work with the ʻohana on erosion control and revegetation projects; (2) the ʻohana established a permanent base camp on the northeast side of the island or Kahioawa as well as three temporary camps along the north side of Kuheia and Ahupu and on the west side at Keanakeiki; (3) hiking trails were

cleared, water catchments installed, and soil conservation and revegetation projects initiated; (4) ancestral shrines and temples were re-dedicated; and (5) new cultural sites, such as a traditional meeting house, a hula platform, and a memorial for kūpuna who had passed on, were established. (Social Science Research Institute 1998)

The following year, 1981, the island of Kaho'olawe was listed on the National Register of Historic Places under ID number 81000205, which fell under the prehistoric and historic-aboriginal criteria. A comprehensive archaeological survey of the whole island, sponsored by the navy and initiated in 1976, was completed in 1980 (Hommon 1977, 1980a, 1983). Hawai'i Marine Research Inc., the firm hired to do the archaeological work, recorded 544 cultural sites containing 2,337 features, all of which formed a body of information that was significant enough, under criterion D, to place the entire island on the National Register of Historic Places on March 18, 1981 (Hommon 1980b). That same year, the construction of the first modern traditional *hale* in Hakioawa began as a way to reassert traditional practices.

On October 22, 1990, after a decade of persistent, dedicated, and focused work for Kanaloa under the consent decree, "the bombing of Kaho'olawe stopped" (McGregor 2007, 274). The Democratic senator from Hawai'i, Sparky Matsunaga, passed away in office in April 1990. The National Republican Party and President George H. W. Bush himself urged Congresswoman Patricia Saiki to run for the deceased senator's seat as part of the national campaign to win a Republican majority in the US Senate. According to Saiki's Native Hawaiian campaign manager, Andy Anderson, Bush asked the congresswoman what it would take for her to get elected. She said it would take a miracle for her as a Republican to get elected from the Democratic state of Hawai'i. Asked what such a miracle might be, Saiki's campaign staff suggested that stopping the bombing of Kaho'olawe would win her the support of the general public in her bid for the US Senate. The conversation goes as follows: Anderson said, "What can I do for you to give you a hand here, to help with the state and get your election looked at positively?" I said, "No, I, you've got to stop the bombing of Kaho'olawe. It is an island that has been devastated by the impact exercises. Although the exercises are very worthy, it is an assault and an insult to the Hawaiian people" (oral history with Congresswomen Patricia Saiki, 2018).

As a result of this conversation, and as a gesture to launch the campaign of Congresswoman Saiki for the US Senate, Bush issued the "Memorandum on the Kahoʻolawe, Hawaii, Weapons Range" on October 22, 1990, directing the US military "to discontinue use of Kahoʻolawe as a weapons range effective immediately and to set up a commission with the state of Hawaiʻi to examine the future status of Kahoʻolawe and related issues" (McGregor 2007). The next day he set out for Hawaiʻi to personally campaign and attend fundraisers for the congresswoman.

In order to keep his competitive edge in the race for the US Senate seat, Saiki's challenger, Democratic congressman Daniel Akaka, worked with Democratic senator Daniel Inouye to do more for Kahoʻolawe than Saiki and Bush had done. In November 1993, the US Congress passed the bill, and President Bill Clinton signed an act that recognized Kahoʻolawe as a national culture treasure and stopped the use of Kanaloa for any military training for two years and 120 days. It also established the Kahoʻolawe Island Conveyance Commission (KICC) to make recommendations for the future use of the island. This was a more significant and permanent measure. A presidential memorandum could be rescinded or overridden at any time in the future, unlike a Senate bill that had been passed into law.

The KICC conducted hearings statewide to receive testimonies about the future use of the island of Kahoʻolawe and conducted nineteen studies yielding reports about the history, resources, and uses of the island. As part of one of the studies, navigators from the voyaging canoe *Hōkūleʻa* visited Kahoʻolawe and affirmed that the island is a good place for navigation training (KIRC 2009).

In 1992, E kahoʻolawe E hoʻomau Ana i ka Mauli Ola healing ceremony took place with the decision-makers and kūpuna. There was also a dedication of a Mua Hai Kūpuna Kahualele, or memorial platform, on the island. In this ceremony there were officials that represented federal, state, and local government, including the Office of Hawaiian Affairs, kūpuna, and leaders of the Protect Kahoʻolawe ʻOhana. Each person was served *ʻawa*, a ceremonial drink, by Parley Kānakaʻole, the *kahu* of the ceremony. Each person was asked to make a decision and commit to doing whatever was in their power to heal the island of Kahoʻolawe. The Edith Kānakaʻole Foundation composed special chants to open the ceremony at dawn and to acknowledge the genealogy of the decision makers and kūpuna upon their stepping onto the *mua*. A genealogical history of the island and numerous chants in honor of George Helm and Kimo Mitchell were included to represent the people and effort of the movement.

As the sun came up in the East, participants chanted "E Ala E," a chant that is known throughout the islands as a protocol for starting the day in a Hawaiian frame of mind. The read as follows:

E ala e, ka lā i ka hikina	*Awaked/Arise, the sun in the east.*
I ka moana, ka moana hohonu,	*From the ocean, the deep ocean,*
Pi 'i ka lewa, ka lewa nu 'u,	*Climbing to heaven, the highest heaven,*
I ka hikina, aia ka lā, e ala e!	*In the east, there is the sun, arise!*

(Kanaka'ole 2017 [Kanahele 2017])

The cultural ceremony in 1993 affirmed support for the recommendation of the commission to US Congress to permanently end military use of the island, turn title over to the state of Hawai'i, and appropriate $400 million to clear the island of ordnance, and to begin the healing and restoration of the island's cultural and natural resources. The final report from the KICC confirmed that the island be returned to the people of Hawaii as a cultural reserve (KICC 1993).

The Conveyance Commission recommended that the title of Kaho'olawe be turned over to the state of Hawai'i along with congressional appropriation of $400 million to conduct a ten-year omnibus ordnance cleanup of the island (KIRC n.d.a). In response, the US Congress set aside the island under Title X for the following purposes: (1) cultural, (2) historical, (3) archaeological, and (4) educational. Ownership of the island was transferred from the US Navy to the Hawai'i State government in ceremonies held at Palauea Maui, in sight of the island, on May 7, 1994. As Davianna McGregor recalls in an interview about this day, "It was just a long period of commitment and dedication. You have to work slowly and build up that broad base of support across the spectrum of society to get to where there is enough to change the hearts and the minds" (Cerizo 2019). Members of the Protect Kaho'olawe 'Ohana reflect on the people who were significant in this process, such as "U.S. Senator's Daniel K. Inouye and Daniel K. Akaka, President H. W. Bush, Governor John Waihee, and Maui Mayors Hannibal Tavares and Elmer Cravalho, and many more government officials" (Cerizo 2019). The first president of KIRC, Emmett Aluli, gave a speech during this ceremony, "It was an unsurpassed cultural event. We were just jubilant. It was wonderful to have so many people who were part of the effort to return the island to the people to be able to witness it happen" (Cerizo 2019). And as Governor John Waihee recalls, "It was a very moving moment. I know for myself and for many people who were there, we remember the struggle. That is what I thought about that day—all the things we had been through and all the people who had been involved. And to realize that—despite everything—we won" (Cerizo 2019). Obviously, the joy of this event left everyone who was so deeply involved in the process happy about the transfer of Kahoʻolawe from the US Navy to the state of Hawaiʻi. All of their hard work had paid off, and they were able to celebrate that enormous moment together.

The Kahoʻolawe Island Reserve—HRS 6-K

In 1993, the Hawaiʻi State Legislature established the Kahoʻolawe Island Reserve, consisting of Kahoʻolawe and the submerged lands and ocean out to two miles around the island. The establishing of the reserve ensured that the island would be "solely and exclusively and reserved in perpetuity for the preservation and practice of all rights customarily and traditionally exercised by Native Hawaiians for cultural, spiritual, and subsistence purposes; for the preservation and protection of the Reserve's archaeological, historical, and environmental resources, rehabilitation, revegetation, habitat restoration and preservation; and for education" (KIRC n.d.a).

Statute §6K-9 of the Hawaiʻi Revised Statutes set forth the composition of the Kahoʻolawe Island Reserve Commission (KIRC). It states in part that the resources and waters of Kanaloa shall be held in trust as part of the public land trust, provided that the state shall transfer management and control of the island and its waters to the sovereign Native Hawaiian entity upon its recognition by the US and the state of Hawaiʻi. This measure set a precedent for Native Hawaiian sovereignty in that the state of Hawaiʻi acknowledges that there will be a sovereign Native Hawaiian entity and that repatriated federal lands can be part of the land base of the sovereign entity (KIRC n.d.a).

Cleanup and Restoration: 1994–2004

The US Navy received $460 million in appropriated funds from the US Congress in 1993, signing an agreement with the state of Hawai'i to clean 30 percent of the island's subsurface ordnances (McGregor 2007, 302). Parsons-UXB Joint Venture was hired by the US Navy to clean the island, thus making this project the largest remediation in unexploded ordnances. Parsons would eventually retrieve "10 million pounds of metal, 370 vehicles, and 14,000 tires from the island" (302). The project did not complete its goals of clearing 30 percent of the island and instead cleared only 9 percent and / or 2,650 acres of subsurface with a depth of four feet.

This result means that access to the island will be limited because of having only 9 percent of the subsurface cleared. Those areas include historical sites and areas for revegetation projects. Those areas and their significance are as follows: Hakioawa and Kahioawa Iki are the PKO base camp, where they have restored shrines and *heiaus* and created new sites for cultural practices. Moa'ulanui is where KIRC has its staging area for their revegetation projects on the island. Moa'ulanui had the highest priority for clearance because of the traditional site where navigators trained in traditional wayfinding skills. Honokanai'a was one of the first areas cleared and became the center of the communications system and housed the main staging area for the cleanup. Kealaikahiki was cleared because of the significance in voyaging that this location held. It would be here that long voyages between Hawai'i and Kahiki would start, and it has become the most suitable location for training today in celestial navigation. This location was recognized as significant because it is possible to precisely observe the position of the North Star and Southern Cross from over the horizon in relation to the central point of Kealaikahiki at this location. A navigational platform was created in 2004 by Master Navigator Mau Piailug, the PKO, KIRC, and crewmembers of the Hawaiian voyaging canoes because of this significance.

Other areas of significance in the cleared section were at Keanakeiki Beach, where the Makahiki closing ceremonies occur; at Kūhe'eia, the center for ranching during the twentieth century; and at Kaulana, a site of the Kingdom's prison and school and current-day staging area for planting projects. Other areas that were cleared in this 9 percent of area included a ranch in Ahupū, where the island's largest petroglyph field and obsidian glass quarry were found (McGregor 2007, 303). Honoko'a is known for the fishing shrines and the landing area that King Kalākaua visited in the nineteenth century. "A cross section road connected Hakioawa and Kuhiʻeia to the central part of the island over to Honokanaiaʻa and out to Kealaikahiki and Keanakeiki" (303). Another pathway of significance was the trail around the island at Kanapou Bay and the cliffs nearby, which are great areas to kilo the weather and elements of reference. "Activities will continue to focus on the healing and restoration of the cultural and natural resources of Kanaloa and reviving Native Hawaiian spiritual and cultural customs and practices. The limited clearance of ordnance means that the island will not be open for general recreational or commercial activities, nor for resorts, golf courses, or subdivisions" (302).

On November 11, 2003, the transfer of access control from the US Navy to the state of Hawaiʻi ceremonies at Hakioawa and ʻIolani Palace grounds took place. "This transfer marked a new beginning in the history of the island and its surrounding waters" (KIRC 2008). "He Ula Hou O Kahoʻolawe" (Rebirth of a Sacred Island) is written in the KIRC Kahoʻolawe Island Reserve Strategic Plan 2009–2013, with a mission as follows: "Our mission is to implement the vision for Kahoʻolawe in which the kino of Kanaloa is restored and nā poʻe Hawaiʻi care for the land. We pledge to provide for meaningful, safe use of Kahoʻolawe for the purposes of the traditional and cultural practices of the Native Hawaiian people and to undertake the restoration of the island and its waters. Established 1993" (KIRC 2008).

Protect Kahoʻolawe ʻOhana—Kahuʻāina (Steward) of Kanaloa Kahoʻolawe

With the transfer of control of access to the island from the US Navy to the state of Hawaiʻi on November 11, 2003, the Protect Kahoʻolawe ʻOhana signed a Palapala ʻAelike Kahu'aina stewardship agreement with KIRC to sustain its ongoing access to the island and ability to bring community members to experience a safe and meaningful cultural learning experience in the sacred space of Kanaloa Kahoʻolawe.

Participants who travel to Kanaloa Kaho'olawe with the ʻOhana sign a set of forms to be considered volunteers for KIRC. The ʻOhana, in its orientation packet, states, "We go to the island to strengthen our relationship with the land. We are involved in activities to revegetate, re-green and restore the island. We pay our respect to the ancient spirit of the land and recognize a response to our nurturing. We encourage and take to Kanaloa Kaho'olawe interested individuals, students, church and community groups to experience for themselves the beauty and spirit of the island" (Protect Kaho'olawe n.d.).

The story of the healing of Kanaloa Kaho'olawe is the story of a generation of Native Hawaiians assuming responsibility to end abuse of Native Hawaiian lands and in the process reclaim ancestral cultural and spiritual beliefs, customs, and practices. This is reflected in the words of founder and leader of the 'Ohana, Noa Emmett Aluli:

> On Kaho'olawe, we've been able to live together as Hawaiians. We've been able to practice the religion and to carry on the traditions we've learned from our kupuna, our elders. In doing this, we connect to the land, and we connect to the gods. We call them back to the land and back to our lives . . . We commit for generations, not just for careers. We set things up now so that they'll be carried on. We look ahead together so that many of us share the same vision and dream. To our next generations we say, Go with the spirit. Take the challenge. Learn something. Give back. (Levin et al. 1995)

The work to heal the island is also the work to heal as a people and a nation. As it tells of the first lands set aside to be returned to the reestablished Native Hawaiian nation, the story of Kanaloa Kaho'olawe will continue to develop to new stages and levels, inspiring new generations (McGregor and MacKenzie 2015).

The Role and Importance of Kua'āina in the Kaho'olawe Aloha 'Āina Movement

Kua'āina translates as "countryside; person from the country, rustic, backwoodsman; of the country, countrified, rustic, rural," as *kua* means "back" and *'āina* means "land." In the context of the Native Hawaiian Cultural Renaissance of the late twentieth century, kua'āina came to refer to those who had actively perpetuated the Hawaiian culture, living in the cultural *kīpuka*, or rural Hawaiian cultural pockets, throughout our islands. Families who lived in this manner, such as the Kukahiko 'Ohana and the Mitchell 'Ohana, spent their time in and around the ocean and shared their knowledge with the 'Ohana about where to best anchor to safely unload and load their boats. They guided the ʻOhana transport boats using the best routes through the Alalakeiki Channel between Maui and Kahoʻolawe.

The kuaʻāina also shared their knowledge about subsistence fishing around Kahoʻolawe and the various marine resources available there (McGregor 2007). Aunty Alice Kuloloio and her ʻOhana are examples of this dynamic, as they would share fishing traditions and how to gather limu and where to fish around Kahoʻolawe. The PKO continued the ancient practices associated with fishing koʻa, or feeding grounds, and shrine markers and dedicated to Kuʻula, the deity for fishing. "Early native Hawaiian settlers constructed sixty-nine coastal fishing shrines around the island to mark separate fishing grounds for distinct varieties of fish that thrive in the ocean offshore. In addition, there are numerous inland shrines which also appear to have a connection to fishing" (253). In 1976 Kuʻula protocols were reopened by those who fished on the island for subsistence. In ancient times, altars were constructed by placing a single special stone or group of stones or a piece of wood inside a ring of smaller stones or by piling up stones and coral into a mound. Such constructions were found throughout the islands along the coasts. The piles of stones and coral seem to imitate the *koʻa*, or coral mounds in the sea where fish congregate; those altars are called by the same name, koʻa, or *koʻa kuʻula*, or simply *kuʻula*; however, not all koʻa were erected for Kuʻula-kai. Kamakau notes that Kuʻula, "a great fisherman of ancient times," was "the main ʻaumakua of fishermen," but there "were a great many fishing ʻaumakua, each related to his descendants, and each raised above [all others] by his own descendants" (Kamakau 1976, 61). The first fish caught would be an offering for the male, Kūʻula, and the second fish would be the offering for the female, Hina. The son, ʻAiʻai, shared this practice throughout the islands to honor his parents that are honored as the chief fishing deities of Hawaiʻi.

Other kuaʻāina from Maui would share what to pack and how to prepare for the waters around Kahoʻolawe. "Those who go to Kanaloa bring sufficient supplies of fresh water and cook their food on propane burners and in traditional imu. It is an amazing experience in living with the ʻāina, one that transforms the lives of those who make the open ocean crossing" (McGregor 2007, 266). There are many chants, *moʻolelo*, and place-names that confirm Kahoʻolawe as a *wahi pana* and a *puʻuhonua*. We know about this history because of kuaʻāina like Uncle Harry Kunihi Mitchell of Keʻanae on Maui. He would share with the Protect Kaho'olawe 'Ohana interpretations of the place-names of Kaho'olawe the location and uses of important sacred and cultural sites on the island and chants that his kūpuna taught him about Kaho'olawe. For example, Harry Mitchell learned the following chant from his ancestors entitled "Oli Kuhohonu o Kaho'olawe Mai No Kūpuna Mai" (Deep chant of Kaho'olawe from our Ancestors). "This chant connects Kanaloa to navigators returning from a transpacific voyage" (254).

Wehewehe mai nei kahi ao	*Dawn is breaking.*
Kū mai nā wa 'a kaulua	*Two double-hulled canoes are sighted.*
Pūē ke kānaka mai ka wa 'a mai	*The men cheer from the canoe.*
Kūkulu ka iwi o ka 'āina	*Land is sighted.*
'Āilani Kohemalamalama	*To your left it is like heaven all lit up.*
Ho 'ohiki kēia moku iā Kanaloa	*We dedicate this island to Kanaloa.*
Aku a'o ka moana 'ili, moana uli	*God of the shallow and deep ocean.*
Ke holo nei me ke au kāhili	*We are running in an erratic current.*
'Ōhaehae mai ka makani	*The wind is blowing from all directions.*
'Alalā keiki pua ali 'i	*The chief's child is crying.*
Ka piko hole pelu o Kanaloa	*The island of Molokini is shaped like the navel of Kanaloa.*
Kahua pae 'ili kohonua ahua	*The channel between Molokini-Kanaloa and Maui Kahiki Nui is shallow.*
Puehu ka lepo Mou 'ula	*Dust is spreading over Mount Moa 'ula.*
Pū 'uhonua mo 'okahuna kilo pae Honua	*Gathering place of the kahuna classes to study astronomy.*
Pōhaku 'ahu 'aikūpele kapili o keaweiki	*Stone of deep magic of Keaweiki.*
Ka'ū li lua ka makani ke hae nei	*The wind is chilly.*
Kāwele hele nei 'o Hineli 'i	*Light rain is falling.*
Nāpo 'o ka lā i Kahikimoe	*The sun is setting toward Kahiki.*
Nue mai ke a'o Lanikau	*The glow after the sunset is like the colors of the rainbow.*
Kapu mai ka honua kūpa 'a loa	*The world seems to be standing still.*
Pau ka luhi 'ana o ka moana	*We shall no more labor on the ocean.*
Mana 'o hālana pū i ke Akua	*My thoughts are enlightened toward God.*

He aloha pili ka ʻu no kēia ʻāina	*My love for this land will always be deep within my heart.*
Aloha nō ka mana o nā kūpuna	*I love the knowledge and power of my ancestors.*

(Aluli and McGregor 1992)

In analyzing this chant, we find there are six names mentioned for Kanaloa. The first name is Kohemalamalama, which means "to your left and lit up like heaven" Hineliʻi means "light rain," Kahiki Moe means "the sun sets in Kahiki" (McGregor and MacKenzie 2019), and/oor can also mean "horizon; legendary place, one of the five divisions of the sky" (Ulukau Dictionary n.d.). The fourth name is Kanaloa, which is the name of the four primary Hawaiian gods known for the deep sea and navigation. The fifth name is Kohemalamalama o Kanaloa and joins "Kohemalamalama" and "Kanaloa" together to mean "the southern beacon of Kanaloa" (Reeve 1995) and also "the shining birth canal of Kanaloa." The modern name for the island, Kahoʻolawe, means "to take and to embrace" (McGregor 2007, 255).

Among all of the *ʻike Hawaiʻi* (Hawaiian knowledge) given to the Protect Kahoʻolawe ʻOhana, as discussed earlier, was the advice of Aunty Edith Kānakaʻole, from Hawaiʻi Island, to organize their protest in the Hawaiian manner and as an ʻOhana protecting the land (KIRC n.d.b.). In doing so, traditional protocol was included as a way to connect back to the land in modern times.

The kūpuna from Molokaʻi would "reveal that Kahoʻolawe had served as a refuge for native Hawaiian spiritual customs and practices and that it was a center for training in the arts of non-instrument navigation involving the sighting of heavenly bodies" (McGregor 2007, 252). With the guidance and *ʻike* from these kuaʻāina, a sacred island is recognized and the connection to the Native Hawaiian gods is discussed. Native Hawaiian kūpuna discuss the island as a tangible manifestation of Kanaloa, the Native Hawaiian god for the ocean and voyaging.

Ko'ihonua or Genealogy of Kaho'olawe

Origin chants for the Hawaiian islands attribute the mating of Papanuihānaumoku and Wākea for the origin of the island. There is the Papanuihānaumoku and Wākea creation chant by Kaleikuahulu, Kamehameha I, genealogist and son of Kumukoa (King of Moloka'i & grandson of Keawe, King of Hawai'i). Verses 15 and 20 connect Hawaiian cosmology to the island of Kaho'olawe (Ulukau, pt. 3, "The Chiefs Papa and Wakea"):

> *Papa was weakened at the birth of the island Kanaloa. It was born beautiful as a birdling and a*
> *nai 'a,*
> *It was the child born of Papa.*
> *Papa forsook her husband and returned to Kahiki; Returned to Kahiki she lived at Kapakapakaua.*

Abraham Fornander records a chant from the Kumulipo that was translated by Martha Beckwith.

This chant speaks of the birth of Kanaloa.

Kaahea Papa iā Kanaloa, he moku,	*Papa was prostrated with an island*
island, Kanaloa, I Hānauia he pūnua he nai 'a,	*Who was born as a birdling; as a porpoise;*
He keiki ia nā Papa i Hānau,	*A child that Papa gave birth to,*
Ha 'alele Papa ho 'i i Tahiti,	*Then Papa left and went back to Tahiti,*
Ho 'i a Tahiti Kapakapakaua	*Went back to Tahiti at Kapakapakaua.*

(Fornander 1916)

In another account, Fornander writes of Pu'uoinaina; in this legend the *mo'owahine* lived on Kanaloa. This description of Kaho'olawe is said to be revered that it is a sacred island: This daughter of theirs was placed on Kaho'olawe; the name of Kaho'olawe at that time, however, was Kohemalamalama; it was a very sacred land at that time, no chiefs or common people went there" (Fornander 19161).

In *Hawaiian Antiquities*, "Haloa 'O Wākea" is a genealogy chant describing the birth of the Hawaiian Islands. An English translation was done by

Emerson (Malo 1951). David Malo recalls this chant as follows:

'O Wākea noho ia Papahanaumoku	*Wākea lived with Papa, begetter of the islands*
Hānau 'o Hawai'i, he moku	*Begotten was Hawai'i, an island*
Hānau 'o Maui, he moku	*Begotten was Maui, an island*
Ho'i hou o Wākea noho ia Ho'ohōkūkalani	*Wākea made a new departure and lived with Ho'ohōkūkalani*
Hānau 'o Moloka'i, he moku	*Begotten was Moloka'i, an island*
Hānau 'o Lana'ikauka, he moku	*Begotten was Lana'i, an island*
Lili- 'ōpū-punalua o Papa la	*The womb of Papa became jealous at its*
Ho'o-hoku-ka-lani	*partnership with Ho'ohōkūkalani*
Ho'i hou o Papa noho iā Wākea	*Papa returned to live with Wākea*
Hānau o O'ahu, he moku	*Born was O'ahu, an island,*
Hānau o Kaua'i, he moku	*Born was Kaua'i, an island,*
Hānau o Ni'ihau, he moku	*Born was Ni'ihau, an island,*
He 'ula 'ā o Kaho'olawe	*Glowing fiery red was Kaho'olawe.*

In Hawaiian mythology, Martha Beckwith records an account of the sea first arriving to Kanaloa. Beckwith recalls the chant in her writing,

> "Chants of Pele, Hawaiian god of the volcanoe, and her family of deities reinforce the significance of Kanaloa as a wahi pana and pu'u honua. Pele was born in Kapakuela. Her husband, Wahieloa, was enticed away from her by Pele-Kumuhonua. Pele traveled in search of him. With her came the sea, which poured from her head over the land of Kanaloa." (Kepelino and Beckwith 1932)

A sea! A sea!
Forth bursts the sea,
Bursts forth over Kanaloa,
The sea rises to the hills.

In Kua'āina, Davianna Pomaika'i McGregor writes about this mo'olelo as she records Kepelino's version of the sea coming to Kanaloa (2007). This mo'olelo is one example that connects land and sea together in Hawaiian cosmology. The chant reads as follows: It is said that in ancient times the sea was not known here. There was not even fresh water, but with the coming of Pele the sea came also. It was thus that Hawai'i got the sea. Her parents gave it to her, and she brought it in her canoes to the land of Pakuala and thence to the land of Kanaloa, and at this place she poured the sea out from her head. As the sea burst forth her brothers' chant begins:

A sea! A sea!
The sea bursts forth,
The sea burst forth on Kanaloa
The borders of the sea reach to the hills, Gone is the restless sea,
Twice it breaks forth Thrice it breaks forth,
The sea borne on the back of Pele.

Another important mo'olelo that connects Kaho'olawe to its history can be read in the version of Kamohoali'i, Pele's brother, the navigator and shark god. There are two sites that are associated with Kamohoali'i on Kaho'olawe—Kahua Hale o Kamohoali'i and Lua o Kamohoali'i. Kaho'olawe is one of four identified pu'uhonua, or places of refuge for the deity Kamohoali'i in Hawai'i, and therefore holds significance. As McGregor writes, "It is located in a deep cave that opens onto the ocean on the north-east side of the island. No one has explored it in modern times" (McGregor 2007). In the story of Lauka'ie'ie (Racoma 2008), Kamohoali'i, is believed to be living at Kanaloa. In modern times, shrines put in place for Kamohoali'i have been in places such as Kanapou Bay, a site known as a breeding location for sharks. This mo'olelo confirms that Kaho'olawe is also a wahi pana in way-finding traditions.

In oral cultures, place-names connect to history and stories of the beginnings. The first name for Kaho'olawe is Kanaloa, and later the name changed to Kohemalamalama o Kanaloa, which means "the shining birth canal of Kanaloa" or "the southern beacon of Kanaloa" (KIRC n.d.b). Kaho'olawe is the only island in Pacific that is named for a major god. The numerous names connects Kaho'olawe to its role as a traditional center in the training of way-finding between Hawai'i and Tahiti. In order to know how to navigate, a person must know the main gods in the native Hawaiian culture and what they represent in the elements of reference. To do so is to become knowledgeable in understanding the stars, wind pathways, ocean channels, moon phases, and sun directions. Kaho'olawe is the ideal location to immerse oneself within the natural elements related to sailing and navigation.

Recognizing Hawaiian Culture

In 1978, the Hawai'i State Constitutional Convention recognized Hawaiian language, access, gathering rights, and culture. In 1980, as a result of a civil suit filed in 1976 by Aluli et al., the PKO reached an out-of-court settlement with the US Navy called a consent decree (Goodyear-Ka'ōpua 2011).

Ancestral Spirits of Kanaloa

The leaders of the Protect Kaho'olawe 'Ohana from the beginning sought answers from kua'āina and kūpuna to better understand the connection to Kaho'olawe and spirituality that they felt on the island. The following is the chronological order from McGregor that discusses how the 'Ohana went about connecting and revitalizing the spiritual realm. In 1976, Aunty Emma DeFries did a *kanikau*, or lamentation chant, for the 'āina acknowledging the neglect of the island, which caused its devastation. In Hakioawa, Kahuna Sam Lono and Emma DeFries of O'ahu conducted a ceremony that would open the religious sites of the island to receive offerings. In 1979, John Anuenue Ka'imikaua of O'ahu and Moloka'i conducted a ceremony with his *halau hula*, or schools that teach traditional Hawaiian dance and chant, to give life to the land by burying offerings of food in the ground and dancing the *hula kahiko*. Many other kūpuna came forth to offer prayer with the same intention of opening up the space for revitalizing the ancestral spirits. In 1981, the PKO asked Aunty Edith Kānaka'ole and her daughter Nalani Kānaka'ole of Halau o Kekuhi to train them to conduct a Makahiki ceremony. The Protect Kaho'olawe 'Ohana placed the healing and regreening of the island under the care of Lono, Hawaiian god of agriculture.

The Edith Kānaka'ole Foundation and the Halau o Kekuhi are influential in the sacred ceremonies and rituals of Kanaloa and in contemporary Hawai'i as a whole. Aunty Edith Kānaka'ole was trained in the hula by her mother, Mary Ahi'ena Kanaele Fujii, who was born in the 1880s and raised in the *hula kapu*, or sacred hula, in the Puna District of Hawai'i Island. The *halau* is known and celebrated for its mastery of the 'Aiha'a style of hula and chant, which is a low postured, vigorous, bombastic style of hula that springs from the eruptive volcano personas Pele and Hi'iaka. The halau is known for being rooted in seven generations of family practitioners who are seen as leaders in hula and oli.

Reclaiming Makahiki Ceremony and Practice

In January 1982, the Protect Kaho'olawe 'Ohana revived an annual celebration called Makahiki (Lum 2003) in honor of the god Lono, the Hawaiian god of agriculture. This celebration is believed to have been the first modern-day Makahiki celebration since High Chief Kekuaokalani conducted the Makahiki ceremonies in 1819 before going into battle in defense of Hawaiian religion, the year of the 'Ai Noa, or abolishment of the *kapu*. The Makahiki ceremony ends up spreading throughout the *pai'āina* and is seen and practiced throughout the islands. The purpose of the ceremonies was to attract the Akua, Lono, to Kanaloa in the form of rain clouds to soften the earth and ready it to receive young plants to revegetate the island. Every year since 1982 the 'Ohana has opened the Makahiki season in November after the appearance of the starline called Makali'i, or Pleiades constellation, is seen on the horizon at sunset and has closed the Makahiki season in January or late February. What the Kānaka'ole family did for the ceremony was to offer 'ike on the various *kino lau*, or body forms of the Akua. These can be found in certain foods that represent and are kino lau to the gods. Nalani Kānaka'ole composed the chants of prayer to Lono, and the Edith Kānaka'ole described the different chants and the purpose for them (Kanahele 2017, 2). "Nalani Kanaka'ole composed the chants of prayer to Lono which was the first formal prayer chant composed for a formal modern day Makahiki ceremony" (McGregor 2007, 273). Through these practices, the Hawaiian religion began to be revived.

At the same time, construction of the first modern traditional hale in Hakioawa began, and monthly accesses to Kaho'olawe were occurring (1982–1990). Negotiations with the navy were conducted every six months. In May 1986, ceremonies were opened for Kanaloa in which the central chant asked Kanaloa to give strength and skill to those united in the goal of protecting and giving life to the island. This ceremony provided focus and inspiration to those involved in the ongoing work to stop the bombing and restore the life of the island. A year later, in 1987, memorial services were held for George Helm and Kimo Mitchell, upon the official declaration of their death, the two having been missing for ten years. Plaques were placed in their honor on a *pōhaku* (rock) in Hakioawa to remember their efforts in the fight to save Kaho'olawe.

Hula Is Dedicated to Laka

In 1982 Kumu Hula Hokulani Holt Padilla of Maui, a member of the Protect Kahoʻolawe ʻOhana, built a *pā hula*, or hula platform, at Hakioawa to have a formal area for the hula practices. The pā hula was dedicated to Laka and named Kaʻieʻie in November 1987 during the Makahiki season. Kumu Padilla led the ceremony along with kumu hula Pualani Kānakaʻole Kanahele and kumu hula Kealii Reichel. A chant composed by Pualani Kanahele in 1992 for the healing ceremony, "He Koʻihonua No Kanaloa He Moku," chronicled the origin and history of the island, provides a poetic summary of the process of reviving religious practices on the island, and is an example of what they did to make the religious ceremonies happen. It is quoted here.

Ua ala Hawai ʻi mai ka moehewa nui	*The Hawaiian woke from the nightmare*
Ho ʻomaopopo i ke keiki i ʻa a Papa	*Remembered was the child of Papa*
ʻO Kanaloa	*O Kanaloa*
Ke moku hei Haumea	*The sacred land of Haumea*
ʻO Kohemalamalama	*O Kohemalamalama*
Ke Kino o Kamohoali ʻi	*The body form of Kamohoali ʻi*
E ho ʻōla kākou iā Kaho ʻolawe	*Save Kaho ʻolawe*
Ola i ka lani a Kāne	*To live in the heavens of Kāne*
Ola i ke kai a Kanaloa	*To live in the sea of Kanaloa*
Ua Kahea ʻia ʻo Lono i ka makahiki hou	*Lono was summoned for a new year Ma ka*
Hale Mua o Lono i kahea ʻia ai	*At the Hale Mua of Lono, he was called Ua*
Kanaloa ʻo Kanaloa i Kohemalamalama	*Kanaloa was reconfirmed to Kohemalamalama*
Puka hou a ʻe ka mana o Kanaloa	*The energy of Kanaloa was revitalized*
Ua kani ka leo pahu i ka Mālama o Hoku	*The voice of the drum sounded in the care of Hoku*
Kuwawā i ka houpo a Laka	*Resounding in the bosom of Laka*
Ua ala ʻo Lako ma Ka ʻie ʻie i Kanaloa	*Laka awoke at Ka ʻie ʻie at Kanaloa*

(PBR Hawaiʻi 1995)

The chant is to revive traditional and ancient ceremonies of Kanaloa and recognizes the Protect Kaho'olawe 'Ohana as a pro-Hawaiian and cultural organization. Over time, cultural protocols strengthened the efforts of the Protect Kaho'olawe 'Ohana and brought together the community in protesting the bombing of Kaho'olawe.

Changing Times

In 2001, the PKO contacted the Polynesian Voyaging Society (PVS) to celebrate the twenty-fifth anniversary of the founding of both organizations in a ceremony to be held at Honokanai'a and Kealaikahiki, Kaho'olawe. This proved to be a historical event, as they were previously two independent movements that ran parallel to each other, with very little intermixing. Moreover, the coming together was a symbol of reopening and elevating Kaho'olawe to its former sacred island status. This event also marked the first visit of *Hōkūle'a* to Kaho'olawe.

In October of 2004, after the completion of the ordnance cleanup and the permanent departure of the US Navy from Kaho'olawe, the Kaho'olawe Island Reserve Commission and the Protect Kaho'olawe 'Ohana organized the Ho'i Hou: Gathering of Early Warriors and Navigation Schools, at Honokanai'a, Kaho'olawe. On this occasion, the Kuhike'e Navigational Observation Platform at Kealaikahiki was blessed and dedicated by Master Navigator Mau Piailug. The location of the navigational platform was selected by PVS navigators Nainoa Thompson and Chad Baybayan. The building of the platform was overseen by Atwood Makanani. Makanani, or "Maka" as he is called, had been an active crewmember for the voyaging canoe, *Hōkūle'a*, since 1975 and is well versed in voyaging traditions. The platform was designed to include a star compass for students of navigation to learn how to way-find, utilizing the compass. The significance of this site is that it connects Hawaiian voyagers to other Oceanic voyagers with a shared compass, thereby connecting Oceania through similar traditions and synchronized worldviews that bring together a Satawal and Hawaiian perception. The platform also brought together the two parallel movements of the PKO and the PVS and mended a rift between the two organizations that had occurred in the 1970s, when the Polynesian Voyaging Society would not add its voice to the protest of the US bombing of Kahoʻolawe. Members of the PVS apologized for not being a part of the effort to stop the bombing. Moving forward, all schools of navigation are invited to come to the island and to train in way-finding to learn how to become navigators.

Elevating Kanaloa Kahoʻolawe as a Cultural Learning Center

The Protect Kahoʻolawe ʻOhana has continued to open and conduct new ceremonies and protocols for the natural life forces the Native Hawaiian ancestors honored as akua or deities. For example, in August of 2008, there was training of *moʻopapa* to open ceremonies for Papanuihānaumoku.

In February of 2009, the Kukulu Ke Ea A Kanaloa Culture Plan was made for Kahoʻolawe (Kanahele 2009) by the Edith Kānakaʻole Foundation. It introduces the Papakūmakawalu approach to Native Hawaiian science and provides a guideline for training of Hawaiian cultural practitioners in the sacred space of Kahoʻolawe. The plan recommends that the island, which is traditionally an Ahupuaʻa of the *moku* of Honuaʻula on Maui, be acknowledged as an island, or moku, in its own right. It also recommends that the island be called Kanaloa Kahoʻolawe, in acknowledgment of its ancestral name and its status as a *kino lau*, or body form, of the deity Kanaloa. The plan also lays the foundation for KIRC and the ʻOhana to work together to elevate Kanaloa Kahoʻolawe into a cultural learning center for the mastery of Hawaiian science, culture, religion, arts, and practices.

On November 11, 2009, the ʻOhana dedicated Namakapili Hale Halawai in Hakioawa. It is a traditional hale for the ʻOhana and *huakaʻi* participants to learn about Hawaiian culture and history. In 2011 the *Faafaite*, a voyaging canoe from Tahiti, launched off of Kealaikahiki for its return voyage back to Tahiti. This was the first time that a waʻa kaulua had launched its voyage to Kahiki in the traditional manner, from Kealaikahiki, since AD 1400.

Kahoʻolawe Aloha ʻĀina and the Cultural Renaissance

The Kahoʻolawe Aloha ʻĀina Movement also ignited a bigger and broader cultural revival, one that reverberated throughout the Hawaiian islands from 1976 to the 1990s and challenged other institutions of American colonization. A general cultural renaissance developed as the number of halau hula expanded and the number of dancers of both Hawaiian and non-Hawaiian ancestry increased. Hawaiian music gained new popularity, and new songs, styles, and rhythms were created. Lā'au Lapa'au, traditional herbal and spiritual healing practices, were recognized as valid and significant. Traditional Hawaiian healers began to train new generations in the Hawaiian healing arts. For international significance, traditional navigational skills were revived through transpacific noninstrument navigation in traditional Hawaiian double-hulled sailing canoes such as *Hōkūle'a, Hawai'i Loa,* and *Makali'i.*

Another aspect of the Hawaiian Renaissance is in the new generation of young Native Hawaiians who are pursuing livelihoods involving the cultivation of taro. We have also started to see Native Hawaiians seeking careers in natural resources management and protection of land. This was a time in Hawai'i's history that resort and industrial developments threatened to expand into the rural districts that had served as the last strongholds of Native Hawaiian custom, belief, and practice; communities began to organize to protect their lands and natural resources and Hawaiian way of life (Trask 2000). Native Hawaiians on Molokai continued to organize as Hui Ala Loa to stop resort development that threatened to divert limited water resources away from community-based economic development and to destroy subsistence resources. Native Hawaiians in Ka'ū organized against plans to launch rockets from Hawaiian Home Lands at South Point and to develop a spaceport at Kahilipali and Palina Point.

They argued that these massive projects would destroy Native Hawaiian cultural sites in the district, bring in newcomers, and transform the Native Hawaiian way of life. Native Hawaiians on Hawai'i Island organized against geothermal energy development in the Wao Kele o Puna rainforest of Puna. Industrialization of the volcano threatened to destroy the largest expanse of lowland tropical rainforest in the United States. The Pele practitioners asserted that geothermal energy would desecrate and destroy the life force and manifestations of their deity (Faulstich 1990). Native Hawaiians on Maui organized against sprawling resort development that blocked access to the beaches of Makena for subsistence fishing and gathering of marine resources. Native Hawaiians on all islands organized to protect their traditional burial grounds from destruction by various forms of development, a movement sparked by the controversy at Honokahua in Maui, where over 1,000 graves were dug up and relocated to build a Ritz-Carlton hotel (Merwin 1989).

Kohemalamalama O Kanaloa / Protect Kaho'olawe Fund

Before George Helm died, he and Noa Emmett Aluli founded the Kohemalamalama o Kanaloa / Protect Kaho'olawe Fund (PKF) (Corbin 2014). Together, Aluli and Colette Machado, an 'Ohana member and member of the PKF board, networked with national funding groups supportive of Native American culture, land rights, and sovereignty, among them the Seventh Generation Fund, the Tides Foundation, and the Gerbode Foundation. The PKF board included representatives of grassroots communities on every island and therefore did more than raise money for the work of stopping the bombing of Kanaloa and restoring its cultural and national resources. The PKF also supported and funded grassroots organizations engaged in aloha 'āina struggles on Kaua'i, Maui, Lana'i, Moloka'i, and Hawai'i, while continuing to expand support for Kanaloa Kaho'olawe (McGregor 2007, 268).

In the 1980s, the PKF helped Hāna Pōhaku on Maui raise funds for self-sufficiency projects in taro cultivation and fishing, research into protecting their land from federal condemnation for a national park, and protection of their water rights from diversion for hotels. The Hui Ala Nui o Makena on Maui was assisted by the PKF in the research and legal work to keep access to the Makena coastline open for fishing and gathering by local people. On Kaua'i, the fund assisted the Niumalu-Nawiliwili Tenants Association with developing an alternative land use plan that included their new homes. For Lana'i, monies were raised for research of kuleana lands and water concerns. Hui Ala Loa on Moloka'i received assistance for its litigation and organizing work to protect that island's cultural, natural, and agricultural resources from overdevelopment.

On the island Hawai'i, the PKF assisted the Mālama ka 'Āina Hāna ka 'Āina community organization to get monies to develop a plan to settle Hawaiian Home Lands at King's Landing by families desiring to pursue traditional Hawaiian subsistence livelihoods instead of building standard residential houses on lots. Ka 'Ohana o KaLae at South Point worked with the PKF to receive monies for a community curatorship program to protect the historic sites and rich natural resources of the Ka'ū District from industrial development. Efforts of Pele practitioners to protect her and the Kilauea Volcano and rainforest from geothermal development were initially funded by grants to the PKF until the Pele Defense Fund branched out from the Protect Kaho'olawe Fund (McGregor 2007, 268–270).

Aloha 'Āina Philosophy

This movement brought about a revival of the traditional Hawaiian value of aloha 'āina, or love and respect for the land. (McGregor 2007, 264)

The first significant outcome from the violent history that Kaho'olawe endured was bringing back the aloha 'āina philosophy into the Native Hawaiian consciousness. In 1893 Queen Lili'uokalani was illegally overthrown by the US government, and her book *Hawai'i's Story by Hawai'i's Queen* (Liliuokalani 1898) describes the pain she felt. In 1897, Annexation was attempted through the adoption of a Treaty of Annexation and failed. Then the US settled on a Joint Resolution within their own government policies to add Hawai'i to their collective possessions. Under international law, this was an illegal option for the annexation of a country, and yet the political status of Hawai'i continues to be under US occupation. Because of this history, loyal Hawaiian nationals called their cause to fight for justice "Aloha 'āina." The interpretation or definition of this term during that troubled time period was "patriot." The person identifying themselves as an aloha 'āina referred to themselves as being loyal to their Queen and were against the US illegally occupying Hawai'i.

This term continues to be used today in the same way: however, through education and a consciousness of Hawaiian identity and language, the term references much more than just being a patriot of our Queen. The philosophy of aloha 'āina and/or "love of the land" can be traced back through genealogy and finds its natural place in Hawaiian cosmology. In Hawaiian cosmology, Papa (Mother Earth) and Wākea (Sky Father) are the creators of the islands in the Hawaiian Archipelago.

Mo'olelo of Papa and Wākea; Birth of the Hawaiian Islands

Here is the genealogy of these islands. Kahiko was the husband, Kūpūlanakehau was the wife. A son was born to them, Wākea. Wākea is known as sky father.

Kūkalani'ehu was the husband, Kahakanakoko was the wife. A daughter was born to them, Papahānaumoku. For short, we call her Papa and she is known as earth mother.

> Wākea lived with Papa. Hawai'i, the eldest island and their eldest child, was born to them. Papa gave birth to Maui, an island, and then to Kanaloa, an island also known as Kaho'olawe. Then, Papa left Hawai'i and traveled to Tahiti.
>
> Wākea took a new wife, Ka'ula, and she gave birth to Lāna'ika'ula.
>
> Wākea took another new wife, Hina. Hina gave birth to Moloka'i, an island which is also known by the name of Moloka'inuiahina.
>
> Papa returned from Tahiti and was furious and jealous of the two new wives. So Papa took Lua as a husband. Born was the island of O'ahu, also known as O'ahulua, an island child.
>
> Papa returned to Wākea. Born were the islands of Kaua'i, Ni'ihau, Lehua, and Ka'ula.
>
> It was Wākea who established the eating kapu. Wākea also placed restrictions on certain foods that women were forbidden to eat. Wākea built numerous religious sites for the gods: for Kū, for Lono, for Kāne, and for Kanaloa. (Malo 1951, 188–190)

The lesson here is that we (Hawaiians) come from Papa and Wākea. We are connected to the land because they are our older siblings. The belief system is one where humans take care of the land and the land, in turn, takes care of humans.

Mo'olelo of Hāloa; Birth of the First Man and/or First Chief

> Papa and Wākea gave birth to a daughter named Ho'ohōkūkalani. When she became an adult, Wākea's desire for her welled up within him. So he lived with his own daughter, and she became pregnant.
>
> A premature infant was born to them and they gave him the name Hāloanakalaukapalili, They buried this child near the back wall of their house and from that spot grew a taro plant. He was the source of all the taro plants in Hawaii.
>
> Wākea paired with Ho'ohōkūkalani again, and they had another male child, whom they also named Hāloa. This Hāloa was the ancestor of the Hawaiian race.
>
> Therefore, both the taro and the land are older siblings to Hawaiian people, just as Hawaiian people are the younger siblings to the taro and the land.
>
> Older and younger siblings have responsibilities to each other. It is the responsibility of the older siblings to feed the younger siblings, and it is the responsibility

> of the younger siblings to care for the older siblings. Thus, the needs of both are fulfilled.
>
> This relationship continues to this very day. It is important to remember the lesson of this story in all that we do. (Malo 1951, 188–190)

Therefore, aloha ʻāina refers to the connection between humans and land that lives in a cyclical relationship as foretold in our Hawaiian cosmology. The aloha ʻāina movement picks up again and is used in practice in this new generation. In essence, by reclaiming the island of Kanaloa Kahoʻolawe, we, as Hawaiians, have also reclaimed our genealogy and cosmology. This consciousness of our cosmology allows us to follow the same philosophy that our ancestors followed. This is also an example of the depths that we can achieve if we understand that our Hawaiian language contains answers within itself. The answers in the language and in the moʻolelo are there waiting for us to retrieve. Therefore, when a person speaks of going back in time in order to move forward, what they mean is to go back to Papa and Wākea to understand where we fit in to our modern-day Hawaiian identity.

Lessons of Stewardship from Kanaloa Kahoʻolawe

The vision statement from KIRC encompasses the physical and spiritual restoration of Kanaloa, both the island and the god.

> The kino (physical manifestation) of Kanaloa is restored. Forests and shrublands of native plants and other biota clothe its slopes and valleys. Pristine ocean waters and healthy reef ecosystems are the foundation that supports and surrounds the island. Nā poʻe o Hawaiʻi (the people of Hawaiʻi) care for the land in a manner, which recognizes the island and ocean of Kanaloa as a living spiritual entity. Kanaloa is a puʻuhonua and wahi pana (a place of refuge, a sacred place) where native Hawaiian cultural practices flourish. The piko of Kanaloa (the navel, the center) is the crossroads of past and future generations from which the native Hawaiian lifestyle is spread throughout the islands. (KIRC 1995)

It projects activities on the island that revolve around restoration. The isolation of the island provides a historic opportunity to revegetate it with native plants. It also envisions a protected marine sanctuary that can serve as a pool for restocking marine life for the ocean in and around Maui Nui. The statement presented Kanaloa as a cultural learning center where traditional cultural and spiritual customs, beliefs, and practices of Native Hawaiians such as way-finding, fishing, and healing can flourish and spread out to all the islands. Native Hawaiian culture exists nowhere else in the world, and Kanaloa will play a role in its perpetuation. In order to implement this vision, KIRC worked with the protect Kaho'olawe 'Ohana and the Edith Kānaka'ole Foundation to develop traditional kua'āina stewardship principles for guiding the development of a land use plan for the island.

The following are the principles seen in Native Hawaiian stewardship. The first understanding is that the Ahupua'a is the basic unit of Hawaiian natural and cultural resource management. An Ahupua'a runs from the sea to the mountains and contains a sea fishery and beach; a stretch of *kula*, or open cultivable land and, higher up, the forest. The island was divided into twelve *'ili*, or watersheds. Restoration will start at the central point of the island and proceed down to the ocean, 'ili by 'ili, recognizing the integral relationship between soil disturbance, water flows, wind, erosion, and runoff (KIRC 2009).

The next principle concerns the natural elements, as land, air, fresh water, and ocean are interconnected and interdependent. Hawaiians consider the land and ocean to be integrally united and that these Ahupua'a also include the shoreline as well as inshore and offshore ocean areas such as fishponds, reefs, channels, and deep-sea fishing grounds. The sixty-nine fishing *ko'a* that had been constructed on the island were also markers for offshore fishing grounds. These fishing grounds are also part of 'ili and must be considered in restoration activities on the island (KIRC 2009). The third principle looks at the natural elements and views fresh water as the most important for life and as needing to be considered in every aspect of land use and planning. The Hawaiian word for water is *wai*; the Hawaiian word for wealth is *waiwai*. In Hawai'i, water is the source of well-being and wealth, and the wealth of the land is based upon the amount of fresh water available (KIRC 2009). The fourth principle is the acknowledgment that Hawaiian ancestors studied the land and the natural elements and became very familiar with the land's features and assets. Ancestral knowledge of the land was recorded and passed down through place-names, chants, and legends that evoke the winds, rains, and features of a particular district (KIRC 2009). The fifth principle recognizes that an inherent aspect of Hawaiian stewardship and use of cultural and natural resources is the practice of aloha ʻāina and *malama ʻāina*, or respect and conservation of the land to ensure the sustainability of natural resources for present and future generations (KIRC 2009). Taken together, these principles—learned through the collaboration of kua'āina, scholars, Native Hawaiian activists, and planners in projecting future uses of Kanaloa—provide an excellent foundation for the stewardship of the Hawaiian islands as a whole.

What Has Evolved

The Protect Kahoʻolawe ʻOhana is credited as starting the second Hawaiian Renaissance because of the social movement that started as a result of the bombings of Kahoʻolawe (McGregor and MacKenzie 2015). The movement started a cultural revival in religion, hula, and navigation that spread throughout the Hawaiian islands and continues to do so today. An example of what has come out of the movement can be seen at the Bishop Museum. An exhibit of Kahoʻolawe was on display, and 187,000 visitors came to see and learn the history of this movement. Kahoʻolawe is a key example that shows the dynamics of collaboration between many parties in an effort to not only stop the bombing of the island but also restore the island back to its natural space. By bringing back the religion, the ʻOhana has brought back the connection to the foundation of the Hawaiian culture. In that space, the cultural beliefs, ceremonies, and practices are reconceptualized for modern practices and are key to showing how a thriving people adapts to change. The ʻOhana remained rooted in the founding principles of aloha ʻāina, kūpuna leadership, ʻOhana or collective decision making and action, accountability to the grassroots kuaʻāina, and a clear focus on healing and restoring the life of Kanaloa itself (McGregor 2007, 268). The ʻOhana continued to follow the philosophy of George Helm, which was to "follow your naʻau, but do your homework" and made it a committed organization of political action guided by an informed and sophisticated strategy. Moreover, "the Molokaʻi kuaʻāina kept alive the memory and vision of George Helm for Kahoʻolawe to be regreened and restored as a puʻuhonua for the Hawaiian culture, so that the sacrifice of Helm's life would not be in vain" (268).

Today, the island of Kahoʻolawe holds an esteemed place for Hawaiians to visit to and to be a Hawaiian without judgment and/or criteria. There are two ways to enter the island: with the Protect Kahoʻolawe ʻOhana (PKO) access and/or with Kahoʻolawe Island Reserve Commission (KIRC) access. I have been to the island with both agencies and find the path with PKO more of a spiritual journey than just a mere visit to the island. Before venturing to the island, there are protocols and two *oli* that need to be remembered before you are allowed entrance. The traditional way is observed and sets a tone for the duration of your presence on the island. Once there, all one has to do is just be silent because you become aware that you are not on the island with only those who came over on the boat ride with you, but, rather, you feel the presence of those who have come before you and have been awaiting your trip. I have been told that one cannot prepare for Kahoʻolawe but rather Kahoʻolawe prepares you for a journey powered by the aloha ʻāina philosophy and Hawaiian consciousness.

While on the island, you work with the group that you came with as they become your immediate family and community. The work is completed in the daylight hours so as to plant endemic plants and to move *pōhaku* (rock) to make the Ala Loa an obvious pathway for those people that hike up the mountain. The Hawaiian words of Lōkahi (together) and Laulima (many hands) are practiced because work is carried out easier and faster if completed together.

This teaches us today how to navigate within a colonial and occupied nation. The actions that the PKO took against the US allows modern-day Hawaiians to see that it is okay to stand up and speak out against a clashing colonial system if our values and spirituality are attacked by these colonial agents. This action tells us that if we do not say anything, then who will? Or as Dr. Kekuni Blaisdell told me in our many conversations together, "If not you, then who?" as he referred to not waiting for anyone else to speak up but rather if there is a need to say something, then say it.

The example of the Kahoʻolawe struggle also shows us that we are able to be diplomatic with the powers of today. There is a lot to learn from the elders that communicated with those in the highest positions of the US government and collaborated in a diplomatic fashion to change the destiny of Kahoʻolawe. That act recalls how our ancestors communicated in the nineteenth century by protesting the US Congress–forced Annexation.

By discussing Kaho'olawe with President Bush and members of the US Congress, Hawaiians demonstrated that we were capable of following along in their ancestors' footsteps by taking a place at the table to discuss those issues pertaining to ourselves, our belief systems, and our future as a people. It also shows us that we can all come together and collaborate on issues that are current and life-changing for one group of people. We can all learn the lessons of how we can work together and collaborate with others. This example has shown us how to effectively navigate the system through collaborations, sometimes even with those who were once deemed the enemy.

This social movement has its own story of moving from the margins to the center in terms of negotiating pathways of knowledge by reclaiming, reasserting, and reconceptualizing Hawaiian identity in modern times. This movement was extreme in the beginning stages because of the bombings and the disappearance of Mitchell and Helm. Because of Mitchell, Helm, and the PKO, this movement unfolded into a dynamic transformation of empowerment and agency for Hawaiian people. The call to organize showed how a community-led, grassroots movement can be just as powerful as a political change if not more powerful and life changing. My own personal story can attest to this affirmation that was life changing for me. Each time as I revisit Kaho'olawe, the affirmation of Hawaiian identity is strengthened as each trip to the island is special and spiritual. This affirmation is seen as an act of liberation for myself and empowers my Native agency in my relations with my family and community. Within this same dialogue of liberation, Kaho'olawe continues to be a place to reconnect and thrive as a Hawaiian in modern times.

References

Aluli, N., and D. McGregor. 1992. "Mai ke Kai Mai Ke Ola, From the Ocean Comes Life: Hawaiian Customs, Uses, and Practices on Kaho'olawe Relating to the Surrounding Ocean." *Hawaiian Journal of History* 26:231–254 (Honolulu: Hawaiian Historical Society).

Cerizo, K. 2019. "25 Years Hence, Recovery Work Continues on the Island of Kahooalwe; Anniversary of Sign-Over Ceremony Is a Time for Reflection and Vision." *Maui News*, May 5.

Charlton, L. 1974. "Hawaiians Call for Reparations." *New York Times*, June 25.

Corbin, A. 2014. "Kahoʻolawe." *Sacred Land Film Project*. https://sacredland.org/kaho%ca%bbolawe-united-states/.

Duerksen, C., D. Bonderman, and S. Dennis. 1983. *A Handbook on Historic Preservation Law*. Washington, DC: Conservation Foundation.

Faulstich, P. 1990. "Hawaii's Rainforest Crunch: Land, People, and Geothermal Development." *Cultural Survival Quarterly* 14 (4) https://www.culturalsurvival.org/publications/cultural-survival-quarterly/hawaiis-rainforest-crunch-land-people-and-geothermal.

Fornander, A. 1916. "Kamahualele's Chant. Moʻikeha Story." *Fornander Collection of Hawaiian Antiquities and Folk-Lore: the Hawaiians' Account of the Formation of Their Islands and Origin of Their Race, with the Traditions of Their Migrations, Etc., as Gathered from Original Sources*. Honolulu: Bishop Museum Press.

Gilbert, M. 2009. *The Second World War: A Complete History*. London: Orion Publishing Group.

Goodyear-Kaʻōpua, N. 2011. "Kuleana Lahui: Collective Responsibility for Hawaiian Nationhood in Activists' Praxis." *Sociology* (August 31).

Graves, M., and A. Kehaunani. 1993. "Preservation of Historical Resources on Kahoʻolawe: Responsibilities, Natural and Cultural Impacts, and Priorities." Kahoʻolawe Island Conveyance Commission, city of Wailuku. http://www.kahoolawe.hawaii.gov/KICC/7%20Preservation%20of%20Historical%20Resources%20on%20Kaho'olawe.pdf.

Green, T., and Judge Advocate General's School. 1943. *Martial Law in Hawaii December 7,—April 4, 1943*. Library of Congress. https://www.loc.gov/item/2011525474/.

Hommon, Robert J. 1977, 1980a, 1983. "National Register of Historic Places Multiple Resource Nomination Forms for the Historic Resources of Kahoʻolawe." Hawaiʻi Marine Research Inc.

Hommon, Robert J. 1980b. "National Register of Historic Places Multiple Resource Nomination Forms for the Historic Resources of Kahoʻolawe." Hawaiʻi Marine Research Inc.

Kamakau, S. 1976. *The Works of the People of Old = Na Hana a Ka Po'e Kahiko*. Honolulu: Bishop Museum Press.

Kanahele, P., Kanahele-Mossma, H., Kanakaʻole, N., Kanakaʻole, K., Kealiʻikanakaʻoleohaililani, K., Mossman, K. K., Mossman, K., Tangarō, T., Stewart, R. 2017. "Nā Oli no ka ʻāina o Kanakaʻole (The Chants for the Kanakaʻole lands): A Compilation of Oli and Cultural Practices." Edith Kānakaʻole Foundation. https://edithkanakaolefoundation.org/docs/NaOliNoKaAinaOKanakaole.pdf.

Kanahele, P., H. Kanahele-Mossma, A. Nu'uhwa, and K. Keali'ikanaka'ole. 2009. "The Culture Plan for Kanaloa Kaho'olawe." Edith Kānaka'ole Foundation. https://kahoolawe.hawaii.gov/downloads/CULTURAL%20PLAN.pdf.

Kepelino, and Martha Warren Beckwith. 1932. *Kepelino's Traditions of Hawaii*. Honolulu: Bernice P. Bishop Museum.

KICC. 1993. *Kaho'olawe Island: Restoring a Cultural Treasure: Final Report of the Kaho'olawe Island Conveyance Commission to the Congress of the United States*. https://evols.library.manoa.hawaii.edu/items/c5e3dfed-5622-490c-bda3-f1bd24640a6f.

KIRC. n.d.a. "Hawai'i Revised Statuses." *Kahoolawe Island Reserve Commission Legal Documents*. Accessed February 25, 2023. http://kahoolawe.hawaii.gov/legal.shtml.

KIRC. n.d.b. "Kaho'olawe History." *Kahoolawe Island Reserve Commission History*. Accessed February 25, 2023. https://www.kahoolawe.hawaii.gov/history.shtml.

KIRC. 1995. *Kahoolawe Island Reserve Commission Strategic Plan 2004–2008*. Kahoolawe.hawaii.gov/plans/EE10-StrategicPlan2.pdf.

KIRC. 2008. *Kahoolawe Island Reserve Commission Strategic Plan 2009–2013*. https://www.kahoolawe.hawaii.gov/plans-policies-reports.shtml#strategic.

KIRC. 2009. *Palapala 'Aelike Kahu'āina Stewardship Agreement Pertaining to the Kaho'olawe Island Reserve Commission and the Protect Kaho'olawe 'Ohana through its Non-profit Corporation and Fiscal Agent Kohemalamalama O Kanaloa / Protect Kaho'olawe*. http://kahoolawe.hawaii.gov/plans/Stewardship.pdf.

Levin, W., R. Reeve, F. Salmoiraghi, and D. Ulrich. 1995. *Kaho'olawe : Nā Leo o Kanaloa : Chants and Stories of Kaho'olawe*. Honolulu: 'Ai Pōhaku Press.

Liliuokalani. 1898. *Hawaii's Story*. Boston: Lee and Shepard.

Lum, B. 2003. "Kaho'olawe and the Makahiki Ceremony: The Healing of an Island." *California Journal of Health Promotion* 1 (SI): 23–25.

MacKenzie, M., S. Serrano, and K. Kaulukukui. 2007. "Environmental Justice for Indigenous Hawaiians: Reclaiming Land and Resources." *Natural Resources and Environment* 21 (3): 37–79.

Malo, D. 1951. *Hawaiian Antiquities (Moolelo Hawai'i)*. 2nd ed. Honolulu: The Museum.

McGregor, D. 2007. *Na Kua'aina: Living Hawaiian Culture*. Honolulu: University of Hawai'i Press.

McGregor, D., and M. MacKenzie. 2015. "Mo'olelo 'Eā O Nā Hawai'i: History of Native Hawaiian Governance in Hawai'i." https://downloads.regulations.gov/DOI-2015-0005-4290/attachment_1.pdf.

McLeod, C. 2013. *Islands of Sanctuary, Standing on Sacred Ground*. Film. Distributed by Bullfrog Films, Oley PA.

Merwin, W. S. 1989. "The Sacred Bones of Maui." *New York Times Magazine*, August 6.

PBR Hawai'i. 1995. "Palapala Ho'onohonoho Moku'aina O Kaho'olawe: Kaho'olawe Use Plan." https://www.kahoolawe.hawaii.gov/plans/Use%20Plan%20Page.htm.

Racoma, Robin Yoko. 2008. *Lauka'ie'ie: A Hawaiian Legend Retold. Kamehameha Schools*. Honolulu, HI.

Reeve, R. 1995. "Kaho'olawe: Ka Mokupuni O Kanaloa." *Manoa (Honolulu, Hawaii. 1989)* 7 (1): 203–220.

Social Science Research Institute. 1998. "Ho' Ola Hou I Ke Kina O Kanaloa: Kaho' olawe Environmental Restoration Plan." https://kahoolawe.hawaii.gov/plans/KIRC_98_Restoration%20Plan.pdf.

Trask, H. 2000. "The Struggle for Hawaiian Sovereignty—Introduction." *Cultural Survival Quarterly* 24 (1).

Ulukau Dictionary. n.d. "Kahiki." Accessed March 1, 2023. https://wehewehe.org/?l=en.

12

Resisting Colonialism within Sustainability in Higher Education

The Intercultural Sustainability Leaders Program at the University of Minnesota Morris

CLEMENT LOO AND TROY GOODNOUGH

"When I hear about 'sustainability,' I think of buildings and managers. Sustainability isn't a topic for me." That's what one of our students, J, said when we asked her why her friends weren't more engaged with sustainability efforts on campus. She spoke those words paraphrasing one of her friends, K, explaining why he wasn't interested in sustainability.

We would learn later that K was actually deeply concerned with sustainability but correctly understood that the way "sustainability" is often defined and conceived of (as about infrastructure and resource efficiency without much consideration for social equity and thriving communities) is thin. Sustainability, as it has been most commonly understood, is usually informed by assumptions reflective of a very narrow range of perspectives and is not a topic that's particularly worthy of K's attention.

We share this anecdote because in this chapter we want to introduce you to a program we (Troy and Clement) created (in collaboration with our colleague Tammy Berberi) with the support of the University of Minnesota's Institute on the Environment (IonE). That program is the Intercultural

https://doi.org/10.5876/9781646425105.c012

Sustainability Leaders (ISLe). The ISLe program is a cohort of students who are for the most part persons of color and/or Indigenous, who work together to consider how the sustainability efforts at our campus could become more reflective of the full range of cultural worldviews that are found at University of Minnesota (UMN) Morris.

Through the ISLe program, we hope to accomplish three goals: (1) to create a more culturally robust and representative approach to sustainability on our campus, (2) to support the building of a community/network of students who work together to promote culturally informed sustainability initiatives at our university, and (3) to create alternative discourses and dialogues about sustainability that better match the interests, concerns, and worldviews of students who have been alienated from earlier sustainability efforts at UMN Morris.

In pursuit of such goals, ISLe students participate in a paid fellowship where we meet once every two weeks throughout the academic year to (a) have conversations with regional leaders working at the intersection of sustainability and equity, (b) reflect upon and discuss how cultural lenses affect how sustainability is conceptualized, and (c) consider how we might better integrate different cultural perspectives and knowledges into UMN Morris's sustainability efforts.

The idea of ISLe found its start with a recognition that UMN Morris is one of (if not the) most racially diverse campuses within the University of Minnesota system and that the students who were most actively involved in campus sustainability efforts were not representative of the diversity found in the broader campus population. We also realized that while UMN Morris is an international leader in campus sustainability, the way sustainability was conceptualized on campus often wasn't adequately informed by the perspectives and cultural understandings of many of our students.

While nearly 40 percent of UMN Morris's student population are persons of color or Indigenous, with the largest group (approximately 27%–28%) identifying as either Native American or First Nations, until recently the vast majority of students serving as interns within the UMN Morris Office of Sustainability (MOOS) identified as white. The Office of Sustainability was created in 2006 and is the first sustainability office established within the University of Minnesota system. The office is coordinated by one full-time staff member and typically houses five to ten student interns.

The sustainability office typically funds internships via several mechanisms, including federal work-study (FWS) funds, internal grants, external grants, and philanthropic funds. Federal work-study funds are the most reliable source of funding for many offices, including MOOS, for providing meaningful campus work experiences. Other funding streams are far more variable. Students who participate in UMN Morris's Native American tuition waiver (which we discuss at greater length later in the text), however, are not eligible to receive FWS funding to support their internships.

Given the structural challenge of FWS and the perception that sustainability (as it has been traditionally understood) is excessively narrow in its scope, it has been the case that overwhelmingly the interns who have served in MOOS have been students who identify or present as white and female. Overall, there have been very few students of color who have served in the MOOS. Though even prior to ISLe, MOOS has made fledgling efforts to incorporate more BIPOC+ students into internships.

For example, using philanthropic funds, MOOS hired student interns focused specifically on outreach to marginalized student groups on-campus to open a dialogue about sustainability (which did not work well). A second internship experiment focused on encouraging Indigenous students and students of color to explore sustainability from their own cultural lens, with some focus on making connections between Indigenous language and sustainability and environmental concepts. This approach has been a way to begin a dialogue about Native languages, like Dakota and Anishinaabe languages, and how they incorporate phenology-related concepts into their calendars.

A few years ago, UMN IonE launched a new grant program that focused on support for new projects that worked to integrate sustainability and DEI work. This new grant program is consistent with the evolving conversation and focus on diversity, equity, inclusion, and justice (DEIJ) work within higher education during recent years. With more than a decade of history, MOOS has the benefit of seeing the trajectory of many alumni who served as interns grow into sustainability careers across the United States. The organization realizes that these efforts need to expand to include more representation in sustainability careers in and outside of Minnesota. And, so, the conditions were ripe to create ISLe.

In the case of UMN Morris, our efforts to better engage students of color and Indigenous students in our sustainability efforts through ISLe are consistent with our university's mission. This mission is in important ways defined by an obligation to respond to and begin to make recompense for the historical oppression of Native American boarding schools within the United States.

University of Minnesota Morris is built on lands that—in addition to being home to the Dakota and Ojibwe—also previously housed buildings that were part of and have a history that is inextricably linked to, a Native American boarding school. Between 1887 to 1909, at the site of our campus, stood a boarding school that was first established by the Sisters of Mercy and then later became the Morris Industrial School for Indians operated by the US federal government. When the location of our institution was transferred to the University of Minnesota, it was with the requirement that any campus built here would provide a tuition waiver to all Native American students.

Our campus continues to meet that obligation, offering full tuition waivers to (a) enrolled members of a federally recognized American Indian tribes, Alaskan Native Villages, or Canadian First Nations; (b) direct descendants of a parent or grandparent who is an enrolled member of a federally recognized American Indian tribe, Alaskan Native Village, or Canadian First Nation; or (c) direct descendants of a tribally verified member of a federally recognized American Indian tribe, Alaskan Native Village, or Canadian First Nation, other than parent or grandparent.

However, simply offering tuition waivers is on its own not enough. A tuition waiver to an institution that centers settler colonial worldviews, pedagogies, and values would be a continuation of a history of oppression. That being so, UMN Morris has since the late 1980s developed partnerships with regional Indigenous leaders and nations to work toward reckoning with the obligations that arise from our institution's history and becoming better as an institution that appropriately serves Indigenous students and communities.

One way we do this is through the American Indian Advisory Committee (AIAC), a body consisting of members that reflect regional Native American communities that advises our university's chancellor and helps our campus set priorities for better serving our Native students and neighbors. The guidance of the AIAC has led our institution to develop language revitalization programs, improving financial and student service supports for our Indigenous students, created and improved programming aimed at improving sense of place and community among our Native students, and better integrated cultural programming that enhances the college experience of Indigenous students.

More recently, UMN Morris has also been growing partnerships with the nations and communities that have been most impacted by the boarding school that previously occupied the site of our campus. Through such partnerships, we hope to determine the best ways to proceed to identify and grapple with the full impact of the boarding school (such as identifying whether there are unrematriated remains on our campus and, if so, how best to honor and respect those remains) and to, hopefully, engage in more robust healing and reconciliation.

University of Minnesota Morris has also worked to be and has become recognized as a Native American Serving Nontribal Institution by the US Department of Education. And, recently, our institution has made an explicit commitment to more robustly acknowledge and respond to its history by "recogniz(ing) the unique obligation and opportunity at UMN Morris for greater equity in education for Native American students fostered by the history of this place; provide indigenized support for student learning, health, wellbeing, and success; and produce graduates from all backgrounds who have a greater understanding of and appreciation for Native American history, cultures, and lifeways" (University of Minnesota Morris 2021).

To meet this commitment, our campus has in the past several years taken our first steps in becoming an institution that better serves Indigenous students. We have begun centering discourse (informed and guided by Indigenous partners) about what it means to be a predominantly white institution that works to resist ongoing colonization and to support the efforts of Indigenous folks to reclaim and revitalize culture, language, and traditions that have been suppressed. While we have certainly not figured it all out, we have been perhaps making progress. And, one of the ways that we've been working toward such progress is through the ISLe program.

We would also like to add that even for institutions and organizations not sharing UMN Morris's specific history and mission, having representative participation in sustainability efforts as well as conceiving of sustainability in ways informed by and reflective of the full range of cultural perspectives within one's community are important for a number of reasons.

First, sustainability is unavoidably a value-laden concept. The word "sustainability," has been defined in terms of meeting present needs without undermining the ability of future generations to meet their needs (World Commission 1987) or in terms of thriving or flourishing (Ehrenfeld and Hoffman 2013). However, needs, thriving, and flourishing are all to some degree dependent on what we hold to be important, worthwhile, and necessary for a good life—all things that are influenced by culture (Loo 2015).

Second, as the mantra often repeated by disability advocates (Charlton 2000) states, "nothing about us without us." As scholars of justice argue, social justice requires participative or procedural justice (Shrader-Frechette 2002). That is, decision making and discourse that are about and impact a group of folks should never occur without those folks being at the center of the conversation.

And, third, nature abhors monocultures (perhaps even more so than vacuums), and shouldn't those of us who are attentive to nature recognize such when it comes to how we approach our sustainability work? Like how genetic diversity leads to healthier species and functional diversity often leads to healthier ecosystems, having more robust and culturally inclusive discourse offers us healthier conversations. When we are informed by a broader range of cultural perspectives and worldviews, we can collectively reflect and plan in ways that are richer in regard to how we understand the relationships we have with one another and the land, offer more options for how we conceptualize problems and objectives, and allow us to be more responsive to a broader range of factors and concerns.

Considering all the factors mentioned, we formed the first cohort of ISLe students in the fall of 2019. For the first two cohorts of ISLe, participation was by invitation only. We specifically identified students who had established roles on campus advocating or actively contributing to efforts related to equity, social justice, or community economic development. For the third cohort we placed an open call to all the students at UMN Morris. The students from these three cohorts represented a broad range of racial and cultural identities. Four of the students are Black (with three being immigrants or the child of immigrants). Two are Asian American. Four are Latino, one of whom is also Dakota. And, six are Native American, being Dakota, Lakota, and Anishinaabe.

When we began envisioning the program, we invited students to visit with the planning team to discuss what an "ISLe" program might look like. Several initial ideas emerged: (a) work with students to develop a better personal understanding of sustainability; (b) develop friendships amongst ISLe cohort participants; (c) include students in the program development, meeting planning, and implementation of the program; (d) provide opportunities for the ISLe cohort to meet sustainability leaders in and, to a lesser extent, outside of Minnesota from a range of different racial and cultural backgrounds; (e) provide opportunities for team-building and educational travel experiences to amplify the previous themes; and (f) inspire ISLe cohort members to envision themselves in sustainability-connected careers or work.

The foundational aspect of the ISLe program has been storytelling by invited speakers. There are about fifteen ISLe meetings during an academic year, about five of which include an invited speaker. The rest of the meetings focus on reflecting on themes we heard from speakers, relationship building, and discussing our own personal sustainability and wellness.

Another foundational aspect of ISLe has been funding student interns and invited speakers. Interns in the ISLe program are paid to attend each meeting and for the hours they participate in the program to reflect the value and contribution of their efforts. Invited speakers are offered an honorarium to visit with the cohort to demonstrate our appreciation for their expertise, knowledge, and generosity.

To prepare the invited speakers, we make our expectations clear. We invite the speakers to share their own personal life, career, and sustainability journey, encouraging them to interweave these threads however they would like to do so. We let our speakers know that we aren't looking for formal presentations but, instead, hope to relate as potential friends sharing stories and questions. We have found that the students of the ISLe cohorts are extremely interested in hearing the personal stories of the invited speakers and the invited speakers are excited to share at length the themes, ideas, and thoughts that they are inspired to share. Speakers have been very generous with their time and their stories. We have heard stories of tragedy, persistence, failure, and success.

In the first cohorts, we had tried several ways of trying to engage the student interns between the meetings. These experiments included suggested readings and videos. We had also experimented with using Discord, an online platform that allows for threaded discussions. But, ultimately, we settled on less homework, less technology, less structure, and more time in organic conversation. That said, with the COVID pandemic, we have modified how we approach conversation to include a Zoom option for cohort participants who did not want to meet in-person.

Flowing out of our conversations, throughout the ISLe program, we have resisted offering any detailed definitions of sustainability. Instead, we have focused on reflecting and building upon the messages and themes shared by speakers. We have thought about and discussed topics such as (1) how identity and history impact our relationships (as well as how we define those relationships) with the land, other species, and one another; and (2) the impact of language and culture in how we understand the objectives of sustainability. Other topics: (3) We've learned about how sustainability work involves the melding of environmental stewardship and the empowerment of communities (both outcomes that are often inextricably tied to one another). (4) We've examined how we might take space or make space for Indigenous folks and persons of color in movements, institutions, and organizations. And (5) we've gained insights about how to pursue careers that combine sustainability and equity, as well as how young professionals can capitalize or create professional opportunities for themselves.

More important, through our discussions and time spent together, we've built authentic relationships between the students, between the students and the professional staff coordinating ISLe, and between those of us from UMN Morris and the speakers who are among those doing the most important work, creating a more sustainable and equitable world. Those relationships serve as a basis for the coalition and solidarity, a basis necessary to take the next steps of growing sustainability at UMN Morris in better ways. Indeed, we've welcomed one of our early speakers, Michelle Montgomery (the editor of this anthology), more permanently onto our team as an external coordinator. And, doing so has added a great deal of expertise and experience at creating forums for Indigenous folks, knowledges, and ideas to our group.

As our ISLe group grows and develops, we've begun to think about moving forward from our first steps with ISLe to begin to make practical changes that more concretely shift sustainability efforts at UMN Morris to ones that better integrate equity and the empowerment of historically marginalized communities and individuals. Some of these more concrete steps include more conscientiously removing and mitigating the barriers and burdens that place the lion's share of effort to improve equity on the shoulders of those marginalized by the status quo. Other steps involve considering how we might expand our coalition in ways that preserve the authentic relationships, discourse, and sense of community that have been so important to the first three cohorts of our program. Finally, we're taking steps to begin to shift how the broader campus community thinks about our place in the world, and how we might be in better relation with all of our relatives (human or nonhuman) and the land, as well as be more aware and responsive to the fact that many of the assumptions that guide our institution have been ones grounded by a settler colonial worldview.

Starting with the next (i.e., fourth) cohort of ISLe, our plan is to begin to create materials and facilitate conversation that teach about how local Indigenous peoples traditionally reckoned the passage of time through reference to the annual cycles found in nature. We hope that such materials will help all the members of our campus better understand how relationships with the land and with our nonhuman relatives are centered in the languages and worldviews of the Dakota, Lakota, Nakota, and Anishinaabe, who made and continue to make their homes in the land that is now often referred to as west-central Minnesota.

We hope that by providing tools we help the non-Indigenous members of our campus community better recognize their Ameripean assumptions, how those assumptions might inform how they perceive the world, and how those assumptions are not universal. Helping those of us who are non-Indigenous to better see that privilege often obscures will, in turn, helps us to better understand how assumptions can be shifted in ways that help us grow to become a community that centers those who have been marginalized. And, in doing so, we hope these steps help us to become a community that supports the mutual flourishing of all into the future.

At the beginning of this chapter, we quoted one of our students, J, paraphrasing her friend, K, explaining why he wasn't interested in sustainability efforts at UMN Morris or sustainability more generally. K correctly recognized that historically the dominant sustainability movement has been narrow and excluded the interests, concerns, values, and worldviews of Indigenous folks and persons of color. We hope that through the ongoing work with ISLe that we're moving toward an approach to sustainability at UMN Morris that centers equity, resists settler colonial worldviews, and provides a space for folks of all identities to be in relationship and build solidarity to work on achieving the sort of sustainability that is worthy of everybody's attention, time, and effort.

References

Charlton, J. I. 2000. *Nothing about Us without Us: Disability, Oppression, and Empowerment*. Berkeley: University of California Press.

Ehrenfeld, J. R., and A. J. Hoffman. 2013. *Flourishing: A Frank Conversation about Sustainability*. 1st ed. Stanford, CA: Stanford University Press.

Loo, C. 2015. "A More Central Role for Lower and Middle Income Countries in Climate Governance." In *Global Policy: Climate Change and Human Rights: The 2015 Paris Conference and the Task of Protecting People on a Warming Planet*, edited by M. Di Paola and D. Kamal, 86–94. Chichester, UK: John Wiley and Sons.

Shrader-Frechette, K. 2002. *Environmental Justice: Creating Equity, Reclaiming Democracy*. Oxford: Oxford University Press.

University of Minnesota Morris. 2021. Strategic Visioning and Planning. Accessed April 22, 2022. https://Morris.Umn.Edu/About/Organizational-Structure-And-Campus-Governance/Chancellor/Initiatives/Strategic-Visioning-And#:~:Text=University%20of%20Minnesota%20Morris%20Mission&Amp;Text=UMN%20Morris%20is%20committed%20to,A%20deep%20sense%20of%20community.

World Commission on Environment and Development. 1987. *Our Common Future*. Oxford: Oxford University Press.

13

Bifurcation

An Indigenous Perspective on Water Science and Water Justice

RYAN E. EMANUEL

Water is at the heart of some of the most pressing challenges faced by humanity. Climate change alters the odds that droughts or floods will happen, and rising seas threaten to swallow up coastal areas (IPCC 2021). Industrial activities leave streams and aquifers polluted with toxic chemicals and harmful pathogens. Cities outgrow their water supplies and hunt for new ones. As a hydrologist, I find that all these challenges motivate my work. I am especially interested in the societal disparities that accompany these challenges. Disparities exist because pollution, climate change, and other water-related challenges do not affect all places and all people equally.

One of the most tragic aspects of water-related challenges is that communities shouldering the largest burdens are often least equipped to respond, adapt, or otherwise meet the challenges in robust and meaningful ways. These kinds of disparities are well documented for issues that stem from climate change and water pollution (e.g., Hsiang et al. 2017; Neville 2022; Wing 2000). Many of these disparities are also at the fore of discussions about environmental justice, which is often defined in the United States as the fair

https://doi.org/10.5876/9781646425105.c013

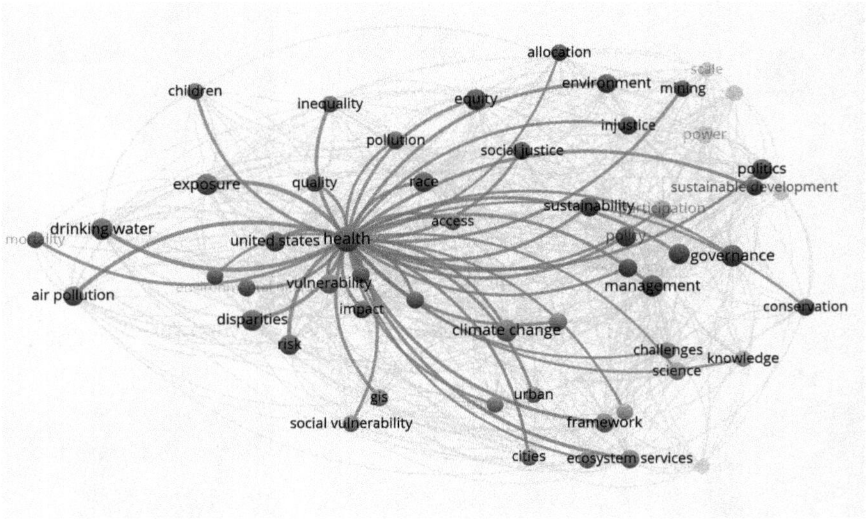

FIGURE 13.1. A bibliometric analysis of keywords in 542 journal articles about water and environmental justice published through 2020. Circles indicate the fifty most-frequent keywords found in these records, with circle size corresponding to keyword frequency. Line widths represent strength of links between keywords. Colors indicate clusters of keywords. Figure generated using VOSviewer bibliometric software (Van Eck and Waltman 2010) applied to records retrieved from a Web of Science search for topics "water" and "environmental justice." Keywords "water" and "environmental justice" are omitted from the visualization because they occur in all records.

treatment and meaningful involvement of all people in various aspects of environmental decision-making (e.g., EPA 2022). The inequitable distribution of environmental burdens (or benefits) is an important aspect of environmental justice, but it is not the only dimension at play. Environmental justice also involves procedural fairness, recognition of distinct identities, and respect—especially respect for marginalized perspectives (Bullard 1996; Schlosberg 2007).

Much of the academic dialogue around environmental justice and water focuses on the health of individuals or communities (figure 13.1). Rightly so: safe, predictable, and accessible water supplies are essential to human health and well-being (Bartram and Cairncross 2010; Hunter, Macdonald, and Carter 2010). But many academic discussions overlook spiritual and cultural aspects of water. These aspects are especially important to Indigenous peoples whose collective identities are tied to water or watery places. Water—in its dual roles as a substance and as a place—shapes the cultures and experiences of Indigenous peoples in ways that may not be captured in health-focused discussions.

Academic literature can sometimes articulate the significance of water for Indigenous peoples, especially literature that focuses on existential threats from pollution, climate change, unsustainable development, or public policies that may harm culturally significant waters (e.g., Arsenault 2021; Bulltail and Walter 2020; Crepelle 2019; Emanuel 2018; Hikuroa, Slade, and Gravley 2011; Laltaika 2022; Mitchell et al. 2020; Moggridge and Thompson 2021; Robison et al. 2018; Van Horne et al. 2021). The work is diverse, insightful, and larger than the representative publications cited here. As a whole, the work emphasizes that for many Indigenous peoples, the nexus of water and environmental justice is about more than individual or community health (although these issues are certainly part of the picture). J. Robison et al. (2018) share an especially diverse set of principles around Indigenous water justice that highlight respect for cultural traditions, inclusive governance, education of non-Indigenous peoples about Indigenous values, and more.

I am excited by the proliferation of scholarly work highlighting Indigenous perspectives on water and on water-related aspects of justice; it enriches academic and policy discourse at the nexus of water and environmental justice. The very act of generating this scholarship can be a form of justice. The latter is true because the work often injects Indigenous voices into discussions that otherwise commodify clean water or watery places such as wetlands, rivers, and coastlines. Without this kind of work, Indigenous peoples' sacred connections to place risk being erased in academic and policy discussions about water and environmental justice (Chief, Emanuel, and Conroy-Ben 2019; Jenkins et al. 2021).

I want to elaborate on the idea of scholarship promoting justice from my standpoint as a hydrologist whose research has bifurcated (and may be bifurcating still) to address issues in my own Indigenous community and in neighboring Indigenous communities on the Coastal Plain of what is now North Carolina. These issues include aspects of pollution, climate change, and land development that I never expected to work on when I became an environmental scientist—histories of racism and oppression, public policies around

FIGURE 13.2. Mr. Danny Bell, Lumbee and Coharie elder. Photo by Cayce Emanuel.

tribal consultation and environmental justice, ethical dealings with tribal nations, and so on. Before I share more, I need to explain where I come from.

I belong to the Lumbee Tribe, a group of Indigenous people who still live in and around our ancestral territories in what is now Robeson County, North Carolina. Our ancestors survived early colonial diseases, conflicts, and dispossession by isolating themselves in remote parts of the Coastal Plain—places that were unmapped, unexplored, and unwanted by settlers until the nineteenth century (Emanuel 2019). Our ancestors may have been isolated from colonial society, but they were not hiding. Mr. Danny Bell, a Lumbee and Coharie elder (figure 13.2), recently put it to me this way: If our ancestors were hiding, they were not very good at it. They appear periodically in historical records—continuing their communal lives, protecting their families, and stewarding their lands as best they could.

The beating heart of our community has always been our namesake river, the Lumbee. The Lumbee River is a blackwater stream; its waters have naturally high concentrations of dissolved organic matter (Neville et al. 2021). Rain that falls on the Lumbee River watershed soaks into deep, organic-rich soils of wetlands that occupy much of the landscape (Emanuel 2018). There, the water steeps until it reemerges into rivers and streams the color of rich, brown tea.

Several decades ago, Lumbee people—who descend from several different contact-era Indigenous peoples—chose to name themselves for the river whose dark water and swampy tributaries insulated us from extractive settler colonialism and white supremacist policies until well into the nineteenth century (Dial and Eliades 1975; Lowery 2018). Settler colonialism and white supremacy still raged around our ancestors, strongly influencing their lives and cultural practices, but the tortuous river and its swamp-strewn watershed buffered Lumbee ancestors from nineteenth-century policies faced by many other tribal nations, including treaty-making, forced removal, and confinement to reservations.

To be sure, Lumbee ancestors faced violence and oppression, but their dealings with outsiders were tempered by the reputation of our homeland as an impenetrable and worthless swamp. In 1871, Giles Leitch, a white official from Robeson County, testified to Congress about the inability of local and federal officials to capture a band of post–Civil War guerrilla fighters made up of Lumbee ancestors and allies. Leitch, who was born and raised only a few miles away from our homeland, could only offer members of Congress a vague and confusing description of our home territory: "That swamp is about three quarters of a mile wide on an average. It is not all swamp, but there are islands in it of an acre, or two acres, or five acres in extent. . . . Upon those islands they have dens and caves in which they hide. Very few people traverse that swamp; there are very few who know where the islands are, or where their caves and dens are" (US Congress 1872).

More than a decade after Leitch's testimony to Congress, outsiders still viewed our homeland as nothing more than a "malarious ooze" that ought to be drained, logged, and converted into farmland (Scientific American 1888). The mere reputation of our river and its tributary swamps shaped our history as Indigenous people; it is no surprise that we call ourselves People of the Dark Water and named our modern-day tribal nation after the river.

The Lumbee River and its tributary swamps dissect sandy uplands that are home to Lumbee communities—which some Lumbees call settlements. My mother is from the Sandy Plains community, near the headwaters of Moss Neck Swamp, and my father is from Saddletree, named after Saddletree Swamp. These are two of a dozen or more Lumbee settlements that still exist today, many of which are named after their adjacent swamps.

In times past, the swamps provided our people with fish and game, firewood, medicines, and more. Our people grew crops and built homes on the sandy plains nearby, far enough from the water to escape flooding but near enough to consider the swamps and the river home. Still today, many Lumbee settlements share their names with the swamps located nearby. Some Lumbees still live close to the land, hunting and fishing along the river and in the swamps, just as our ancestors did. Lumbee people are also living in a time of cultural renewal, and the swamp environments provide us with traditional medicines and materials for practicing our historic lifeways. A few places still hold sacred artifacts and items of patrimony (Knick 2008). Our history, culture, and collective identity as a people are all bound up in the swamps and in the blackwater streams that flow from them.

For decades, decision makers have permitted or even incentivized the damage or destruction of culturally significant places through land use change or pollution in and around the Lumbee River watershed. More than a century ago, government-sanctioned ditching and draining efforts transformed many of our culturally significant wetlands for the purpose of creating more land for cotton, tobacco, and other commercial crops (e.g., Maxwell 2017). In the 1950s, state and federal officials began to allow energy companies to construct large, natural gas pipelines and related infrastructure through wetlands, beneath streams, and in the midst of Lumbee communities—a practice that continues to this day (Emanuel and Wilkins 2020). In the 1980s, state officials and corporate leaders promoted industrialized livestock facilities, which pollute wetlands and streams with nutrients and pathogens (Harris et al. 2021; Martin 2018; Niedermeyer 2020).

Decision makers rationalize each wave of transformation as progress for Lumbees and our neighbors. At the turn of the twentieth century, decision makers said that draining swamps would create more profitable farmland. In the 1950s, pipeline proponents and regulators said that natural gas pipelines would usher in a new wave of economic opportunity. In the 1980s, meat-processing companies and state officials said that industrialized livestock production would feed a growing world. Lumbees and other Indigenous peoples may or may not have benefited from these various forms of "progress," but a more important point is that Lumbee people have never had a formal say in decision-making discussions about any of these transformations to our homeland. This point is important, because each wave of transformation brought new forms of damage and destruction to the streams and wetlands that helped to form our identity as Lumbee people and still bind our communities together today. What is progress to some can be an existential threat to others.

Many of these activities result from policies enacted decades ago, long before the emergence of environmental justice policies, which lay out expectations for meaningful engagement of low-wealth and racially marginalized people in environmental governance (e.g., Emanuel 2017; Yeoman 2021). But some of these activities continue today, more than two decades after federal environmental justice policy took shape, and at a time when state officials regularly reaffirm their commitments to environmental justice. One of the key problems, as I see it, with public policies and affirmations around environmental justice is that they do not actively seek ways to stop the stockpiling of burdens onto marginalized peoples; instead, they often simply create opportunities for people to vent their frustrations. Other times, these policies and affirmations claim to promote justice through economic benefits or other forms of progress that have never been weighed against the cultural costs to Lumbee people. Decision makers perpetuate historic injustices and promote Indigenous erasure when they define progress on their own terms instead of letting Indigenous peoples define progress for themselves.

The emergence of scholarship that highlights Indigenous perspectives on water and justice pushes back against the erasure of Indigenous peoples by decision makers, corporations, and others who insist on talking over us. The body of scholarship is not a full remedy, but it demands that environmental regulators, consultants, and others pay attention. Collectively, this research compels decision makers to recognize that water—as a substance and as a place—cannot be envisioned solely as a commodity in situations where it holds cultural significance to Indigenous peoples. To that end, this body of work promotes justice by pointing back to Indigenous peoples as those who are often most qualified to speak on behalf of water and watery places in their own communities.

Early in my career, I worked to address challenges faced by Indigenous peoples by championing science education and careers in science. I did this mostly by attending college fairs in Robeson County, leading science activities for Lumbee students and serving on local and state advisory groups on American Indian education. I worked with other American Indian educators to raise awareness about issues facing our students, and I helped to create training materials to train non-Indigenous educators about our rich and living cultures.

Eventually, I began to grapple more explicitly with justice-related challenges in my work. In 2014, the North Carolina's Commission of Indian Affairs invited me to join their newly formed environmental justice committee. Over the next few years, we took up issues related to disproportionately high and adverse impacts associated with natural gas infrastructure, we helped state and federal regulators think more critically about the ways in which they engage with tribal nations, and we helped tribes in North Carolina find ways to exert their sovereignty to protect culturally significant lands and waters.

These partnerships with tribal nations and community members caused my scholarship to branch into two distinct paths. On one path, I still lead a group of active hydrologists and environmental scientists, and we partner with other researchers to study interactions between plants and water in various settings. For example, we are currently studying the characteristics of water stored inside of trees; we are especially curious about how much water trees store and how stored water varies through time and in different parts of trees. The characteristics of tree water storage have implications for larger ecosystems and water cycles.

The second, newer, path engages directly with environmental justice and Indigenous rights in ways that cut across traditional disciplinary boundaries of environmental sciences, public policy, and history. For example, I seek out ways to expose structural barriers to Indigenous participation in environmental governance by analyzing regulatory and permitting cases. I also examine the historical roots of connections between Lumbee people and water. Other work on this path is forward looking and contemplates the impacts of climate change on Lumbee homelands.

I sometimes look for ways to resolve the bifurcation—to bring ideas from one realm of thinking into another. But I am not especially concerned about unifying the various strands of my work. I am more concerned about making sure that my work centers Indigenous perspectives, bolsters tribal sovereignty, and finds its way to the right audiences for maximum impact. In other words, I want to produce scholarship that fights the erasure of Indigenous peoples on matters related to water and the environment—the places that shape our cultural identities and bind us together. I am encouraged to know that other scholars are doing the same. I am inspired by the stories of hydrologists, soil scientists, biologists, demographers, historians, artists, and others who have found ways to promote justice for Indigenous peoples through their scholarship and creative endeavors. My bifurcated path is only one small part of this much larger narrative.

References

Arsenault, R. 2021. "Water Insecurity in Ontario First Nations: An Exploratory Study on Past Interventions and the Need for Indigenous Water Governance." *Water* 13 (5): 717.

Bartram, J., and S. Cairncross. 2010. "Hygiene, Sanitation, and Water: Forgotten Foundations of Health." *PLOS Medicine* 7 (11): E1000367.

Bullard, R. D. 1996. "Environmental Justice: It's More than Waste Facility Siting." *Social Science Quarterly* 77 (3): 493–499.

Bulltail, G., and M. T. Walter. 2020. "Impacts of Coal Resource Development on Surface Water Quality in a Multi-jurisdictional Watershed in the Western United States." *Journal of Contemporary Water Research and Education* 169 (1): 79–91.

Chief, K., R. E. Emanuel, and O. Conroy-Ben. 2019. "Indigenous Symposium on Water Research, Education, and Engagement." *Eos 100* (January 24).

Crepelle, A. 2019. "The Reservation Water Crisis: American Indians and Third World Water Conditions." *Tulane Environmental Law Journal* 32 (2): 157–188.

Dial, A. L., and D. K. Eliades. 1975. *The Only Land I Know: A History of the Lumbee Indians*. Syracuse, NY: Syracuse University Press.

Emanuel, R. E. 2017. "Flawed Environmental Justice Analyses." *Science* 357 (6348): 260–260.

Emanuel, R. E. 2018. "Climate Change in the Lumbee River Watershed and Potential Impacts on the Lumbee Tribe of North Carolina." *Journal of Contemporary Water Research and Education* 163 (1): 79–93.

Emanuel, R. E. 2019. "Water in the Lumbee World: A River and Its People in a Time of Change." *Environmental History* 24 (1): 25–51.

Emanuel, R. E., and D. E. Wilkins. 2020. "Breaching Barriers: The Fight for Indigenous Participation in Water Governance." *Water* 12 (8): 2113.

EPA. 2022. "Environmental Justice." Accessed October 15, 2022. https://www.epa.gov/environmentaljustice.

Harris, A. R., E. N. Fidan, N. G. Nelson, R. E. Emanuel, T. Jass, S. Kathariou, J. Niedermeyer, M. Sharara, F. L. De Los Reyes III, and D. A. Riveros-Iregui. 2021. "Microbial Contamination in Environmental Waters of Rural and Agriculturally-Dominated Landscapes Following Hurricane Florence." *ACS ES&T Water* 1 (9): 2012–2019.

Hikuroa, D., A. Slade, and D. Gravley. 2011. "Implementing Māori Indigenous Knowledge (Mātauranga) in a Scientific Paradigm: Restoring the Mauri to Te Kete Poutama." *MAI Review* 3 (1): 9.

Hsiang, S., R. Kopp, A. Jina, J. Rising, M. Delgado, S. Mohan, D. J. Rasmussen, R. Muir-Wood, P. Wilson, M. Oppenheimer, K. Larsen, and T. Houser. 2017. "Estimating Economic Damage from Climate Change in the United States." *Science* 356 (6345): 1362–1369.

Hunter, P. R., A. M. Macdonald, and R. C. Carter. 2010. "Water Supply and Health." *PLOS Medicine* 7 (11).

IPCC. 2021. "Climate Change 2021: The Physical Science Basis." *Contribution of Working Group I to the Sixth Assessment Report of the Intergovernmental Panel on Climate Change*. https://www.ipcc.ch/report/ar6/wg1/.

Jenkins, W., L. Rosa, J. Schmidt, L. Band, A. Beltran-Peña, A. Clarens, S. Doney, R. E. Emanuel, A. Glassie, J. Quinn, M. C. Rulli, W. Shobe, L. Szeptycki, and P. D'Odorico. 2021. "Values-Based Scenarios of Water Security: Rights to Water, Rights of Waters, and Commercial Water Rights." *Bioscience* 71 (11): 1157–1170.

Knick, S. 2008. "Because It Is Right." *Native South* 1 (1): 80–89.

Laltaika, E. 2022. "Indigenous Peoples' Participation and the Management of Wetlands in Africa: A Review of the Ramsar Convention." In *Fundamentals of Tropical Freshwater Wetlands*, edited by T. Dalu and R. J. Wasserman, 711–726. N.p.: Elsevier.

Lowery, M. M. 2018. *The Lumbee Indians: An American Struggle*. Chapel Hill: University of North Carolina Press.

Martin, K. L., R. E. Emanuel, and J. M. Vose. 2018. "Terra Incognita: The Unknown Risks to Environmental Quality Posed by the Spatial Distribution and Abundance of Concentrated Animal Feeding Operations." *Science of the Total Environment* 642 (November 15): 887–893.

Maxwell, W. 2017. "The Back Swamp Drainage Project, Robeson County, North Carolina: Biopolitical Intervention in the Lives of Indian Farmers." *Water History* 9 (1): 9–28.

Mitchell, T. A., N. J. Casper, L. T. Logan, E. Colclazier, and K. J. R. Mitchell. 2020. "Using Traditional Ecological Knowledge to Protect Wetlands: The Swinomish Tribe's Wetlands Cultural Assessment Project." Unpublished manuscript.

Moggridge, B. J., and R. M. Thompson. 2021. "Cultural Value of Water and Western Water Management: An Australian Indigenous Perspective." *Australasian Journal of Water Resources* 25 (1): 4–14.

Neville, J. A., R. E. Emanuel, E. G. Nichols, and J. Vose. 2021. "Extreme Flooding and Nitrogen Dynamics of a Blackwater River." *Water Resources Research* 57 (12). https://agupubs.onlinelibrary.wiley.com/doi/10.1029/2020WR029106.

Neville, J. A., J. Guz, H. M. Rosko, and M. C. Owens. 2022. "Water Quality Inequality: A Non-targeted Hotspot Analysis for Ambient Water Quality Injustices." *Hydrological Sciences Journal* (May): 1011–1025.

Niedermeyer, J. A., W. G. Miller, E. Yee, A. Harris, R. E. Emanuel, T. Jass, N. Nelson, and S. Kathariou. 2020. "Search for Campylobacter Spp. Reveals High Prevalence and Pronounced Genetic Diversity of Arcobacter Butzleri in Floodwater Samples Associated with Hurricane Florence in North Carolina, USA." *Applied and Environmental Microbiology* 86 (20): E01118–120.

Robison, J., B. Cosens, S. Jackson, K. Leonard, and D. Mccool. 2018. "Indigenous Water Justice." *Lewis and Clark Law Review* 22 (3): 841–922.

Schlosberg, D. 2007. "Distribution and Beyond: Conceptions of Justice in Contemporary Theory and Practice." In *Defining Environmental Justice*. Oxford: Oxford University Press.

Scientific American. 1888. "How to Utilize a Cypress Swamp." *Scientific American* 58 (10): 152.

US Congress. 1872. "Testimony of Giles Leitch, July 31, 1871." *Report of the Joint Select Committee to Inquire into the Condition of Affairs in the Late Insurrectionary States*: 283–304.

Van Eck, N. J., and L. Waltman. 2010. "Software Survey: VOSviewer, A Computer Program for Bibliometric Mapping." *Scientometrics* 84 (2): 523–538.

Van Horne, Y. O., K. Chief, P. H. Charley, M. G. Begay, N. Lothrop, M. L. Bell, R. A. Canales, N. I. Teufel-Shone, and P. I. Beamer. 2021. "Impacts to Diné Activities with the San Juan River after the Gold King Mine Spill." *Journal of Exposure Science and Environmental Epidemiology* 31 (5): 852–866.

Wing, S., D. Cole, and G. Grant. 2000. "Environmental Injustice in North Carolina's Hog Industry." *Environmental Health Perspectives* 108 (3): 225–231.

Yeoman, B. 2021. "The Contested Swamps of Robeson County." *Assembly*. September 22, 2021. https://www.theassemblync.com/long-form/the-contested-swamps-of-robeson-county/.

14

Lifting the Voices of Indigenous Students to Empower the Next Generation of Ocean Leaders

MELISSA B. PEACOCK AND MICHELLE MONTGOMERY

The United Nations International Decade of Ocean Science for Sustainable Development began in 2021 and will continue through 2030. The tagline for this program is "the science we need for the ocean we want," and the action plan is to develop globally shared information and knowledge systems to maintain ocean health (Duarte 2018; Ryabinin et al. 2019; UNESCO n.d.a, n.d.b). Within the development of the action plan for the Decade are the acknowledgment of the impacts that the ocean has on multiple stakeholders, and the commitment to increase diversity, equity, and different ways of knowing, including supporting and incorporating Indigenous or Traditional Knowledge in the science planning for now and the future (UNESCO n.d.b). The world stage and announcement of the importance of the ocean provide an opportunity to increase literacy surrounding the complex interactions that we as humans have with the ocean. It also allows an opportunity to spotlight the good work that is already happening with increasing student awareness and literacy of the ocean, and the stewardship that is already going on. While it is timely announcement from the United Nations

https://doi.org/10.5876/9781646425105.c014

Educational, Scientific and Cultural Organization (UNESCO) and the UN, and a lofty goal supported immediately by the UNESCO nations, it needs to be highlighted that Indigenous peoples in the Coast Salish region have been stewards of their oceans since time immemorial and are already working toward this future through the uplifting and support of the next generation of ocean leaders.

In our specific example, the generational leaders who will be present in this action plan for the sustainability of the world's oceans live and complete their research in the Salish Sea. The Salish Sea is a unique coastal environment, with complicated stewardship relationships. With an estimated population of approximately 8 million people (Jones 2021), this natural resource provides undeniable importance for people who live here. Located in the Pacific Northwest, it is an environment rich in diversity, known for its dynamic marine environment and complex ecological interactions (Jones, Keller, and van der Flier Keller 2021). The Salish Sea spans from the Campbell River in British Columbia to Olympia, Washington (see Freelan 2009 online for a map), crossing international and tribal boundaries. The earliest-known occupants along the Pacific Northwest coast are the Indigenous peoples known today as the Coast Salish People, and they were, and are, tasked with the protection and conservation for the Salish Sea. Traditional jurisdiction and stewardship of the Salish Sea have been complicated since the arrival of non-Indigenous settlers (Kew 2010). As J. Jones and colleagues (2021) ask, "Who is stewarding, advocating for, and helping protect and conserve the Salish Sea?" This, of course, refers to the variety of governmental, international, tribal, First Nations, and citizens who work to protect the beauty and resources of the Salish Sea. For the complexity of the region, the Salish Sea is an example of a strong, interactive working relationship between member groups. But, with no simple answer to who should lead the conservation efforts of the Salish Sea, a consensus that there is a necessity to bring in diverse, equitable narratives can be a feature in the conversation. What we highlight now is the often-overlooked subgroup of people and how we prepare our students who will facilitate this—they are the future stewards who will provide guidance and support in this decade of ocean science and beyond.

Through aggressive lobbying, the Geosciences (including Ocean Sciences) are supported at a higher funding rate (NSF 2021) in the United States than they have ever been. Unfortunately, higher education in the US as a whole has been failing to provide opportunities for Indigenous students to participate and excel in the Oceanography/Geosciences (NSF 2016). There are critical barriers to Native Americans in science, technology, engineering, and mathematics (STEM) graduate school or industry pathways to food and natural resource science. In most STEM fields, Native Americans are grossly underrepresented. In 2014, only 0.5 percent of master's degrees in STEM were awarded to persons with Native American heritage, even though Native Americans make up about 2 percent of the population (NSF 2016; US Census Bureau 2015). That number drops to 0.3 percent when doctoral degrees are taken into account, averaging at fewer than 100 degrees awarded in a ten-year period out of almost 30,000 STEM doctorates from US institutions (NSF 2016). The natural world plays a central role in Native American cultures, and young students are drawn to these interactions. Their diverse perspective should be celebrated and represented within the STEM communities but are often missing from higher education. Consequently, the lack of representation in STEM likely has less to do with interest and more to do with institutional barriers (Kelley and Knowles 2016). While there are many papers discussing the pipeline problem where preparation in math and sciences is inadequate to provide the necessary support for students to advance to graduate programs in STEM fields (Russell, Hancock, and McCullough 2007; Pender et al. 2010; Adams et al. 2021), we found from conversations with our students in higher education that this barrier can often extend beyond basic preparedness for upper-division STEM classes, and includes the exclusion of the knowledge, use, and availability of environmentally focused research experiences, also known as Research Education Experiences (REUs).

In the US, there are thousands of REUs, both internal and external, offered through higher education. Not all REUs offered can support our Indigenous students in such a way that they don't need to burden themselves with explaining their history, culture, or worldview. In the Pacific Northwest, located in the heart of the Salish Sea, Northwest Indian College (NWIC), a 1994 land-grant institution, offers a Bachelor of Native Environmental Science degree, that includes hand-on, community-relevant, place-based learning. To facilitate classroom learning and stewardship of the ocean, the Salish Sea Research Center (SSRC), the marine research center at NWIC, offers guided, summer, for-credit paid REU and internships for science students. Students can actively engage in projects related to community-based needs, with input

FIGURE 14.1. The Salish Sea Research Center logo, designed by Thayne Yazzie, with input from Indigenous students and researchers at Northwest Indian College.

from our tribal partners at Lummi Natural Resources, such as water quality, harmful algae, sustainable seafood, and genetics of forage fishes (figure 14.1).

The data are clear: participating in undergraduate summer research increases the likelihood that students will matriculate in graduate school in STEM fields (Bauer and Bennett 2003; Tsui 2007; Nerio et al. 2019). To increase minority participation and retention, many universities have focused their REU experiences to emphasize project-based curricula and independent research. The SSRC expands on this system by incorporating place-based pedagogy, community-focused research projects, and traditional learning (Cajete 1994, 2000, 2005; Deloria, Deloria Jr., and Wildcat 2001; Berardi et al. 2003). The SSRC was developed to increase the presence and influence of Native American leadership in the area of environmental sciences and natural resource management. Solutions to environmental degradation require attention to both science and culture, and more Native Americans need the education and training necessary to carry out these responsibilities. Specifically, the SSRC is charged with increasing the number of Native Americans with science backgrounds in leadership roles that serve their communities. Our students at NWIC have a strong sense of community, which can be lost when they study at nontribal colleges, and this includes leaving

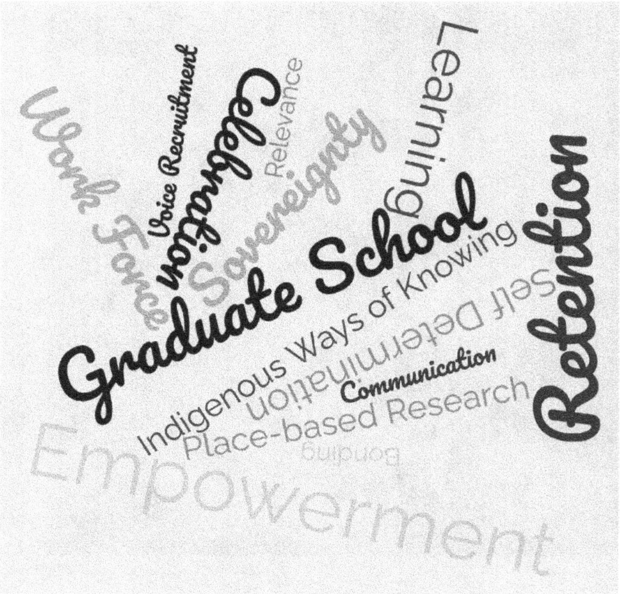

FIGURE 14.2. Word cloud produced by Salish Sea Research Center REU participants highlighting their goals and focus.

their community to participate in a summer REU program. To combat this, the SSRC has created opportunities at NWIC for students to produce guided, community-focused summer research.

Our summer REU and mentorship program at the Salish Sea Research Center follows three guidelines: (1) the research is focused on community research projects, (2) we support tribal nations in food and data sovereignty, and (3) we engage in community knowledge exchanges. The guiding principle is the inclusion of both our students and the community (figure 14.2). As such, we teach what we know, and the research projects that our students participate in are focused to provide the maximum student, mentor, and community engagement. This approach follows other best practices of mentoring undergraduates, including tools to increase persistence and retention in STEM fields (Eby 2007; Crisp and Cruz 2009; Hernandez 2017).

In 2019, the SSRC adapted a nested-mentor model for our summer internship program. Each student has a dedicated graduate student mentor, a research mentor at the Salish Sea Research Center, and an environmental justice mentor. The students are matched based on shared perspectives, which may be key to facilitating the matriculation of Native American

FIGURE 14.3. Research mentor Rachael Mallon teaches water quality monitoring to student intern Tamisha Yazzie in the Salish Sea, Washington.

undergraduates in STEM into a mainstream graduate degree-granting institutions. The graduate student, research, and environmental justice mentors weave a narrative to guide the students in the research that they're doing, to help determine the best pathway to graduation and beyond. Same-race and same-gender mentorship increases that persistence and retention rate of undergraduates (Hernandez 2017), which is especially important when attempting to add underrepresented diverse voices in the STEM fields (Smith et al. 2014; Woodcock, Hernandez, and Schultz 2016). Not all mentor-mentee relationships need to be formalized (Chao 2006; Eby 2007), but we found that there is added benefit from a structured relationship. This way, the layers of mentors enhance the undergraduate's development in academia (figure 14.3).

The mentors pass on knowledge related to scientific ethics in research, scientific method, data collection and analysis, and presentation and dissemination of the projects (Estrada et al. 2011; Woodcock, Hernandez, and Schultz 2016; Hernandez et al. 2017) (figure 14.4). Besides strictly academic mentorship, the peer mentors in our model, the graduate students, often have a

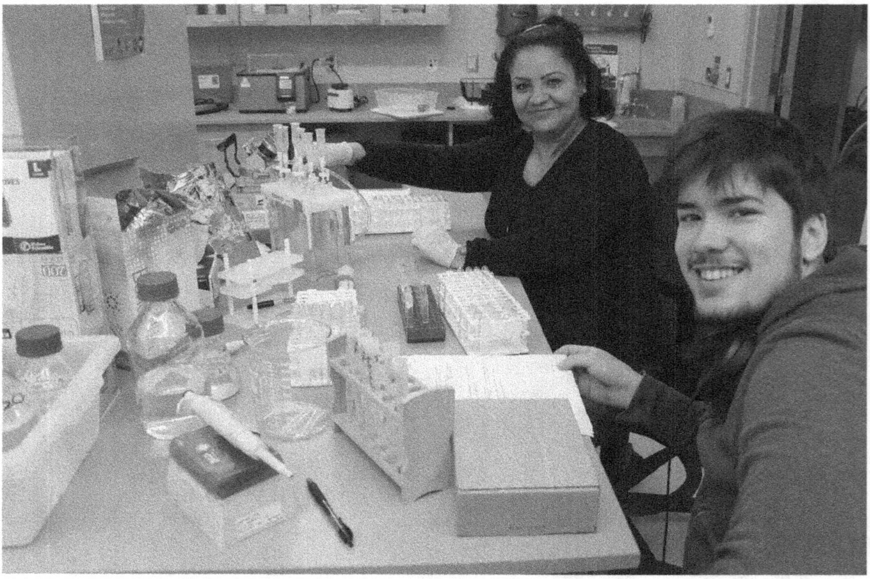

FIGURE 14.4. Rosa Hunter, research mentor, passes on methods for biotoxin analyses to Mikale Milne, student intern.

great social mentorship influence, providing support for the undergraduate students through counseling, encouragement, and modeling behavior (Eby 2007; Hernandez et al. 2017). This type of mentorship can introduce and ready the student for graduate school and STEM careers. Like others, we've found that the three key factors that enhance a successful mentor-mentee relationship include (1) frequent mentor-mentee contact, (2) mentor-mentee demographic similarities, and (3) shared beliefs, in terms of attitudes, outlooks, and values (Harrison, Price, and Bell 1998; Turban, Dougherty, and Lee 2002; Eby 2007; Hernandez et al. 2017; Adams et al. 2021). Above all, quality mentorship is considered to be the most important thing for an undergrad mentee (Kardash and Edwards 2012; Hernandez et al. 2017).

The nested-mentor model supports a multigenerational community learning approach to incorporate both Western Ecological Knowledges (WEK) and placed-based traditional ecological knowledges (TEK). The community approach of placed-based learning resonates strongly with Indigenous ways of knowing by including Indigenous scholars and drawing on known

Indigenous pedagogy to Indigenize and decolonize the western narrative (Montgomery and Blanchard 2021; Montgomery 2022). A predeterminate to support success is when mentees can see themselves and their community infrastructure present and visible in their learning, which makes it easier for them to engage and provides a firm foundation for them to build their learning journey. It is important to utilize Indigenous Knowledges as both a practice and a process to engage with key issues having to do with research, in particular environmental justice issues such as climate change. The advancement of Indigenous persons in the nested-mentor model empowers mentees to express themselves based on their knowledges and experiences. In the community learning approach, the actual engagements themselves weave together WEK and TEK, critique of institutions, respect for Indigenous cosmologies, and ideas for pathways forward for improvement in the future. Through this approach, mentees are also provided an opportunity to build confidence in an academic setting, which can translate to greater opportunities for success beyond academia.

Each opportunity that we use to broaden the diverse narrative in ocean sciences is one step closer to achieving "the science we need for the ocean we want" (UNESCO n.d.a, n.d.b). The REU program at the SSRC gives a microphone to our students, who can use it to guide the science behind decision-making processes that impact ocean resources. Our inclusion of dedicated research mentors and REU experiences with a focus on incorporating cultural knowledge, a lens of sustainability, sovereignty, and environmental justice will provide the next generation of ocean scientists with opportunities to lead in this UN Decade of Ocean Science and beyond.

References

Adams, J. H., D. Bright, D., J. Jackson, and O. S. Simmons. 2021. "A Holistic Model for Black Student Success in STEM: The Case for a Comprehensive and Holistic Approach in Building the Pipeline." In *Social Justice and Education in the Twenty-First Century*, edited by Willie Pearson Jr. and Vijay Reddy Page, 195–219. Diversity and Inclusion Research. Cham, Switzerland: Springer.

Bauer, K. W., and J. S. Bennett. 2003. "Alumni Perceptions Used to Assess Undergraduate Research Experience." *Journal of Higher Education* 74 (2): 210–230.

Berardi, G., D. Burns, P. Duran, R. Gonzalez-Plaza, S. Kinley, L. Robbins, T. Williams, and W. Woods. 2003. "The Tribal Environment and Natural Resources

Management Approach to Indian Education and Student Assessment." *Journal of American Indian Education* 42 (1): 58–74.

Cajete, G. 1994. *Look to the Mountain: An Ecology of Indigenous Education*. Durango, CO: Kivaki Press.

Cajete, G. 2000. *Native Science: Natural Laws of Interdependence*. Santa Fe, NM: Clear Light Publishers.

Cajete, G. 2005. *Spirit of the Game: An Indigenous Wellspring*. Durango, CO: Kivaki Press.

Chao, G. T. 2009. "Formal Mentoring: Lessons Learned from Past Practice." *Professional Psychology: Research and Practice* 40 (3): 314.

Crisp, G., and I. Cruz. 2009. "Mentoring College Students: A Critical Review of the Literature between 1990 and 2007." *Research in Higher Education* 50 (6): 525–545.

Deloria, V., V. Deloria Jr., and D. R. Wildcat. 2001. *Power and Place: Indian Education in America*. Golden, CO: Fulcrum Publishing.

Duarte, C. M., I. Poiner, and J. Gunn. 2018. "Perspectives on a Global Observing System to Assess Ocean Health." *Frontiers in Marine Science* 5 (August 3). https://www.frontiersin.org/articles/10.3389/fmars.2018.00265/full.

Eby, L. T. 2007. "Understanding Relational Problems in Mentoring." In *The Handbook of Mentoring at Work: Theory, Research, and Practice*, edited by Belle Rose Ragins and Kathy E. Kram, 323–344. Los Angeles: Sage Publications.

Estrada, M., A. Woodcock, P. R. Hernandez, and P. W. Schultz. 2011. "Toward a Model of Social Influence That Explains Minority Student Integration into the Scientific Community." *Journal of Educational Psychology* 103 (1): 206–222.

Freelan, S. 2009. *Map of the Salish Sea and Surrounding Basin*. https://maps.stefanfreelan.com/.

Harrison, D. A., K. H. Price, and M. P. Bell. 1998. "Beyond Relational Demography: Time and the Effects of Surface-and Deep-Level Diversity on Work Group Cohesion." *Academy of Management Journal* 41 (1): 96–107.

Hernandez, P. R., B. Bloodhart, R. T. Barnes, A. S. Adams, S. M. Clinton, I. Pollack, E. Godfrey, M. Burt, and E. V. Fischer. 2017. "Promoting Professional Identity, Motivation, and Persistence: Benefits of an Informal Mentoring Program for Female Undergraduate Students." *Plos One* 12 (11): e0187531.

Jones, J., P. Keller, and E. van der Flier Keller. 2021. "Review of Official Responsibility for the Salish Sea Marine Environment." *Ocean and Coastal Management* 211 (October 1). https://www.sciencedirect.com/science/article/abs/pii/S0964569121002313?via%3Dihub.

Kardash, C. M., and O. V. Edwards. 2012. "Thinking and Behaving Like Scientists: Perceptions of Undergraduate Science Interns and Their Faculty Mentors." *Instructional Science* 40 (6): 875–899.

Kelley, T. R., and J. G. Knowles. 2016. "A Conceptual Framework for Integrated STEM Education." *International Journal of STEM Education* 3 (11). https://stemeducationjournal.springeropen.com/articles/10.1186/s40594-016-0046-z.

Kew, M. 2010. "Northwest Coast Indigenous Peoples in Canada." *The Canadian Encyclopedia*. Accessed November 2022. https://www.thecanadianencyclopedia.ca/en/article/aboriginal-people-northwest-coast#:%7E:text=The%20Northwest%20Coast%20cultural%20area,fjords%20and%20snow%2Dcapped%20mountains.

Montgomery M. 2022. "Indigenous Moral Epistemology and Eco-Critical Race Theory." In *Re-Indigenizing Ecological Consciousness and Interconnectedness of Indigenous Identities*, edited by M. Montgomery, 53–63. Lanham, MD: Rowan and Littlefield Publishing.

Montgomery, M., and P. Blanchard. 2021. "Testing Justice: New Ways to Address Environmental Inequalities." *Solutions Journal*. Accessed 2021. https://www.resilience.org/stories/2022-02-17/testing-justice-new-ways-to-address-environmental-inequalities/.

Nerio, R., A. Webber, E. MacLachlan, D. Lopatto, and A. J. Caplan. 2019. "One-Year Research Experience for Associate's Degree Students Impacts Graduation, STEM Retention, and Transfer Patterns." *CBE Life Sciences Education* 18 (2).

NSF. 2016. "Women, Minorities, and Persons with Disabilities in Science and Engineering." Accessed November 2022. https://www.nsf.gov/statistics/2017/nsf17310/data.cfm.

NSF. 2021. "Women, Minorities, and Persons with Disabilities in Science and Engineering." Accessed October 2022. https://ncses.nsf.gov/pubs/nsf21321/report.

Pender, M., D. E. Marcotte, M. R. S. Domingo, and K. I. Maton. 2010. "The STEM Pipeline: The Role of Summer Research Experience in Minority Students' Ph.D. Aspirations." *Education Policy Analysis Archives* 18 (30): 1.

Russell, S. H., M. P. Hancock, and J. McCullough. 2007. "Benefits of Undergraduate Research Experiences." *Science* 316 (5824): 548–549.

Ryabinin, V., J. Barbière, P. Haugan, G. Kullenberg, N. Smith, C. McLean, and J. Rigaud. 2019. "The UN Decade of Ocean Science for Sustainable Development." *Frontiers in Marine Science* 6 (July 31): 470. https://www.frontiersin.org/articles/10.3389/fmars.2019.00470/full.

Smith, J. L., E. Cech, A. Metz, M. Huntoon, and C. Moyer. 2014. "Giving Back or Giving Op: Native American Student Experiences in Science and Engineering." *Cultural Diversity and Ethnic Minority Psychology* 20 (3): 413.

Tsui, L. 2007. "Effective Strategies to Increase Diversity in STEM Fields: A Review of the Research Literature." *Journal of Negro Education* 76 (4): 555–581.

Turban, D. B., T. W. Dougherty, and F. K. Lee. 2002. "Gender, Race, and Perceived Similarity Effects in Developmental Relationships: The Moderating Role of Relationship Duration." *Journal of Vocational Behavior* 61 (2): 240–262.

UNESCO. n.d.a. "Decade of Ocean Science For Sustainable Development (2021–2030)." Accessed November 2022. https://en.unesco.org/ocean-decade.

UNESCO. n.d.b. "Decade of Ocean Science for Sustainable Development (2021–2030) Implementation Plan." Accessed November 2022. https://unesdoc.unesco.org/ark:/48223/pf0000376780.

US Census Bureau. 2015. "Quick Facts." Accessed November 2022. https://www.census.gov/quickfacts/fact/table/US/PST045221.

Woodcock, A., P. R. Hernandez, and P. W. Schultz. 2016. "Diversifying Science: Intervention Programs Moderate the Effect of Stereotype Threat on Motivation and Career Choice." *Social Psychological and Personality Science* 7 (2): 184–192.

15

Na'ałkałi

BRANDI KAMERMANS

Introduction

Environmental DNA (eDNA) is genetic material (DNA) released by organisms in the environment. Quantitative polymerase chain reaction (qPCR) is a molecular method that uses a fluorescent probe in a traditional PCR reaction to monitor the amplification of DNA in real time. A fluorometer detects the fluorescent signal that is produced once a molecular target has been amplified, which allows us to quantify target DNA in the environment of interest. As a molecular researcher at Salish Sea Research Center, I use qPCR of eDNA collected from samples taken in Bellingham Bay, Lummi Bay, and the Nooksack River to monitor the following: (1) harmful algae blooms and (2) a species of anadromous fish, the Longfin Smelt (*Spirinchus thaleichthys*). The goal for the Tiokowe (Longfin Smelt in the Lummi language) eDNA project is to determine where Tiokowe are spawning. In addition to understanding the spawning habitat of Tiokowe, the local Lummi shellfish hatcheries are interested in predicting the onset of Harmful Algal Blooms (HABs). The Salish

https://doi.org/10.5876/9781646425105.c015

Sea Research Center has been monitoring toxin-producing phytoplankton as part of SoundToxins, using traditional microscopy techniques. In addition to cell counts, we are utilizing a qPCR assay to detect genes responsible for producing saxitoxin in Dinoflagellates. This work is important because detecting species using eDNA methods, rather than directly sampling the organisms, can reduce impacts on sensitive species. This work also applies scientific methods for issues that are important to Native American tribes served by Northwest Indian College.

Keywords: environmental, DNA, eDNA, toxin, Lummi, Longfin Smelt, Alexandrium, spawning, Native American.

Na'ałkałi

Mervyn Tano, the President of the International Institute for Indigenous Resource Management, wrote, "The world is not created anew each day, that everyone stands on someone else's shoulders. The wisdom of the tribe is not the wisdom of the wisest sage. It is the collective wisdom of the tribal members" (1999). When I wrote this chapter, I wanted to make sure I wrote about those who have taught me. These are the members of my science community. I stand on their shoulders in the job I currently hold at a tribal college. I am Nihoobáanii (my mother's) clan and Bilagáana (my father's clan). I am Navajo (Diné) from Gallup, New Mexico. My clan has been passed down to me from my mother, grandmother, great-grandmother, and all the mothers before that. I am also the descendent of Cybil Janson and Sarah Cron, Irish and German women. In kindergarten, I was given the Science Award at Chee Dodge Elementary School in Ya'at'teeh, New Mexico (located on the Navajo Nation). My mother picked me up from my classroom. As soon as I saw my mom I asked her, "What is science?" Since the birth of my son, my mother and I have had more conversations about this happening. Recently, she explained that a scientist is *na'ałkałi*, or someone who investigates. I have pursued a life of scientific investigation.

Go My Son

My earliest memories from elementary school are reciting this verse at school assemblies:

Upon the ladder of an education,
You can work to help your Indian Nation,
Then reach, my son, And bring your people up with you. (Nofchissey and Burson 1967)

This verse has been instrumental for my career choices. There are many, many children from Native American communities who heard and recited this song. Giving back to community was instilled in me as an elementary school student and as a high school athlete. My high school cross-country coach, Curtis Williams, taught the front-runners on the team to form a community by forcing each runner to turn around at the finish line to gather the rest of the team. After every training day, the first people to cross the finish line had to turn around and pick up a slower teammate. That engrained in me a sense of teamwork that coincided with the teachings of "Go My Son."

Career Pathway

When I started college, I wanted to be a medical doctor. I enrolled at the University of New Mexico in 2004 as a student in the biology program. When I was a junior, I took a course taught by Dr. Cristina Vesbach-Takacs. She presented a figure showing chemolithoautotrophs. Once I saw this figure, I could not stop thinking about it. I wanted to know how microbial life utilized inorganic carbon sources for metabolic processes. In the same semester I took the course from Dr. Vesbach-Takacs, I also met the director of the Ronald E. McNair program at the University of New Mexico, Dr. Carolina J. Aguirre. With funding from the program, I began work with water samples from the Tierra Amarilla anticline, a geologic feature in northern New Mexico that is a consequence of plate tectonic activity. The anticline hosts carbonate-rich springs that my ancestors traveled across by foot or wagon, and the springs offered them water.

At some point during the time I was starting this research, my grandmother asked what I did for a living. She did not speak English, so my mother told her, in Navajo, "Brandi is studying the bugs and the rocks in the water." My grandmother was happy to know that I was studying the water that gave our family nourishment.

My research career began at the University of New Mexico as a Ronald E. McNair Fellow in 2007 (Crossey 2020). I graduated from the University of New Mexico with a bachelor's in Biology in 2008. As an undergraduate, I was a work study intern with Dr. Crossey in the Department of Earth and Planetary Sciences. I continued to work within the department as a New Mexico Alliance for Minority Participation (New Mexico AMP) graduate researcher. In the AMP program, I formed a community of colleagues and Dr. Crossey was the critical component of the research community. She and the other researchers were my support group. Before the McNair program or the AMP program, I did not know how to pursue science as a career. Over the course of my undergraduate studies and earning my master's, I determined the extent of microbial diversity in the spring at Tierra Amarilla and I characterized the first Zetaproteobacteria in a terrestrial environment (Crossey et al. 2016).

While I finished my degree at the University of New Mexico, I applied for the National Science Foundation Graduate Research Fellowship. When I earned funding from the program, I pursued a doctoral degree in Marine Science. I wanted to go into marine science because Dr. Crossey had encouraged me to participate in a research cruise with Dr. Anna-Louise Reysenbach. In the summer of 2009, I traveled to the Mid-Atlantic Ridge with researchers from the University of Minnesota. After the cruise, I had the goal of teaching other Diné students about oceanography. I wanted to conduct science and mentor others in the fields of Environmental Science and Earth Science. Professor Crossey helped me see that science and my Diné tradition are not necessarily so separate, and that is one of many important wisdoms I would like to offer others.

I attended the University of Minnesota to earn a doctorate in Geobiology. My PhD research described the composition of sulfur-bearing minerals within particles using sulfur 1s X-ray Absorption Near Edge Structure spectroscopy (XANES) (Cron, Macalady, and Cosmidis 2021). The XANES method allowed me to make measurements of sulfur-rich particulates filtered in situ from deep-sea hydrothermal vents. In the time I spent earning my PhD, I learned a lot about geochemistry of hydrothermal vents.

Community

As a PhD student, I battled homesickness every day. Like the experience I had as an AMP recipient, I was lucky that I met people that supported me in Minnesota. I joined the University of Minnesota American Indian Science and Engineering Society (AISES). As a member of AISES, I learned that many of the Native American graduate students were also homesick. I also attended seminars offered by the university about surviving graduate school. Some of the seminars were about how to choose the right PhD program and the right PhD advisor. In retrospect, I realize that the people I met in Minnesota became my extended family. Dr. Brandy Toner was my PhD mentor, and she is still a mentor and a source of knowledge for me. Dr. Toner is from Bemidji, Minnesota. She mentioned that after she earned her degrees at Berkeley, Berkeley felt like home. I now have the same connection with Saint Paul, the location of the University of Minnesota. The AISES community and Dr. Toner were principal components of my research community as a PhD student.

As a postdoctoral fellow at Penn State, I worked with Dr. Julie Cosmidis and Dr. Jennifer Macalady in the College of Earth and Mineral Sciences. I used chemical signatures to decipher between microbial and chemical production of S° in a laboratory experiment (Cron 2019) and from sulfur-rich system, the Frasassi Cave, Italy (Cron, Macalady, and Cosmidis 2021). The research was fascinating, but I envied those who were able to work directly with the community. I sought opportunities to do outreach. It was through outreach opportunities that I found the Penn State Postdoc Society. The society is comprised of postdoctoral fellows. I felt a strong connection to the group of researchers I met. I helped plan the Penn State 11th Annual Postdoctoral Research Exhibition. As a postdoc, I was immersed in a community of researchers. My mentors and my fellow postdocs helped me grow as a researcher.

In 2017, the first year I worked for Penn State, I traveled to the Osservatorio Geologico di Coldgioco, Italy, to collect samples from a sulfur-rich stream deep within the Frasassi Cave System. At Osservatorio Geologico di Coldgioco, I met a group of Carleton College students participating in a program where they were learning Geology and Italian language and culture. The experience of watching the students go out into field and then come back to camp to learn Italian and cook Italian food inspired me to pursue a career path that would allow me to study my own language and culture and teach science at the same time. I began my pursuit of a job where I could teach Diné students about oceanography.

The Scientist

I wrote the following poem as a postdoc at Northwest Indian College.

There once was The Scientist.
The Scientist was a well-meaning scientist.
The Scientist had a toolkit of western knowledge.
Knowledge that was meant to serve the reservation.

The Scientist was a well-meaning scientist.
The Scientist arrived from a foreign land to make the life of the reservation better.
With knowledge that was meant to serve the reservation.
The Scientist had the livelihood of the land and the Indians of the land in mind.

The Scientist arrived from a foreign land to make the life of the reservation better.
For many years, The Scientist did well.
The Scientist had the livelihood of the land and the Indians of the land in mind.
The western science tools did no harm.

For many years, The Scientist did well.
The information collected was harmless.
Then, it seemed like things were good.
The western science tools did no harm.

The information collected was harmless.
Things were done in a good way.
The western science tools did no harm.
Until the livelihood of the Indians was forgotten.

Things were done in a good way.
Then, The Scientist asked a question that was never meant to be asked.
The livelihood of the Indians was forgotten.
Did The Scientist know that asking questions is the start of the downfall of The Scientist?

The Scientist asked a question that was never meant to be asked.
Asking questions means someone will answer.
Did The Scientist know that asking questions is the start of the downfall of The Scientist?
Will the answer be what The Scientist predicted?

Asking questions means someone will answer.
Can The Scientist control the result?
Will the answer be what The Scientist predicted?
The question is answered.

Can The Scientist control the result?
The reservation suffers.
The question is answered.
There once was The Scientist.

Early Career Scientist

I am not within the four sacred mountains, and they are far from the home I reside in. I was hired at the Salish Sea Research Center to study algae in marine and freshwater environments. I was hired to wrangle a molecular method for the Salish Sea Research Center, quantitative polymerase chain reaction (qPCR). Since its development in the 1990s, qPCR has become widely used for detection of nucleic acids in many fields. We use qPCR to detect environmental DNA (eDNA) released by species in the Salish Sea. When I was hired, I decided to study algae in the genus *Alexandrium*. The Salish Sea Research Center lab manager, Rosa Hunter, and I call them Alex. Alex can produce Paralytic Shellfish Toxins, the causative agent for Paralytic Shellfish Poisoning, and is considered a harmful alga.

Bellingham is nestled on the Salish Sea—a network of waterways along the coast of British Columbia, Canada, and the US state of Washington—and is home to the Coast Salish People. Residents, including the Lummi People, rely on shellfish for subsistence harvesting. In collaboration with Washington State Harmful Algal Bloom monitoring program, SoundToxins, the Salish Sea Research Center uses traditional microscopy techniques to identify toxin producing phytoplankton. Alex, or *Alexandrium*, have been observed in Bellingham Bay during the early fall months. I aim to test the hypothesis that we can use qPCR for early detection of harmful algae in the waters along the coast of the Lummi Nation. The occurrence of HAB events in the estuarine and coastal waters negatively impacts sustainable access to safe shellfish, and we hope that early detection will provide data for the Lummi Nation Shellfish hatcheries.

Dr. Rachel Arnold was the first person I interacted with at the Salish Sea Research Center. She was also my boss for the first sixteen months of my postdoc appointment. Dr. Arnold announced her resignation as the Associate Director of the Salish Sea Research Center unexpectedly. I inherited a two-year grant with the National Institute of Food and Agriculture (NIFA) when she left. The project investigates a species of forage fish for the Lummi Nation, the Hooligan. The Hooligan are also known as *Spirinchus thaleichthys*. The Lummi fishing community knew Dr. Arnold, and when her project was passed on to me no one knew who I was. The study relied heavily on communication with the local community and with Lummi Natural Resources department.

My first year as investigator was spent meeting new researchers at Lummi Natural Resources and other institutions, familiarizing myself with the state of the project. It was exciting meeting the community members and the fishermen. It was invigorating spending days out on the boat in the middle of the Nooksack River talking to fish biologists about their jobs and their lives. The first handful of Hooligan I caught in a dip net captured my heart. The instant I saw their shimmering scales in the sunlight, I knew I was hooked. I wanted to know more about the Hooligan. I moved to Bellingham to study algae and stumbled onto a project that has forced me to study something unfamiliar to me, anadromous fish!

As funding the NIFA funding ends, I look to the future. I have hesitancy when I comes to continuing to study the local forage fish, Longfin Smelt (*Spirinchus thaleichthys*). The most recent hesitancy is because I need to learn how to use genetics to compare the local *Spirinchus thaleichthys* to others in San Francisco and Alaska. The worry is that knowing more about the local population could make them become listed as an endangered species, and the Lummi Nation might not be able to catch them anymore. This is an important food source for people, and it would be devastating if they lost it.

The Director of the Salish Sea Research Center, Dr. Melissa B. Peacock, organizes research and teaching opportunities with Native American students at Northwest Indian College. She nurtures the next generation of Native American scientists with equitable and inclusive research opportunities. Dr. Peacock directs community-based participatory research. She communicates with the college and enacts both food and data sovereignty for tribes that are served by the college. She acts as a mentor for me and helps me navigate participatory research in the environmental sciences at a tribal college.

To circumvent any unforeseen challenges with the Hooligan study, based on guidance from Dr. Peacock, I meet regularly with the leadership at Lummi Natural Resources. Meetings are used to discuss the goals of the tribe and the needs of the community for the Hooligan research. From these conversations, I feel comfortable with a document I developed to manage the genomic data that is produced by colleagues and researchers at the Salish Sea Research Center. It is a document that will protect the sovereignty and governance of genetic data. This data will be produced by the Salish Sea Research Center and our colleagues at the University of California, Davis, and the University of Alaska. I made this document to stand to protect Indigenous food and data sovereignty. I am not among the four sacred mountains, but I am protecting and hopefully giving back to a community that has provided me and my family with a home. I want my son to know that his ancestors came from within the four sacred mountains. But, more important, I want him to learn how to care for and protect the people in his life who support him. I am setting an example for my son. I am learning about the Lummi Nation's needs and attempting to support its livelihoods. I am showing my son how to care for and support others.

Culture and Tradition

In the book *Science and Native American Communities* (2001), Keith James mentions that innovation and creativity flow out of culture and tradition and carry culture and tradition refreshed back to themselves. As I have developed an online genomics course, I have learned more about how my creativity flows from my culture and my family traditions. I inherited from Dr. Arnold a National Institutes of Health (NIH) contract to develop a free online course for all tribal colleges to teach genetics from a Native American perspective. Many tribal colleges lack Indigenous professors to teach genomics. This course is intended to give students a core curriculum to learn more about genetics. The course is also meant to empower students to learn how genetics is being used in their communities. Each tribal college or student is to use the material as they need and potentially add to modules genetic ideas or genetic research currently being used in their community. Each community is different; therefore, we also hope that with each college that uses these online modules, the modules will begin to acquire curated content. Hesitancies I have had about designing this course include questions of ownership of traditional knowledge. In a module I designed, I interviewed my mother. The interview includes a discussion of why my mother declined to participate in a genetics study, based on her traditional Diné religious beliefs. It wasn't until I really started discussing the development of genetics curriculum and talking about the ethics of genetics research with my mom and with my community that I knew how important it was to me that it was conducted in an equitable way. Keith James mentions in chapter 2 of *Science and Native American Communities* that many of the needs of Native American communities require expertise in science. He also mentions that science skills should be applicable to the needs and goals of the Native American community. The online course is designed to give students the genetics tools they require to meet the needs of their communities.

Reach Back

As I was growing up, my mom told me creation stories as we made road trips and drove across New Mexico, Utah, and Arizona. My mother's stories taught me that my cultural history was tied to the Earth's history. This included how Diné are tied to the four sacred mountains: Tsisnassjini (White Shell Mountain), Tsoodzil (Mount Taylor), Doko'oosliid (San Francisco Peak), and Dibé Nitsaa (Mount Hesperus). In college, I was an aspiring Geologist, and Dr. Crossey gave me a copy of *Roadside Geology of New Mexico*, a book detailing the more than 1 billion–year history of New Mexico (through the story of rocks). My mother's stories and the roadside map have coalesced in my mind. According to Diné belief, Twins were born from Spider Woman and the Sun. My mother told me of how the Twins once defeated the Great Giant. Now, the Giant's blood is left behind along I-25 between Albuquerque and Gallup, New Mexico. In college, I visited the Monster's Blood as a Geobiologist, looking for life beneath the surface of the Earth.

As a master's student and as a PhD student, I listened to professors explain to me how the Earth was shaped through Western Knowledge. However, I discovered a divide between Western Knowledge and Traditional Ecological Knowledge. It is a divide that I want to bridge. Scientific solutions to climate change (Fixico 2021), conservation efforts (Center For American Progress 2021), water quality (Center n.d.), and uranium and acid mine drainage (Blake 2015) necessitate not only scientific expertise but also understanding of the cultural context in which they occur (Gewin 2021). I am prompted to pursue jobs and research projects that include Indigenous Ecological Knowledge with Western Science. Just as the song I learned in elementary school stated, I want to reach back to my "Indian Nation."

References

Blake, J. 2015. "Elevated Concentrations of U and Co-occurring Metals in Abandoned Mine Wastes in a Northeastern Arizona Native American Community." *Environmental Science & Technology* 48 (14): 8506–8514.

Center for American Progress. 2021. "The Biden Administration's Conservation Plan Must Prioritize Indigenous Leadership." https://www.americanprogress.org/article/biden-administrations-conservation-plan-must-prioritize-indigenous-leadership/.

Center for American Indian Health. n.d. *Water Quality Study*. https://cih.jhu.edu/programs/water-quality-study/.

Cron, B., P. Henri, C. S. Chan, J. L. Macalady, and J. Cosmidis. 2019. "Elemental Sulfur Formation by *Sulfuricurvum Kujiense* Is Mediated by Extracellular Organic Compounds." *Frontiers in Microbiology* 10:2710. https://doi.org/10.3389/fmicb.2019.02710.

Cron, B., J. L. Macalady, and J. Cosmidis. 2021. "Organic Stabilization of Extracellular Elemental Sulfur in a *Sulfurovum*-Rich Biofilm: A New Role for Extracellular Polymeric Substances?" *Frontiers in Microbiology* 12 (August): 720101. https://www.frontiersin.org/articles/10.3389/fmicb.2021.720101/full.

Crossey, L. J. 2020. "Partnering for Success: Leveraging Efforts in Diversity and Inclusion in Undergraduate Research with LSAMP Making a World of Difference, Integrating Research, Education, and Outreach." Carbonate Critical Zone RCN Virtual Workshop Closing Plenary.

Crossey, L. J., K. E. Karlstrom, B. Schmandt, R. R. Crow, D. R. Colman, B. Cron, C. D. Takacs Vesbach, C. N. Dahm, D. E. Northup, D. E., D. R. Hilton, J. W. Ricketts, and A. R. Lowry. 2016. "Continental Smokers Couple Mantle Degassing and Distinctive Microbiology within Continents." *Earth and Planetary Science Letters* 435 (February 16): 22–30.

Fixico, D. L. 2021. "Documenting Indigenous Dispossession." *Science* 374 (6567): 536–537.

Gewin, V. 2021. "How to Include Indigenous Researchers and Their Knowledge." *Nature* 588 (7841): 315–317.

James, K., ed. 2001. *Science And Native American Communities*. Lincoln: University of Nebraska Press.

Nofchissey, A., and C. Burson. 1967. "Go My Son." *Go My Son*. Blue Eagle Records.

Tano, M. 1999. "On Becoming a Tribal Natural Resource Manager: Some Friendly Advice from a Long-Time Observer." Denver: International Institute for Indigenous Resource Management. https://www.iiirm.org/publications/Articles%20Reports%20Papers/Environmental%20Protection/onbecomi.pdf.

16

Enbridge Line 3 Impact on Wild Rice Lakes in Minnesota Using GIS and Remote Sensing

MARY BANNER

Boozhoo. My name is Mary Banner. I am of the Ponca Tribe of Indians and an enrolled tribal member of Mille Lacs Band of Ojibwe. I am the daughter of Sharon Banner, who is Ponca Tribe of Indians, and I was raised with my older brother Ambrose Banner, who is Ponca Tribe of Indians and Mille Lacs Band of Ojibwe. My maternal grandma was a heavy influence in our life, as she helped with raising us alongside our single-parent mother. My grandma Iva May Gayton was a full-blood Indian of the Ponca Tribe of Indians and was just one of many family members who was assimilated and sent to boarding school. My ancestors resisted these assaults by surviving and being alive during the midst of an all-out colonial attack on Indigenous peoples. I was completely unaware of the damages that had been done to my family due to my alcoholic lifestyle that had been lived through most of adolescence to adulthood. I am now six years sober on the red road to wellbriety, and I am proudly reasserting my traditional tribal identity as a Native American Woman who is Two-spirited in that I am healing from historical and intergenerational trauma that has been present in my life and my family's life, and

https://doi.org/10.5876/9781646425105.c016

I am reclaiming and revitalizing my *e-yaa'oyaanh,* my identity, who I am, the way I am living and becoming.

From the historical and intergenerational trauma that has been present in my life and my family's life, we have been disconnected from our culture for generations. I have been lost since I was a child, being brought up knowing very little about my culture. I was born and raised on the Puyallup Tribe of Indians' land. I currently reside on Fox Island in Washington State. I was raised in Western academia with science where Native Studies or Native Environmental Science or Traditional Ecological Knowledge is unknown. It makes sense that when you try to erase an Indigenous person's knowledge, their perspective would disappear as well, but it hasn't nor will it so long as we can continue to learn and understand an Indigenous worldview and respect this knowledge. Our Indigenous ecology has brought relational guided healing of our lands and waterways. We have a responsibility to be stewards to the land, through relationally we can bring needed balance to an ecosystem.

The Anishinaabeg call it Manoomin, or *bagwaji-manoomin,* which has the meaning of "good fruit" or "spirit delicacy," and through Western science we know from the genus *Zizania,* the common name is wild rice. Through oral stories and traditions, more than a thousand years ago, seven spirits, my ancestors, were guided by the prophecies that led them to the place where the food grows on the water. As they migrated westward through the Great Lakes, displacing the Dakotas, they found Manoomin growing in the waters of tributaries and lakes. They established their new homelands near Mille Lac Lake in current-day Minnesota. They depended on the harvest and preservation of the highly flavorful and incredible nutritional grain to get them through the harsh winters. As colonization happened not just to the Indigenous people but to our trees, flora, fauna, foodways, and systems, we started to see the damage caused to our environment, which had a direct negative impact on Manoomin.

Manoomin is a cultural and economic resource for surrounding Indigenous communities. I have been researching and seeing the environmental conditions affecting Manoomin's growth and reproduction in Minnesota. Manoomin is our sustenance and is the reason we were sent to these lakes, and this sensitive aquatic plant is being eradicated due to water quality changes and global warming. Manoomin beds started fading as our man-made elements started appearing with the mining of copper and uranium, the timber boom with logging camps, dams, and pipelines. The increase in transportation of crude oil through pipelines creates persistent threats of possible oil spills, leaks, and/or explosions. These catastrophes would greatly contaminate Mother Earth, affecting the health of the flora and fauna and humans alike. In addition, the extraction of fossil fuels (oil, natural gas, coal) and uranium has degraded a large portion of Indigenous lands with environmental pollutants through different exposure routes including ingestion, inhalation, and dermal contact. Thanks to the use of geographic information systems (GIS) and Remote Sensing (RS), I was able to research the effects of Enbridge Line 3 pipeline on Manoomin waters in Minnesota. The main objectives of this research can be summarized as follows:

1. Create GIS-based risk maps that will present information visually and communicate risk information to Indigenous communities in a timely manner that'll reduce risks posed by exposure to contaminants (contaminated soil, fish migration, water quality, oil spills) while preserving a traditional tribal lifestyle.
2. Record the impacts of Enbridge Line 3 pipeline on Manoomin lakes in Minnesota using GIS and RS applications (ArcGIS Pro) to map the pipeline's crossing methods and identify hotspots.
3. Highlight social impacts of Line 3 and Missing and Murdered Indigenous Women (MMIW)+ on Indigenous lands.

The creation story for Mille Lacs Band of Ojibwe is where we were told by our prophets, the Anishinaabe people who lived on the eastern seaboard, and we were instructed by our prophets that we should follow a shell that appeared in the sky. In following this shell in the sky, we'd appear where the food grows on the water. That food is Manoomin, or wild rice. We were instructed by the creator to move to Lake Mille Lac, Minnesota. (figure 16.1). Wild rice is sacred. It is the first food given to a newborn, and the last food given before you pass into the spirit world. It is given at all feasts and ceremonies. Food comes from our relatives, whether they have wings, or fins or roots, but indeed, that is how we consider food. Food has a culture. It has a history. It has stories; it has relationships that tie us to our food. The oral history passed down from generation to generation represents the traditional knowledge from my ancestors about the connection to water and how water

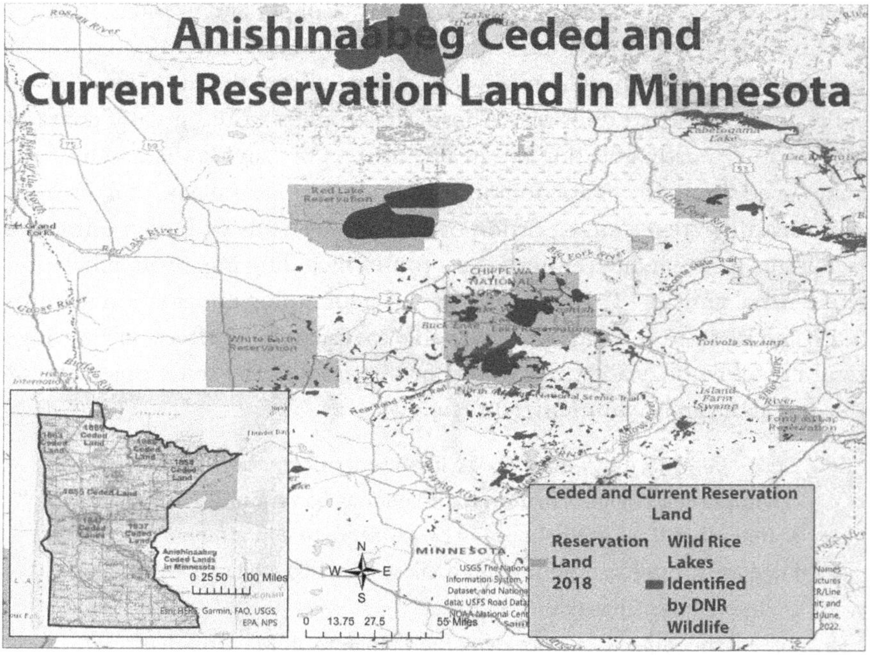

FIGURE 16.1. Anishinaabeg locations of ceded territory in Minnesota using ArcGIS Pro. Mary Banner.

is sacred. Water will tend the seeds to help them grow where humans, flora, and fauna alike will survive on.

My ancestors of Mille Lacs Band began migrating from the Atlantic coast of North America to "where the food grows on water." It was around the mid-1700s when they started settling in and establishing themselves around Mille Lacs Lake. We know it today as East Central Minnesota. This move started what is now a 250-year-old relationship with the region. A tribal member from Mille Lac Band once said, "This part of Minnesota—where the seasons of the year bring cycles of great beauty to the Lake and the land—has been the setting of our history for more than two centuries. For miles in every direction, there is hardly a place untouched by some large or small event from our past. Our homelands are a place where the past touches the present and connects our life with the people who came before and left a rich tribal heritage" (https://millelacsband.com). Being able to look over an area where there is just so much history and past that connect us to the present is absolutely astonishing and can bring healing as long as we sustain her care.

Over the next century, the white settlers started occupying our lands, and they also brought many diseases with them, such as smallpox around the late 1790s and malaria around the 1830s. "The Treaty of 1837, my ancestors of the Mille Lacs Band of Ojibwe had ceded millions of acres of land to what is now Minnesota and Wisconsin, but kept the rights to hunt, fish, and gather on ceded lands" (Mille Lacs n.d.). The 1854 Treaty established other reservations in Minnesota such as Fond du Lac, Grand Portage, and Bois Forte Bands, and in exchange 2 million acres of land were given up, but those tribes maintained their rights to hunt, fish, and gather on ceded lands. "In the Treaty of 1855, the United States government set aside 61,000 acres of land south and west of Mille Lacs Lake, which is our current day reservation land, Mille Lacs Band of Ojibwe Reservation" (Mille Lacs n.d.). This was relatively pointless as non-Natives kept coming, and tribal members became landless, ultimately forcing them to be removed from their homes. Homes they had occupied for millennia.

Soon after forced removal came the era to conform and assimilate into Western Society, to act like non-Natives. Little Mille Lac children were forced from their homes into boarding schools, where they were forced into mainstream society. They were forbidden to speak the Ojibwe language, just as my grandma I was raised with was forbidden to speak her Ponca language. They were stripped of their identity, couldn't practice cultural or religious anything, and were forced to conform. Our relationships to the land are also being displaced, as it was stolen and given to settlers. "Indian tribal self governance was passed in 1934, but shortly after came the Indian Termination and Indian Relocation policies which overruled the tribal self-governance during that era" (Mille Lacs n.d.). By becoming sovereign nations, American Indian tribes started establishing laws to govern their reservations and provide infrastructure to accommodate our own health and needs of tribal members. The Ojibwe have rights to hunt, gather, and fish throughout Northern Minnesota as they are guaranteed by treaties signed by the federal government and acknowledged by the Supreme Court.

As goes for many Indigenous peoples, through these very same treaties both land and rights have been given and taken away. I believe that these injustices and the feeling of displacement from lands are creating havoc in the Indigenous community. My whole entire genealogy has been colonized on both sides of my family. Even the family that I do not know, yet I am writing my whole capstone on, has been colonized. There is an enormous amount of trauma and lived experiences from the endless amount of suicide, which comes in all ages and forms; drugs and alcohol over education; mental health issues linked to depression; anxiety; addicting behaviors; eating disorders; domestic violence issues that have ruined entire lives to families—conditions that are very much be linked to patriarchy, historical, and intergenerational trauma.

I was completely unaware of the damages that had been done to my family due to the alcoholic lifestyle I had lived through most of adolescence to adulthood. By maintaining my sobriety and not living that stereotypical drunken Indian lifestyle, I am en route to *mino bimaadiziwin*, the art of living the good life because I once again have feeling. With all the trauma that has been present in my life and my family's life, we have been disconnected from our culture for generations. I have been lost since I was a child, being brought up knowing very little about my Indigenous e-yaa'oyaanh.

I am now a first-generation college graduate beginning with an Associate of Arts, emphasis in Sociology, where I was met with firsthand colonial resistance. I did have a few opportunities arise while I was at Pierce College. That work led me into obtaining a Bachelor's degree in Native Environmental Science and a Certificate in GIS from Northwest Indian College (NWIC). My future work will be dealing with Indigenous communities and nonprofits from a holistic, place-based emphasis.

I was able to work and serve communities as far away as Puerto Rico to Peru, even got to experience Kenya, and had my recent community adventure in Mexico, twice. Pierce College offered a program called Raiders Serve, and for a week in between quarters a group of about ten students were sent on a community giveback trip. The first trip I applied for and went on was in 2018 for a Hurricane Maria disaster relief project in Puerto Rico. This is the trip that saved and altered my life, even kicked off my potential future career in community place-based programs. We have done environmental restoration, mangrove restoration, and reforestation at El Yunque National Forest. We worked on local conservation projects for the ecosystem that had been ripped apart by back-to-back hurricanes that year. I took this trip after I lost my British brother to suicide, and in so many ways the land, the community, the waters, the sun, and the environment had helped heal me in ways I had yet known. I created bonds and friendships that have turned into my chosen family, which will last a lifetime. These relationships are in a community so far away from my homelands, yet these bonds happened. This trip and the community meant so much to me that I returned to Puerto Rico twice that same year, and even applied for the program that following year.

In 2019 I reapplied for the Raiders Serve program; only this time the trip was set to head to La Florida, Peru, to assist the Fuller Center for Housing Global Builders in building homes in a migrant community that is susceptible to earthquakes. I was selected to go on this trip, and yet again it left a huge impact on my soul. We worked with the local community and assisted them in stabilization of existing homes, and while lacking the local language, which is Spanish, we still excelled. Even though the majority of the group couldn't speak Spanish, we did great at following verbal and visual instruction. I would love to go back to Peru and continue this work. I may have found the courage to sign up for a group. Time is all I need now. I know there is work in other ways regarding resources like food and water that could get groups together to help locally and within Indigenous communities. Someone just needs to take the initiative, for Native People by Native People. I can relate epistemology by living my life and being that example. I have done so many things that I shouldn't have. Thanks to my wellbriety I am growing from all the different experiences, and I am becoming stronger.

I believe that through those experiences, I received my first internship with Bonneville Power Administration and Yakama Nation Fisheries. I was a fish culturist for the summer on site at Cle Elum Fish Hatchery in Cle Elum, Washington, during the lockdown and first summer of the coronavirus. This was my first time being able to spend a summer with a local tribe from my home state too. I have always been considered an outsider, and this experience was the complete opposite. I was part of the Sockeye reintroduction program in the Yakima Basin. We transported 10,000 fish to Lake Cle Elum, collected samples of DNA, and tagged fish. I was part of a Snoqualmie Pass Fish survey and a fish rescue of Bull Trout. Last but not least, I was very privileged to be on and see Yakama Nations closed land and forest. We stocked over 10,000 Rainbow Trout at two different lakes—Howard Lake and Mt. Adams Lake—for the community to go and fish. This land we were on was never ceded by the Yakama during the Treaty eras. I felt honored being on that sacred land and hope I return one day. This experience brought my culture and that familiarity back into my e-yaa'oyaanh.

I can apply ontology to my past life events such as the mental health, physical well-being, and health and diet, life experiences that ultimately brought me to writing this chapter. I wasn't living a healthy life in my past life. My diet was horrid, I wasn't healthy, I was extremely overweight, and I got sick a lot. I began changing my ways and once I removed the alcohol, my diet and health started coming back. The risk of diabetes dropped significantly, and I do not get high blood pressure as often. This is just the health and physical aspect, right? Through my health and diet, I am reclaiming my identity as a Native woman with my culture.

Axiology is how I will react and be accountable. It is mainly through humility but also ethics, generosity, courage, compassion, honor, wisdom, bravery, respect, reciprocity, and responsibility. The land has started healing me and in healing myself, I am healing my family. I want to relearn these creation stories in relation to the land, where they are most likely in the local Indigenous language and not English, and insert ourselves into stories that have relationships with the land. Indigenous thought can only be learned through this personal experience because our greatest influence is on ourselves, and because living in a good way is an incredible disruption of the colonial metanarrative in and of itself. We have this intimate relationship with the land: how we live in it, we take care of her, and there are feelings. This is who we are as we are tied to the land. Land is spiritual, and she has saved my soul. Somehow, figuring my e-yaa'oyaanh, I am creating an act of resurgence simply by being Native. I want to live in a way that promotes rebirth, which is what I am currently going through, reciprocity, renewal, and having respect. I have begun the regeneration process and for the first time in my life, I am focused on myself where I have found healing in my sobriety, and education because this change has helped guide me into regenerating my culture. I am choosing to find roots in my spiritual aspect, in my body, emotionally, and in my physical well-being, and these are just some of many ways to resist colonialism. Understanding the reciprocity of relationships with the land, the forests, the water, the ecosystems heals all communities.

I want to focus my energy on Indigenizing energy and have that sustainable clean solar and wind instead of pipelines, mining, dams, pollution, and fossil fuels. In our current society, money is extremely valued as well as overconsumption and materialism; because of this Mother Earth is suffering. We need to break away. It is our responsibility to be caretakers, incorporate ancestral teachings of traditional knowledge and song and dance with ceremonies in our traditional languages despite a lot being lost. Hypothetically, what would happen environmentally if we lost Manoomin and our water sources due to pollution from oil? Manoomin is an ancient food with an entire ecosystem, and a fifth of the world's fresh water is in imminent danger. Clean water for future generations where there are untouched places, the headwater of the Mississippi River that'll pass through all Treaty territory in Minnesota, and forty-one Manoomin watersheds.

These ecosystems are in imminent danger, which violates Anishinaabeg rights to harvest food and medicine, and this affects all livelihood, homes, rights, clean water, culture, climate change impacts, and people of Minnesota, plus our relatives' flora and fauna because Enbridge Line 3 pipeline is expanding the oil industry, and it is meant for a foreign economy. The oil isn't even meant for a Minnesota economy. The Keystone XL, Trans Mountain Pipeline, and Enbridge Line 3 are all designed to get oil to the coast from Canada. It seems that many of our reservations were physically put there to save Manoomin beds. We are here to live a life of Manoomin and protect us all.

With modern technology, GIS can be used for spatial modeling capabilities and can be applied in innovative ways to environmental decision-making, tribal resource management, land and food sovereignty, and climate justice, and these skills could be utilized and used for all Indigenous peoples or those less fortunate, or no longer with us. Geographic information systems can be designed for Indigenous communities to depict both environmental and cultural information with consideration of who is given the data and whether they are publicized due to their being potentially culturally sensitive information. The use of geospatial technologies, such as RS, can help us take a deeper look at the Earth's surface without being physically present to detect certain impacts such as pipeline leaks and what the environmental damages would look like when they occurred, which could be invisible to the naked eye. Applications of GIS and RS help provide visualization, analysis, and display when a person isn't physically present. They can be used as tools to identify sources and potential routes of exposure of harmful agents in the air, water, and food, and even dust; evaluate the spatial relationships between diseases and environmental hazards; and visualize these results of spatial analyses.

Maps based on GIS can be respectful of tribal culture and traditional subsistence lifeways by including traditional language of the tribal communities involved. If elders do not know English, this is a better visual to help with the language barrier. Geographic information system–based research involving Indigenous tribes requires a long-term commitment to establish trusting relations. Mutual agreements between researchers, tribal experts, and the tribal community can cultivate new programs that benefit the whole community. Trust, informed consent, data ownership, and sovereign rights all have to be a part of the dialogue in order for the risk information to be communicated in a culturally appropriate manner.

Why should I continue to learn and research GIS and RS applications? Indigenous peoples are always at the front lines protecting the environment. Where you live has a bearing on your well-being, with certain communities at a constant threat of exposure to ecological hazards and degraded environments at risk from environmental catastrophes. When you're living in out-of-the-way invisible communities that lack a voice and are invisible to the government, often your voice isn't heard. Race is the most important factor in where toxic waste site locations will end up, or where and what pipelines will cross over Manoomin waters or what waterways they'll go under, where nuclear testing sites happen, or rubbish and recycling facilities are located, and what waterways will be polluted. There are many different settler-colonial megaprojects that have catastrophically affected Indigenous peoples' lives, health, and culture from the past to our current day and age, and they will affect future generations if this constant exposure of pollution is continued. Environmental racism is a problem of disproportionate exposure of Indigenous, Black, and other communities of color to environmental burdens to pollutants and contaminants.

Water is Life. In Anishinaabeg, we honor the water. It is who we are, for water is alive. Water (her) is a living spirit. Water is the blood of Earth. Water is a part of the greater interconnected whole. We must respect the earth and take responsibility for caring for the land, water, and its resources. Without water we cannot live. Water is our relative and is guided by spirits. Through ceremony we give thanks. This is true for us all. No matter where we come from, water is the essence of life. There are water issues all around our world simply because water does not know any boundaries, especially if a drought were to happen because it could cause famine throughout the region. Would that happen on our ancestral lands? Highly doubtful on the famine part.

We begin in water and our bodies are 69 percent water, and therefore we need it to survive. We are all equal, and all life must be respected as we are in reciprocal relations. If there was no water, what would survive? We wouldn't have our flora and fauna, let alone any humans alive to be the stewards of the land, so water is life. No garden. No food. No rivers. No oceans. No life. What would happen to life if it weren't dependent on water? By listening to the origin story of the Ojibwe and what and how we came into being, and a creation story told about how we were brought to the place where food grows on the water, Manoomin.

The summer of 2021, I was able to intern virtually with NWIC's research center, Salish Sea Research Center, which is partnered with NASA Ames Research Center, where I was able to choose my research project. I began my research by learning the history of the land and culture of Anishinaabe Peoples, gathered shapefiles and data regarding Enbridge Line 3 pipeline, Manoomin lakes, ceded Treaty lands, and current reservation lands in Minnesota. My tribes are resisting against nonrenewable energy megapipeline extraction projects carrying around Mother Earth's dirtiest fossil fuel, tar sands oil. Canadian Oil corporations are wreaking havoc on the lands where the boreal forest once stood in Canada, as the First Nations communities are at ground-zero witnessing their livelihood contaminated by destruction and devastation for years to come. The Ponca Tribe of Indians were protesting the Keystone XL expansion pipeline in Oklahoma as Anishinaabe Peoples were and still are fighting multiple pipelines from Enbridge corporation, and the original Enbridge Line 3 pipeline went through Mille Lacs reservation and Treaty lands, which is why I chose my summer internship on Enbridge Line 3 "replacement" pipeline. Where all this destruction begins, you have complete devastation of the land that directly affects the First Nations communities, all flora and fauna alike; to the middle or somewhere in between the start and the ending of these pipelines, there are direct impacts on Manoomin lakes in Minnesota, which are being eradicated due to water quality changes and global warming from anthropogenic activities.

At the start of my internship, Enbridge Line 3 "replacement" pipeline in Minnesota was only 60 percent completed, and in my two months of interning the company had rushed construction in every aspect to nearly complete the megaextractive project, which was fully operational October 2021. At stake are persistent threats and risks of possible oil spills, leaks, frac-outs, pierced aquifers, and/or explosions that would contaminate Mother Earth's soils and waters, increase air pollution, affect or jeopardize the health of all flora and fauna, and humans alike. Enbridge Line 3 "replacement" project poses a huge threat to our environment, Manoomin lakes, land, waters, ecosystems, Treaty and Indigenous rights, social justice issues such as MMIW+, and even Minnesota's economy. The oil isn't for Minnesota, but the risks are.

Manoomin is an important part of the ecosystem to many lakes, waterways, and streams—a cultural and economic resource in Minnesota. Enbridge pipelines have a track record of spills and leaks, and they can release liquid hydrocarbon into the atmosphere amongst other failures, contaminating the environment, the surrounding ecosystems, and where our Manoomin lakes are (Greenpeace 2018). Enbridge's current plan for the sixty-year-old pipeline, Line 3, is to abandon it and create an entirely new pipeline corridor with the same name. They are calling it a "replacement." What Line 3 is, is 340 miles of new thirty-four-inch diameter pipeline, which is now wide enough to ship crude oil from the tar sands region of Alberta, Canada, to Superior, Wisconsin (Stopline 3a n.d.). "It spans northern Minnesota, crossing the Leech Lake and Fond du Lac Reservations and the 1855, 1854, 1837 and 1842 treaty areas" (Stopline 3a n.d.). It is said that the "new Line 3 will cross more than 200 water ecosystems and tunnel under 20 rivers including the Mississippi River—twice—the source of drinking water for millions of people" (Stopline 3a n.d.). Once completed, and it is now, "Line 3 will ship up to 915,000 barrels of tar sands crude oil a day" (Stopline 3a n.d.), with constant threats of oil spills; habitat and environmental destruction; climate damage that may be irreversible; and harm to Indigenous communities' health, culture, and livelihood.

"The tar sands region in northern Alberta, Canada contains a form of fossil fuel. It is a tar-like substance called bitumen mixed with dirt, sand, and rock. It can be either strip-mined that will completely destroy ancient boreal forests, or the bitumen can be melted underground using superheated steam generated by burning huge amounts of natural gas, and then pumped out" (Stopline 3a n.d.). It is more extremely energy intensive than oil, very similar to that of asphalt, and must be diluted with cancer-causing chemicals known as benzenes and called diluent. It is then mixed with those chemicals and pumped through a pipeline with very high pressure. You have to dig deep underground into the surface, which uses up an unreasonable amount of water: "It takes four to six barrels (124 to 186 gallons) of water to produce one barrel of tar sands oil, which is four times more water than it takes to produce oil from conventional reserves" (Missalla, Schneider, and Anastasijevic 2010), and they have holding "lakes" for the toxic waste. Yes, holding "lakes" of toxic waste where a spill could happen at any given moment.

Enbridge Corporation is known for the largest inland oil spill to date. Transporting oil to and from oil refineries creates a constant risk of environmental destruction across Turtle Island. Oil spills are ecosystem destroyers. "In July 2010, at Marshall, Michigan, 'corrosion fatigue' opened a six-and-a-half-foot-long rupture in a pipeline carrying diluted bitumen from the Alberta tar sands. The failure allowed 843,000 gallons to spill into Talmage Creek, just upstream from where it enters the Kalamazoo River. Once in the river, the constituent parts of the oil separated—the lighter 'diluents' evaporated while the heavier bitumen sank" (Place and Gustafson 2021). A pipeline leak or rupture is a complete environmental and ecological disaster to all.

One of the project's objectives was to create vulnerability maps (heat maps) showing the weighted risks based on the different pipeline construction methods of the proposed Enbridge Line 3 route (Enbridge 2018). That route crosses Manoomin lakes and/or streams as well as current reservation lands and ceded Treaty lands (figure 16.2). It violates sovereign rights. I created a weighted scheme for the crossing methods risk assessment and plugged it into a risk assessment map of Enbridge Line 3 pipeline in or near direct relation with Manoomin water beds.

First, I mapped Enbridge Line 3's proposed "replacement" pipeline with other crude oil pipelines to the original Line 3's route on or near ceded Treaty territory and reservation land that are in the presence of Manoomin lakes in Minnesota, and the construction crossing methods. I created spatial heat maps to see the proposed construction crossing methods to see the damages that are near Line 3 within ceded Treaty land, and within reservation land, and whether Manoomin was present. I was able to find and identify the locations (hotspots) as well as cold spots where Enbridge Line 3's construction crossing methods have the most impacts on water quality and Manoomin's ecosystem.

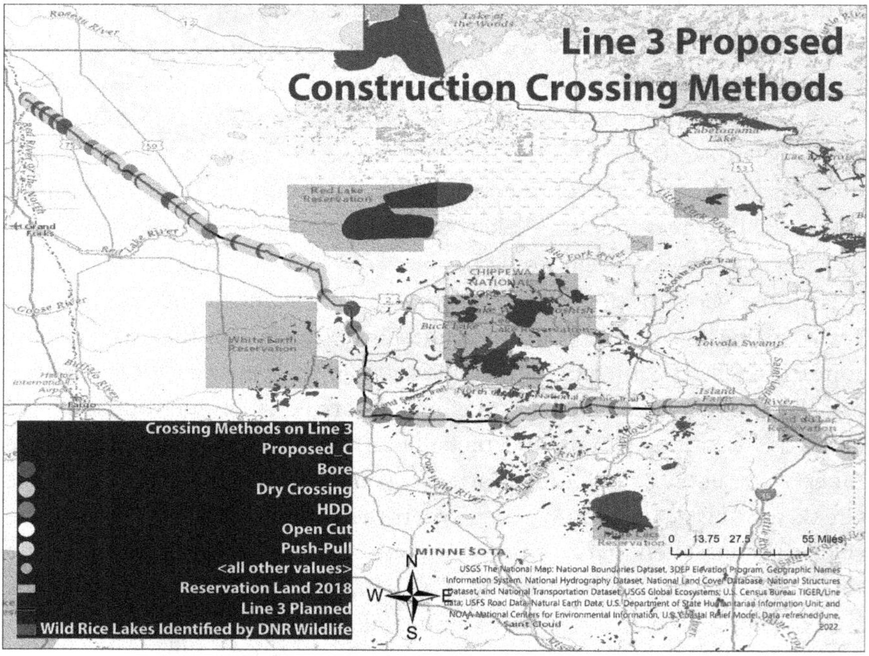

FIGURE 16.2. Map of Line 3's proposed "replacement" pipeline route and construction methods located on or near ceded Treaty territories or reservation lands that are in presence of Manoomin beds. Mary Banner, ArcGIS Pro.

On my map, I color-coded it from reddish to orange because everything is a risk, and some will have a higher risk impact on water quality and the Manoomin's ecosystem. Blue will still have risk; whether it'll have a risk to the environment, ceded land, Manoomin, Treaty land, or social health, Enbridge Line 3 will always carry a risk and threat to Indigenous peoples.

A Line 3 pipeline waterbody crossing table was found which specifies the types of proposed construction crossing methods and whether Manoomin was present (Stopline 3b n.d.). I cross-referenced the table of the proposed construction crossing methods, and I created my own fields in the attribute table, adding ceded Treaty lands, wild rice waters, and current reservation lands. Once that was complete, I created my own weighted method for the construction crossings methods. A weighted sum table allows you to apply different weights to individual categories (e.g., crossing method type, wild rice presence or absence, presence or absence of Native lands). The most invasive or riskier category has a higher weight.

Horizontal Directional Drilling (HDD) is drilling under water and was given the highest weight because it has the most impact on water quality and consequently on Manoomin beds and waterways. This method requires three stages: drilling a small pilot hole, enlarging it, and then pulling the pipeline through. Enbridge planned to use this method on twenty-one of the water crossings for this project. My last step was to create spatial heat maps. Heat maps are usually created to visualize concentration patterns (e.g., density, cluster). In our case, and because of the weighted sum method, they help us visualize the hottest or the coldest points in terms of environmental impacts. I was able to find and identify the spatial patterns and hotspots where Enbridge Line 3's construction crossing methods have the most impacts on water quality and Manoomin's ecosystem. The hotspot map indicates where the riskier and more invasive construction crossing methods along the pipeline route are located (figure 16.3). Horizontal Directional Drilling represents the highest risk.

Indigenous communities have been caught in the middle of oil infrastructure expansion, sexual violence, and human trafficking. Our Indigenous women and girls are at the front of these acts of violence. There is a direct correlation between oil extraction and mining industries and sexual violence all over the world but specifically in Indigenous communities on Turtle Island. These pipeline constructions mean bringing in thousands of temporary out-of-state workers into rural and remote communities called "mancamps," which led to MMIW+, Girls, Two-spirit, and relatives. So-called Man-camps are temporary housing facilities that welcome predominantly male workers. "While oil infrastructure poses an enormous threat to environmental safety and protection, it also greatly impacts the communities in its vicinity, often underdeveloped Indigenous communities and reservations" (Dahanayaka 2021).

Native Women and girls living near the pipelines are in danger, with limited help and resources. Enbridge corporation has a track record with not only leaks but with workers getting caught up in stings to lure out potential abusers too. The Line 3 corridor would violate the Treaty rights of the Anishinaabeg by endangering primary areas of hunting, fishing, wild rice harvesting, and cultural resources. Through my lens as a Native Woman,

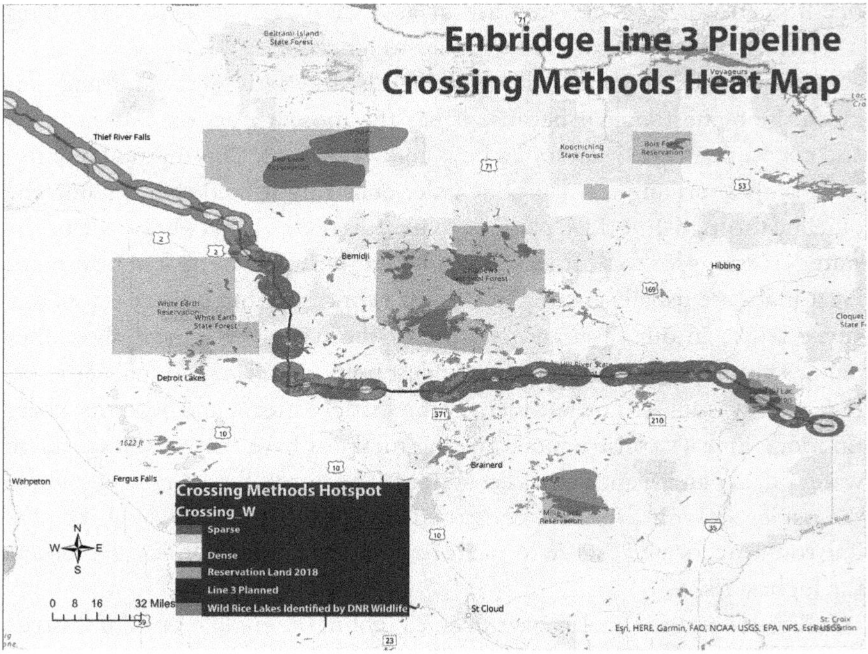

FIGURE 16.3. Heat / Risk Map for Indigenous lands and Manoomin water. Mary Banner, ArcGIS Pro.

I look at this map and I see different risks, not just to our Manoomin and our lands. I see a risk in every circle or chance that a relative and/or a friend or a family member could go missing or get murdered. I see that there is a risk that another Native might "pick up" the bottle or choose that drug over an education. I see a potential domestic violence disturbance. I see another lost soul to colonization. I see another loss of life or bad health from lack of local fresh food. Will these pipelines ever stop? At what cost will it take? Violence on Mother Earth directly correlates to violence against this ongoing epidemic.

My final map was created to point out Fond du Lac reservation where Enbridge Line 3 is going through the land. My final hotspot map indicates there are riskier and more invasive construction crossing methods than others. High Density Drilling presents the highest risk. Blue is still a risk, just perhaps a more social-health one. As you look at the map, the risks are

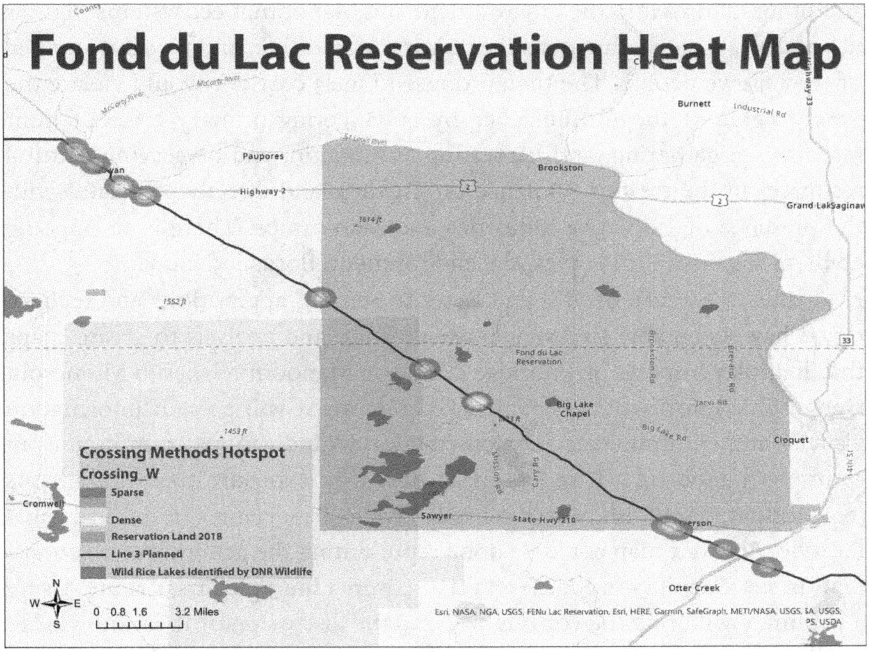

FIGURE 16.4. Fond du Lac reservation Heat/Risk map. Mary Banner, ArcGIS Pro.

located along the proposed Line 3 pipeline route near Manoomin beds (figure 16.4). However, the pipeline has become a social-health issue that will affect Indigenous peoples by allowing the pipeline straight through the reservation. As an Indigenous woman, I find this terrifying. This presents a high social threat of MMIW+, which is what we all should have our focus and attention on. Loopholes in the federal and tribal laws allow perpetrators who work in the extractive industries to commit violent crimes on tribal land and not be tried or convicted. Women and girls experience extreme adverse effects from these extractives industries. All women, men, children, and Two-spirit people who live in areas where extractive industries are located could very well benefit from my map and my research into Enbridge Line 3 pipeline.

All crossing methods pose a risk to the environment, ceded lands, Manoomin lakes, Treaty land, and sovereign rights, and increase threats to social health in Minnesota. This study further highlights spatial patterns that exhibit some degree of clustering where there is a higher risk of spills, leaks, and other failures into the environment and Manoomin ecosystems (figures 16.3 and 16.4). Line 3 threatens the culture, way of life, and physical survival of the Ojibwe people. The then-proposed Line 3 corridor would violate the Treaty rights of the Anishinaabeg by endangering primary areas of hunting, fishing, gathering, and harvesting Manoomin, and preserving cultural resources in the treaties. Violence on Turtle Island directly correlates with the presence of extractive industries and Man-camps. There is an ongoing epidemic against our Peoples, the environment, flora, and fauna.

Thanks to the use of GIS and Remote Sensing applications and technology, I have been able to provide visualization and analysis to create maps that'll display impacts of Enbridge Line 3 on Manoomin lakes in Minnesota. Geographic information system–based risk maps will present information visually and communicate risk information to Indigenous communities in a timely manner that'll reduce risks posed by exposure to contaminants (contaminated soil, fish, water, oil spills) while preserving a traditional tribal lifestyle. Another map could be done representing the groundwater contamination susceptibility in Minnesota that covers Line 3 pipeline's route. Using a risk-map will bring the community into the discussion of their knowledge of the land because those communities are at risk of potential harm.

I am not local to Minnesota or Oklahoma, where my tribes are located, yet I am able to research and study these megacompanies from my current homelands in Washington State. By being connected to the internet and putting a computer to use, I am working to benefit Indigenous peoples all over Turtle Island. We are all connected and have been battling colonization together, and perhaps each's own battle is where it really begins and grows, as it has with me.

Patriarchy impacts our landscapes and our relationships with the land. Our relationships with natural resources have been commodified, and reclaiming these relationships with the land and waters will bring healing, so long as we continue to have reciprocity; nature will protect us if we protect nature. It is about finding a balance while we push back and uphold our values because we live in a settler society where there are constant stereotypes and consumerisms. Indigenous science has kinship that can heal and mitigate issues in a holistic approach. These systems of control and domination must be critiqued and destabilized from their narratives while engaging in resurgence, sovereignty, and healthy relationships with the land.

Enbridge Line 3 pipeline was indeed an entirely new pipeline project. Line 3 pipeline has gone through a name change and is now Line 93 pipeline, which can officially carry tar sands oil due to that increased couple of inches of its diameter. Our fight isn't done until we get rid of these nonrenewable energy megacorporations, let alone private international Canadian corporations that show no ethical or humanitarian boundaries but rather are straight focused on the money and the greed. We are done with these fossil fuels. Now is the time to focus on sustainable and renewable energy.

Manoomin is a sustainable economy and has been for a thousand years. It is an economic development and creates jobs that do not require fossil fuels that have to be hauled around the world. Cleaning up Line 3's corridor, where the abandoned pipeline is, would create local jobs within the community. We are in a post-fossil-fuels economy where fires are getting hotter and larger, the rising of the sea is sending humans off their traditional homelands, and countries are running out of water. Red Lake Wind is creating energy security and energy sovereignty that meet the needs of tribes and communities, and this should very much have support of the state. This approach is an excellent way of doing future work within the communities.

We need to decolonize and break free from the environmental contamination. From the moment America was founded, there has been a very concentrated effort to destroy Indigenous peoples livelihood, culture, and food systems. Food systems were targeted as a way of politically weakening Indigenous peoples and culture (e.g., buffalo massacre in the 1870s). It is our ability to respond to our own needs for healthy, culturally adapted Indigenous foods where we seek to restore these Indigenous nationhood's, cultural practices, and homelands, which are all at risk from an increase of transportation of crude oil through pipelines. The growth of Manoomin has been endangered due to colonization through dams and pipelines.

My education has led me to research Indigenous methods and ways of resistance to environmental destruction from corporations such as Enbridge. Geographic information system and Remote Sensing applications offer a visual way to communicate the effects that Enbridge Line 3 pipeline will have on Manoomin waters but also highlight the social impacts of MMIW+ along or near the pipeline route. I was able to create risk maps to communicate issues such as potential exposure to contaminants that'll help benefit and support Indigenous communities while preserving a traditional tribal lifestyle. I was able to record the impacts of Enbridge Line 3 pipeline on Manoomin lakes using the pipeline's crossing methods and to identify the hotspots near or along the pipeline route. I was able to focus on Fond du Lac reservation, where Line 3 pipeline has a social impact on MMIW+ on or near sovereign lands. I believe that this is only a start of my Indigenous research and could be carried on with me for a lifetime. Sovereign nations can adapt through modern technology, and the use of GIS and Remote Sensing can help in communicating issues and needs more promptly.

With my research, I wanted to ensure my best was done for myself and my Indigenous community so this project could benefit and allow others to potentially utilize this information. There is future work that could be done with ArcGIS and creation of maps through analysis of water quality indicators that are disrupting Manoomin growth (e.g., include cyanobacterial blooms in a risk assessment model). An assessment could include threatened wildlife such as beavers, migration birds, and fish using a habitat suitability model. Another risk assessment could be done on the spill impacts on soil through the local hydrology of rivers, lakes, and streams. Being the voice of social threats of MMIW+ and for new and changed laws regarding pipeline abandonment, I will be able to engage with the community through GIS Tribal Story Map and ArcGIS Story Map to promote and encourage food security, health equity, ecological justice, land sovereignty, and human rights.

I have gained the courage to be the ripple in the water, to be the change not only for myself but for my family and my Indigenous community, and I have begun my Indigenous resurgence into mino bimaadiziwin, the art of living the good life.

I want to thank Dr. Michelle Montgomery and Ciarra S. Greene for this opportunity to be published alongside other Indigenous authors. It is an honor to be given the chance to be read and to be heard through my research that I find to be heart work and to have the possibility to create change. I never imagined being able to represent my own Indigenous peoples, and I hope that more Indigenous peoples do come out of the shadows that have been cast over us. I am continuing my schooling for a Master's in the Environment at Evergreen State College in Olympia, Washington. Anyone can be and create the change—you just have to be willing. Miigwech for all of your support.

I want to thank Dr. Sylvie Arques, Dr. Sherry L. Palacios, and Dr. Melissa D. Peacock. You all have forever influenced me to be better and have helped with creating that ripple in the water to create change for myself and the community. Miigwech.

References

Dahanayaka, J. 2021. "Enbridge's Line 3 Pipeline: Mixing Oil and Sexual Violence." *McGill International*. November 1. https://www.mironline.ca/enbridges-line-3-pipeline-mixing-oil-and-sexual-violence/.

Enbridge Energy. 2018. "Summary of Construction Methods and Procedures for Wetland and Waterbody Crossings." US Army Corps of Engineers.

Greenpeace Reports. 2018. "Dangerous Pipelines Enbridge's History of Spills Threatens Minnesota Waters." Greenpeace. https://www.greenpeace.org/usa/reports/dangerous-pipelines.

Missalla, Michael, Guenter Schneider, and Nikola Anastasijevic. 2010. Patent issued. Process and plant for refining oil-containing solids.

Mille Lacs Band of Ojibwe. n.d. "Welcome. History. Recognition of Self-Governance." https://millelacsband.com/.

Place, E., and Z. Gustafson. 2021. "The Danger of the Pipelines and Trains That Serve Refineries." *Sightline Institute*. https://www.sightline.org/2021/10/27/the-danger-of-the-pipelines-and-trains-that-serve-refineries/.

Stopline 3a. n.d. "Stop The Line 3 Pipeline for Water, for Treaties, for Climate." https://www.stopline3.org/#intro.

Stopline 3b. n.d. *Pipeline Maps*. https://static1.squarespace.com/static/58a3c10abebafb5c4b3293ac/t/608c0b7ffe9bfc2bc0ea2089/1619790719686/L3R_Waterbody+Crossing_Table.pdf.

17

The Issues of Climate Change and Variability and Indigenous Peoples' Science, Technology, and Society Study

An Indigenous Anticolonial Lens

PAULETTE BLANCHARD

In the past two decades, US federal policies and funding have increasingly encouraged and supported the application of climate science to local, state, national, and tribal decision-making. Climate scientists predict severe impacts of climate change on many tribal lands in the US West, Alaska, and coastal communities. Tribes are uniquely vulnerable to climate change impacts, both because many Native cultures and economies are associated with plants, animals, and ecosystems threatened by climate change and because of land loss and limited control over tribal lands resulting from long-standing US policies and tribal land mismanagement.

Many scientists agree that climate is changing and is human-influenced (IPCC 2013; Wuebbles 2017). All life will feel the impacts, but the most vulnerable will be poor and marginalized peoples, which includes Indigenous peoples worldwide (Wildcat 2009; Nakashima et al. 2012; Maldonado et al. 2013; T. M. Bull Bennett et al. 2014; Maldonado, Colombi, and Pandya 2014). Peoples in the Arctic and most northern regions have already felt the extreme impacts of climate change in the form of ice sheet depletion,

https://doi.org/10.5876/9781646425105.c017

shoreline erosion, and sea level rise for longer than science has documented the phenomenon (Maynard et al. 1998; Cameron 2012; Cochran et al. 2013).

In the past, Native American peoples have experienced climate changes but have been able to adapt over time or move to a more suitable region. Due to governmental restrictions, many Native Americans are tethered to place through jurisdictional boundaries, which increases vulnerability (Lueck 2011) to increasingly shrinking land bases. A. Martin (2011, 1) stated that "for American Indians, the effects of climate change are neither geographically nor temporally distant." Through subsistence-based livelihoods and cultures, Indigenous people have traditionally experienced more direct contact with the environment and nonhuman beings, which has made them the first to undergo the consequences of climate change (Maldonado et al. 2013). Furthermore, the mobility restrictions imposed on American Indians through the reservation and allotment system made adaptation disproportionally difficult (Weinhold 2010). Once again, American Indians are experiencing a removal from their land, but this time it is the land that is changing, leaving tribes with severely altered forms of what they had come to know throughout generations (Wildcat 2009; Lueck 2011; National Wildlife 2011; Maldonado et al. 2013).

Climate variability and extremes are worsening this economic disparity; impacting spiritual traditions (Wildcat 2009; Blanchard 2015); and creating problematic social, political, and environmental dynamics. Indigenous peoples' relationship with the environment is a major aspect of tribal sovereignty (Krakoff 2008) and identity (Sakakibara 2010). Climate extremes and variability are altering the physical geography and thus affecting tribal rights in the areas of subsistence, economics, culture, and intellectual property. Climate change also is a human rights issue (Crate 2011). Indigenous peoples must be afforded a voice in the climate change decision-making process especially in relation to adaptations and mitigation.

This point of having a voice and self-representation in the decision-making process of regulations, policies, and adaptation is sovereignty and is imperative to Indigenous peoples. Indigenous Nations should have the opportunity to provide input regarding decisions and policies that affect them. Each Nation should reevaluate its traditional laws and create its own policies on how it will respond to climate change issues. Native American leaders should be deeply concerned and on the forefront of climate change adaptation and mitigation alternatives for themselves and as an example to the rest of society on sustainable living. "The Indian voice in this issue is both a right and an asset, and there are conceptual and pragmatic spaces where Indigenous and western knowledge can and should be integrated, in order to form environmentally, socially, and economically sustainable solutions to climate change" (Martin 2011).

There are others who consider the inclusion of Indigenous perspective to supplement and enhance understanding of many disciplines of science, both social and physical. Many articles make this point by showing the value of interdisciplinary research with, for, and by Indigenous peoples (Agrawal 2009; Berkes 2009; Murphy 2011; Wildcat 2013; Williams and Hardison 2013) and the wealth of knowledge coproduced through such collaborative research. Indigenous peoples not only possess an incredible wealth of local place-based ecological information; they also have their own forms of science and wisdoms specific to them (Deloria Jr. 1997; Cajete 2000). The possession of these assets then begs the question, How are climate scientists using the Indigenous Knowledges they have collected? Are scientists using the information and, if so, how? If not, what is prohibiting them from benefiting science and tribes with knowledge obtained from tribes?

Federal Institutions and Climate Change

In response to the 1998 Kyoto Protocol, President William J. Clinton issued Executive Order (EO) 13175, in 2000. This EO required federal departments and agencies to consult with Indian tribal governments when considering policies that would impact tribal communities. EO 13175 attempted to reaffirm the federal government's obligation to support tribal sovereignty, self-determination, and self-governance. Its purpose was to ensure that all executive departments and agencies consult with Indian tribes and respect tribal sovereignty as they develop policy on issues that impact Indian communities. Climate is one such issue. This was one of several documents directed at making the relationships between tribes and the federal government better while respecting responsibilities, relationships, and sovereignties with tribes.

In 2009, the Department of the Interior's Secretarial Order 3289 pushed for "addressing the impacts of climate change on America's water, land and other natural and cultural resources" (U.S. Department of the Interior 2009). These federal mandates while on the surface suggest supporting tribes in issues of government-to-government relationships, SO 3289, for example, pushes for oversight on climate changes on "*America's water, land and other natural and cultural resources*" (emphasis in original). This simple order signed by Secretary Salazar started a push for more research in climate science and insofar as climate affects tribes, it mandated that any relevant federal department needed to consult with tribes on policies impacting tribal communities. Another aspect of these orders made production and every Noble Energy drill on public lands a priority for the departments. SO 3289 establishes a "Department-wide approach for applying scientific tools to increase understanding of climate change and to coordinate an effective response to its impact on tribes and on the land, water, ocean, fish and wildlife, and cultural heritage resources that the Department managers."

SO 3289 uses science blatantly to "fulfill our nation's vision for a clean energy economy" and states that the "Interior is now managing America's public lands and oceans not just for balanced oil, natural gas, and coal development, but also—for the first time ever—to promote environmentally responsible renewable energy development," clearly acknowledging an agenda for energy exploration woven into protecting "our country's water, land, fish and wildlife, and cultural heritage and tribal lands and resources, from the dramatic effects of climate change." This entire section suggests the earlier EO 13175 mandates for nation-to-nation relationships are shallow promises over deeper agendas.

Climate Science Centers

In response to the government mandates for more and better climate science, and protection over "water, land, and other natural and cultural resources," the Department of the Interior (DOI) created eight regional Climate Science Centers (CSCs) to be managed by the United States Geological Surveys' (USGSs') National Climate Change and Wildlife Science Center (NCCWSC) with their first objective being that because "our Nation's lands, waters, and ecosystems and the living and cultural resources they contain face myriad challenges," the newly established centers will provide "scientific information and tools" and "while CSCs specialize in providing the fundamental science to support decision-making, LCCs apply that science to specific management challenges" (O'Malley 2012).

While the CSCs and LCCs are responsible for creating the science and tools to disseminate and distribute, the consortium members and stakeholders are supposed to identify the science needs to then be applied to "real world problems." While in theory and thought the picture painted seems rosy, in fact the entire system is based on old "top-down" government methods of science.

Problematic Good Intentions

When looking at this federal top-down model from a Feminist Postcolonial Science and Technology Studies (STS) lens, it is realized that perspectives and interests of the Indigenous Americans' constituencies are not well served by modern western science and technology philosophies, policies, or practices (Harding 2009). Donna Haraway (1991) brings attention to how the claim of objectivity allows western science to perform what she calls the "God trick," or the ability to see everything from nowhere and determine who may be considered a subject with little mention of who decides.

What this governmental approach does for Indigenous peoples is relegate them to subjects of study, or subjects to speak on behalf of, or for. Both Harding and Haraway have made significant contributions to science, pushing equality by exposing inequalities. "Scientific claims to objectivity and rationality developed in a sordid colonial (and gendered) past can," according to Feminist Postcolonial STS, "obscure power relations that define and redefine subjectivity" (Schnabel, Breitwieser, and Hawbaker 2016, 320). Subjective objectivity is using personal opinions, assumptions, interpretations, and beliefs to situate your observation of measurable "facts." Basically, this framework embraces thinking that someone is capable of being completely unbiased in their research/data collecting, which is false, as everything influences how the world and its phenomena are observed and interpreted (Ratner 2002).

To say that the federal institutions are capable of nonbiased views that qualify them to make decisions for multiple groups at multiple scales is ambitious and hubris based in imperialistic, colonial control and power. The feminist view added space for women in sciences such as climate science, as is evident in the number of women employed or doing research at the CSCs. The challenge remains to recognize, respect, and reciprocate the knowledge exchanges between Peoples of Color, especially American Indians, who are not well represented, if at all, in higher science levels. Indigenous peoples are often cast in supporting roles as "consortium members" or "collaborators," who often are recognized as being a valuable contributor earning mention in acknowledgments, yet rarely if ever in authorship as knowledge holders and producers.

Coproduction Collaborative Efforts

There has been a good many attempt at bridging the climate cultures of Native Americans, Alaska Natives, First Nations, and Aboriginal Peoples with science and scientists. Some of these partnerships started long before climate was the big science issue, back when the problems were localized to environmental degradations, pollution, waste, and other "regionally smaller" difficulties. Some of the earlier work between science and Native / Indigenous peoples were discovered in workshops like Native Peoples Native Homelands (Wisdom 1998), where workshop dialogue between Native Peoples and scientists allowed for meaningful discussions of local and regional climate difficulties felt and observed. The reports that came out of these meetings and subsequent others that followed were in many ways groundbreaking. With the tenuous relationship between western scientists and tribes based on historical exploitations and abuses, the ability for a non-Native such as Dr. Nancy Maynard to reach out to Indigenous communities offering opportunity and a platform to share their experiences, knowledges, and sciences with others, especially the government by whom they are and were conquered and colonized, was forward thinking.

The Native Peoples Native Homelands workshops and others like it such as Rising Voices, to name a couple, are changing how science was being done "on" tribes and shifting to doing work "with" or "in service of" tribes at the institutional levels. Native People Native Homelands had multiple sponsors supporting collaborative efforts such as the National Aeronautical and Space Administration (NASA) and Rising Voices working closely with the National Center for Atmospheric Research (NCAR) and the National Science Foundation (NSF), with goals of facilitating discussions of the needs of tribal communities from the communities and working together to address their issues.

Rising Voices has worked with a state-recognized tribe in the bayous of deep southern Louisiana on the impacts climate change has on sea level rise, erosion, storm surge, and a multitude of other things. All the collaborators in attendance worked in groups to identify potential solutions and possible policies supporting the "relocation" of the community. With an announcement in January 2016, the Department of Housing and Urban Development announced grants totaling $1 billion in thirteen states to help communities adapt through resettlement to climate change, as well as building stronger levees, dams, and drainage systems (Davenport and Robertson 2016).

The system of using science and technologies to advance the agenda of an institution by assisting or collaborating with a marginalized group impacted by climate change would fall easily into some Feminist Postcolonial theory in STS. The researchers from NCAR (both of whom are non-Native, white women) collaborated with self-identifying Native men, to expand networks to some of the best Native / Indigenous academic scholars, who used science and technology to advance the opportunities and better the lives of a desperate and deeply marginalized group, the Isle de Jean Charles Band of Biloxi Chitimacha Choctaw. Feminist Postcolonial STS argues that research will be less biased (and less destructive) if subjectivity is extended to all humans, not just rational, disembodied western scientists (Schnabel, Breitwieser, and Hawbaker 2016). Strong objectivity maximizes objectivity by building upon a multitude of diverse subjectivities instead of only the limited perspectives and interests of a few western scientists (Harding 1991, 2009). As valuable as early Feminist Postcolonial work is, it remains that early feminist philosophies further benefited already-advantaged white women but further marginalized Indigenous peoples, especially women (Harding 2009, 2015; Barker 2015).

Indigenous Ways of Doing

As with many subjects, there are multiple ways to address a situation. With climate changes and extreme weather events, Native and Indigenous peoples have been forced to adapt fast, move, or disappear altogether. Instead, Native and Indigenous researchers, community members, leaders, and spiritual leaders have joined together in solidarity to support themselves and their communities as best as possible with limited or no resources. There are larger, more successful tribes that have partnered with government agencies and institutions such as the Chickasaw and Choctaw Nations partnering with the South Central–CSC, becoming consortium members. Most smaller tribes are struggling with dire immediate problems, and to attempt something as daunting as addressing climate change is still small in comparison to issues of safe water, food, and shelter.

Even with such odds against them, there are some Native/Indigenous peoples networking together and designing their own research, research questions, and grants, and getting funded to do it. Groups like Dr. Dan Wildcat's Indigenous Peoples Climate Change Working Group not only unites Native leaders in different communities across the United States to address local climate issues but also supports bright Native/Indigenous students from tribal colleges, creating space for these often-overlooked intelligent students to access sciences and technologies related to climate change and variability. These working group meetings put tribal college students on the stage talking on a panel, engaging in a poster session on their research, or being connected to mentors in their fields to be supported and guided through their educations. These relationships are often lifelong and based in reciprocity, respect, relevance, and redistribution tied to a loosely common set of ancient Indigenous philosophies.

WIS2DOM (Johnson, Louis, and Kliskey 2013) is another workshop designed by Indigenous peoples to address Indigenous Science and the immediate needs of Indigenous peoples in sciences. The idea is to come up with Indigenous solutions for Indigenous problems. This is so important because it is about so much more than science or technology; it becomes about solidarity and sovereignty. It is nation building on a smaller scale, allowing Indigenous peoples to advocate for their people as well as their homelands.

Queer Ecologies and Methodologies

Queer ecologies challenge human exceptionalism through contestation of the nature/culture binary. Indigenous methodologies of science and technologies consist of stories that avoid the hierarchical nature-culture and animal-human split that has enabled domineering human management, naming, controlling, and "saving" of nature (TallBear 2015, 234). Queer ecology, very similar to Indigenous theories, challenges human exceptionalism through contestation of the nature/culture binary (Schnabel, Breitwieser, and Hawbaker 2016, 321). Indigenous peoples are often deeply connected physically and spiritually to place. This intersectionality is lacking in western methodologies and completely absent in western methods, especially in the importance placed on the scientific method and control.

To accomplish its reconceptualization of subjectivity, queer ecologies draw heavily upon Haraway's (2003) notion of "nature-cultures." In this framework nature and culture (often erroneously reduced to the material in the discursive, respectively) are inseparable, both being constructed by and through the other. By problematizing the nature/culture binary, queer ecology significantly troubles anthropocentrism that dictates subjectivity. An Indigenous methodology encourages us to rethink subjectivity or the quality of being a subject.

According to feminist STS the conferral of subjectivity has been rationalized, racialized, and sexualized, and the influence of nonhuman life and nonliving matter has been underemphasized. Fitting with some feminist postcolonial STS scholars, technoscientific practices and knowledge about human nature and the natural world have been generated by gender and racialized systems of power built upon a violent history of colonial expansion. Heavily influenced by anticolonial and Women of Color feminism is feminist postcolonial STS. Feminist postcolonial STS asserts that race, gender, and colonialism intersect with a modern traditional binary. Binary privileges some knowledge producers while devaluing other potential knowledge producers, mainly women, People of Color, and Indigenous populations.

Science grounded in the linear notion of knowledge accumulation in progress generates vulnerabilities to simplistic and dualistic thinking. "There is no privileged scientific method that can translate nature into knowledge and no technological nothing that can translate knowledge into artifacts" (Sismondo 2010). So, then my issue when reading postcolonial STS research is that even as the supposed overarching goals claim to advocate for gender/sex equality, social issues are often presented as independent from colonial, imperial, neocolonial, and neoimperialistic social issues, and they are still based on the perspectives of mostly non-Indigenous men and women. While presenting the still present gender equality, the larger issue of deterministic otherness is hugely problematic, as we Native and Indigenous peoples are still in some manner the subject or the voice they need to amplify. Colonization still has us subjugated in science, technology, and society through methods and methodologies of western sciences.

Indigenous Science and Technology Studies

Science, Technology, and Society studies are vastly open to explore how Indigenous Sciences and Technologies have guided Indigenous peoples and their societies to survive and thrive prior to contact and since colonization. An area of interest is how Indigenous Science and Technology (S&T) have historically contributed to and supplemented western science and continue to do so. Indigenous epistemologies and ontologies include tested methods used to survive extreme environmental climactic changes historically and predicted by western science. It is through our own lenses of climate science and the technologies associated that we can start to negotiate a new relationship of reciprocity between not only Indigenous peoples and western sciences but between humans and our extended more-than-human beings. The dichotomies lie not in the differences in humans as much as in the human/nature binary of western science. Indigenous Science finds, "It is not possible to separate Indigenous science from other areas of life such as ethics, spirituality, metaphysics, social order, ceremony, and a variety of other aspects of daily existence" (Peat 1994, 241).

Western science places more emphasis on prediction, while Indigenous Science may place greater emphasis on explanation. Both western and Indigenous Sciences strive for explanation and prediction (Kawagley 1995). Reardon and TallBear suggest "establishing the continued sovereignty Indigenous peoples have over their bodies, their lands, their identities, and through control of their information that are acts of anticolonization/decolonization strengthening sovereignties" (Reardon and TallBear 2012). Science should then be advancements toward sovereignty, and technologies need to advance that objective. If and when science and technologies fall short of this objective, then they are considered to be a tool of continued colonization and oppression.

In binary dichotomies of either/or, so much information or knowledge is lost. Western sciences' perceived supremacy over all other systems of knowledge depends on maintenance of the modern/traditional divide. It is this gendered, racialized, imperialist, and colonial power structure that necessarily dictated and calculated an unequal conferral of modern subjectivity that continues to oppress. Feminist postcolonial STS reminds us of how subjectivities denied, bestowed, and negotiated even in relation to something as objective as modern science (Schnabel, Breitwieser, and Hawbaker 2016). Indigenous methodologies go further than most of the current Feminist Postcolonial STS studies, as it recognizes and respects variables outside of control and things that cannot be measured, ethics, and the metaphysical and spirituality to name a few. It is the recognition of relatedness and relationships that needs to be considered in western science.

"The line between human and nonhuman becomes nonsensical" (TallBear 2015, 231). Indigenous peoples have never forgotten that nonhumans are agential beings engaged in social relations that profoundly shape human lives. Indigenous approaches also critique settler colonialism and its management of nonhuman others. These and other newer approaches clearly link violence against animals to violence against particular humans who have historically been linked to a less-than-human or animal status (234).

Joanne Barker (2015) explains why and how mainstream feminism does not include Native women; not only does this exclusion have critical impacts on how science accepts the feminine, but it directly and especially affects Indigenous feminist relationships. This is because even though we existed in the same place as non-Natives, our experiences of the same incident are not the same. Our science erases human/nature binaries, as the two are one. Spirit cannot and should not be separated from more-than-human "relatives" we have relationships with. "These are our relatives, not our resources. We need to have relationships that are such" (Wildcat 2009). V. Deloria Jr. and D. Wildcat (2001) explained the different relations between many Native Peoples and the places that they identify to and with. The plants, water, rocks, and animals are all part of an extended family, making place sacred, for it is inherent to identity or relationships to the places that they have deeper senses of place reference (Johnson and Larsen 2013).

It all becomes quite clear that there are a number of ways Indigenous peoples use S&T, and to further understand, much more work needs to be done. Another unique aspect of an Indigenous S&T is how it is passed on—through art, song, dance, storytelling, and numerous other ways of sharing knowledge. Indigenous Science is doing. It is an adjective, a descriptive observation, and a verb, active way of being. The knowledge Indigenous peoples maintain is tried and tested for thousands of generations and far older than modern western science systems and philosophies. The wealth of available wisdom in what is left of the forests, the oceans, and life within; the sky above; and everything seen and unseen. There is still much available to learn and to save in the memories, stories, art, and other knowledge-keeping methods Indigenous peoples and their places of belonging encompass. Humans are not the only ones holding wisdom, as animal and plant life possess a wealth of information related to everything related to their places of belonging too, if scientists will allow it to speak to them and understand what they tell us. Not verbally, but through the different responses to the environment. Our elders are passing on, and they take knowledge with them too. Now is an exciting time to study science, technology, and society, especially for an Indigenous Scientist.

References

Agrawal, A. 2009. "Why 'Indigenous' Knowledge." *Journal of the Royal Society of New Zealand* 39 (4): 15–158.

Barker, J. 2015. "Indigenous Feminism." *The Oxford Handbook of Indigenous People's Politics*: 1–17. https://doi.org/10.1093/Oxfordhb/9780195386653.013.007.

Berkes, F. 2009. "Indigenous Ways of Knowing and the Study of Environmental Change." *Journal of the Royal Society of New Zealand* 39 (4):151–156.

Blanchard, P. 2015. "Our Squirrels Will Have Elephant Ears: Indigenous Perspectives on Climate Change in the South Central United States." SHAREOK. MA thesis, University of Oklahoma.

Bull Bennett, T. M., N. G. Maynard, P. Cochran, R. Gough, K. Lynn, J. Maldonado, G. Voggesser, S. Wotkyns, and K. Cozetto. 2014. "Indigenous Peoples, Lands, and Resources." In *Climate Change Impacts in the United States: The Third National Climate Assessment*, edited by T. C. Terese, Richmond J. M. Melillo, and G. W. Yohe. US Global Change Research Program. https://www.cakex.org/documents/indigenous-peoples-lands-and-resources-climate-change-impacts-united-states-third-national-climate-assessment.

Cajete, G. 2000. *Native Science: Natural Laws of Interdependence*: Santa Fe, NM: Clear Light Publishers.

Cameron, E. S. 2012. "Securing Indigenous Politics: A Critique of the Vulnerability and Adaptation Approach to the Human Dimensions of Climate Change in the Canadian Arctic." *Global Environmental Change* 22 (February): 103–114.

Cochran, P., O. H. Hunting, C. Pungowiyi, S. Tom, F. S. Chapin III, H. P. Huntington, N. G. Maynard, and S. F. Trainor. 2013. "Indigenous Framework for Observing and Responding to Climate Change in Alaska." *Climatic Change* 120 (March 26): 557–567.

Crate, S. A. 2011. "Climate and Culture: Anthropology in the Era of Contemporary Climate Change." *Annual Review of Anthropology* 40 (October):175–194. https://doi.org/10.1146/Annurev.Anthro.012809.104925.

Davenport, C., and C. Robertson. 2016. "Resettling the First American 'Climate Refugees.'" *New York Times*, May 2, 3.

Deloria, V., Jr. 1997. *Red Earth White Lies: Native Americans and the Myth of Scientific Fact*. Golden, CO: Fulcrum Publishing.

Deloria, V., Jr., and D. Wildcat. 2001. "Power and Place Equal Personality and Traditional Technology." In *Power and Place: Indian Education in America*, edited by Deloria, 21–28, 57–66. Golden, CO: Fulcrum.

Haraway, D. J. 1991. "A Cyborg Manifesto: An Ironic Dream of a Common Language for Women in the Integrated Circuit." In *The Transgender Studies Reader Remix*, edited by Susan Stryker and Dylan McCarthy Blackston, 429–443. New York: Routledge.

Haraway, D. J. 2003. *The Companion Species Manifesto: Dogs, People, and Significant Otherness*. Vol. 1. Chicago: Prickly Paradigm Press.

Harding, S. 1991. *Whose Science? Whose Knowledge? Thinking from Women's Lives*: Ithaca, NY: Cornell University Press.

Harding, S. 2009. "Postcolonial and Feminist Philosophies of Science and Technology: Convergences and Dissonances." *Postcolonial Studies* 12 (4): 20.

Harding, S. 2015. "Objectivity and Diversity." In *Objectivity and Diversity*. Chicago: University of Chicago Press.

IPCC. 2013. "Summary for Policymakers Climate Change 2013: The Physical Science Basis." In *Contribution of Working Group I to the Fifth Assessment Report of the Intergovernmental Panel on Climate Change*, edited by T. F. Stocker, D. Qin, G.-K. Plattner, M. Tignor, S. K. Allen, J. Boschung, A. Nauels, Y. Xia, V. Bex, and P. M. Midgley, 1–30. Cambridge: Cambridge University Press.

Johnson, J., and S. C. Larsen. 2013. "A Deeper Sense of Place." In *Stories and Journeys of Indigenous-Academic Collaboration*, edited by J. Johnson and S. C. Larsen, 7–20. Corvallis: Oregon State University.

Johnson, J. T., R. P. Louis, and A. Kliskey. 2013. "Weaving Indigenous and Sustainability Sciences: Diversifying our Methods Workshop (WIS2DOM)." National Science Foundation.

Kawagley, A. O. 1995. "Incorporation of the World Views of Indigenous Cultures: A Dilemma in the Practice and Teaching of Western Science." Paper presented at the 3rd International History, Philosophy, and Science Teaching Conference, Minneapolis, October 29, November 2.

Krakoff, S. 2008. "American Indians, Climate Change, and Ethics for a Warming World." In *University of Colorado Law School Review* 85 (4): 865.

Lueck, M. M. 2011. "Vulnerability, Resilience, and Policy: The Challenge of Environmental Migration and Displacement in the United States." In *Source* 15. Bonn, Germany: United Nations University Institute for Environmental and Human Security.

Maldonado, J. K., B. Colombi, and R. Pandya. 2014. *Climate Change and Indigenous Peoples in the United States: Impacts, Experiences and Actions*. Cham, Switzerland: Springer International Publishing.

Maldonado, Julie Koppel, Christine Shearr, Robin Bronen, Kristina Peterson, and Heather Lazrus. 2013. "The Impact of Climate Change on Tribal Communities in the US: Displacement, Relocation, and Human Rights." *Climactic Change* 120 (3): 601–614.

Martin, A. 2011. "American Indian Knowledge: Why Indigenous Participation Is Essential for Effective U.S. Climate Policy." Research paper. Natural Resources and Sustainable Development / International Affairs, the University for Peace / American University, Washington, DC.

Maynard, N., S. Houser, V. Teller, M. MacCracken, R. Gough, and P. Spears. 1998. "Native Peoples Native Homelands—Final Report." In *U.S. Global Change Research Program*, edited by Nancy Maynard, 24–31. Albuquerque: National Aeronautical and Space Administration.

Murphy, B. 2011. "From Interdisciplinary to Inter-epistemological Approaches: Confronting the Challenges of Integrated Climate Change Research." *Canadian Geographer* 55 (4): 490–509. https://doi.org/10.1111/J.1541-0064.2011.00388.X.

Nakashima, D., J. Rubis, A. R. Castillo, K. Galloway Mclean, and H. Thulstrup. 2012. *Weathering Uncertainty: Traditional Knowledge for Climate Change Assessment and Adaptation*. Paris and Darwin, Australia: UNESCO, UNU.

National Wildlife Federation. 2011. "Facing the Storm: Indian Tribes, Climate-Induced Weather Extremes, and the Future for Indian Country." In *Confronting Global Warming*. Boulder: National Wildlife Federation.

O'Malley, R. 2012. "DOI Climate Science Centers: Regional Science to Address Management Priorities." U.S. Geological Survey Fact Sheet 2012-3048, 4.

Peat, F. D. 1994. *Blackfoot Physics: A Journey into the Native American Worldview*. York Beach, ME: Red Wheel / Weiser.

Ratner, C. 2002. "Subjectivity and Objectivity in Qualitative Methodology." Forum Qualitative Sozialforschung / Forum: Qualitative Social Research 3 (3). Berlin: Freie Universität Berlin.

Reardon, J., And Kim TallBear. 2012. "'Your DNA Is Our History': Genomics, Anthropology, and the Construction of Whiteness as Property." *Current Anthropology* 53 (S5): S233–S245.

Sakakibara, C. 2010. "Kiavallakkikput Agviq (Into The Whaling Cycle): Cetaceousness and Climate Change among the Inupiat of Arctic Alaska." *Annal of the Association of American Geographers* 100 (4): 1003–1012.

Schnabel, L., L. Breitwieser, and A. Hawbaker. 2016. "Subjectivity in Feminist Science and Technology Studies: Implications and Applications for Sociological Research." *Sociology Compass* 10 (4): 318–329.

Sismondo, S. 2010. *An Introduction to Science and Technology Studies*. 2nd ed. West Sussex, UK: Wiley-Blackwell.

TallBear, K. 2015. "An Indigenous Reflection on Working beyond the Human / Not Human." *GLQ: A Journal of Lesbian and Gay Studies* 21 (2–3): 230–235.

U.S. Department of the Interior. 2009. *Secretarial Order 3289. Washington D.C.*

Weinhold, B. 2010. "Climate Change and Health: A Native American Perspective." *Environmental Health Perspectives* 118 (2): 2.

Wildcat, D. 2009. *Red Alert! Saving the Planet with Indigenous Knowledge*. Golden, CO: Fulcrum Publishing.

Wildcat, D. 2013. "Introduction: Climate Change and Indigenous Peoples of the USA." *Climatic Change* 120 (3): 509–515.

Williams, T., and P. Hardison. 2013. "Culture, Law, Risk and Governance: Context of Traditional Knowledge in Climate Adaptation." *Climatic Change* 120:531–544.

Wisdom, Circles Of. 1998. "Native Peoples–Native Homelands Climate Change Workshop."

Wuebbles, D. J., D. W. Fahey, and K. A. Hibbard. 2017. "Climate Science Special Report: Fourth National Climate Assessment, Volume I." Washington, DC.

18

On Land and Social Fragmentation

Lakota Values of Unity and Relationality in the Age of Division

JOSEPH GAZING WOLF

Introduction

No matter where you are now, if you observe the world around you, you will note one common theme in human behavior: fragmentation. It seems in our nature to find every means by which to divide ourselves into "us" and "them." Race, ethnicity, sex, gender, nationality, geography, religion, ethics, politics, economics, and professions all provide excellent means to fragment. I am white, you are Black; I am American, you are Mexican; I am woman, you are man; I am red, you are blue; I am gay, you are straight; I am blue collar, you are white collar. There is a "war on terror," a "war on drugs," and a "war on poverty" in a culture where you can "cancel" opposing voices and the people behind those voices. Take a moment to listen to conversations around you and note the methods of vulgarity, gossip, competition, and alienation that people use to assert their superiority or their groups' superiority over others. The minutia gets even more asinine however: are you for this football team or that one, a dog person or cat person, for small dogs or big dogs, for this

https://doi.org/10.5876/9781646425105.c018

electric vehicle or that gas-guzzling beast? If this seems like an overt dramatization, consider that there is an entire academic literature dedicated to sports fans' murderous rage and property damage, even when their team wins (Hilliard and Johnson 2018; Wann 2003). Romantic couples too frame their "love" in terms of "us vs. the world"; and both self-proclaimed feminists and those who value traditional gender roles see heterosexual relationships as the "battle of the sexes." Parents also see their primary role as protecting their children from the big evil world, teaching them that life is an eternal struggle between good people and bad people (Lukianoff and Haidt 2019). Indeed, fragmentation is so ubiquitous, it infects the whole psyche: fragmented attention spans, fragmented memories, fragmented conversations, fragmented beings.

The nature of our minds is projected out into the world. Hence, it comes as no surprise that the face of Earth herself has been scarified beyond recognition in many landscapes. Extensive land fragmentation is blatantly evident across virtually every ecoregion on earth. With ostentatious ignorance of the natural world, Euro-American settlers have divided American Indian ancestral and reservation lands into oblivion. Once cohesive ecoregions have now become scarified by a diversity of human settlement and their accompanying exploitative value systems. Human settlement in turn asserts its particular form of fragmentation depending on the pattern of land use. Permanent buildings are one common form of fragmentation, and more developments are springing up every day. We then needed roads and parking lots to reach those buildings, so we carved out more formerly contiguous land and disrupted animal migrations. By necessity of our greed and callousness, we needed fences to keep out strangers from our properties along with other unwanted animals. Any which way you look across the landscape, humans have had devastating fragmentary impacts.

The interaction between land and social fragmentation is exponential. The general emphasis on the commodification of land, private ownership, geographic migration, and natural resources exploitation has contributed to the social fragmentation mentioned earlier and its legion of negative repercussions. Land and social fragmentation, in turn, interact to make it difficult to address fragmentation-induced crises such as climate change, biodiversity loss, economic inequality, healthcare disparities, and racial/gender inequities, among others. In this chapter, I utilize the example of wildfire mitigation to demonstrate how land and social fragmentation interact to complicate long-term, effective, positive outcomes in land management. I then introduce the Lakota values of unity and relationality as they have been taught to me by my elders. Last, I draw on these teachings along with the literature to provide some pragmatic guidance to address wildfire and other land-based crises.

Wildfire

Like all ecosystem-level, transboundary issues, effective wildfire mitigation requires collective human action across broad ecoregions, which is a barrier in a socially and geographically fragmented society (Brenkert-Smith 2010; Every et al. 2016; Prior and Eriksen 2013). The variety of government officials, land managers, and landowners in any geographic region impacts settlement patterns, management priorities, and potential agreements, which in turn impact landscape conditions (e.g., invasive plant proliferation, fuel type) that determine the scope and intensity of wildfire in a landscape (Dickinson et al. 2015; Sword-Daniels et al. 2018; Syphard et al. 2016). Creating fire-resilient ecoregions, where fire plays a healthy disturbance role, is therefore highly context dependent with no "one size fits all" solution (Canadas, Novais, and Marques 2016; Moritz et al. 2014; Schoennagel et al. 2017). Urban sprawl, for example, the expansion and subdivision of residential property into wildland areas, introduces new human populations that often arrive with different values and relationships to the land than local populations have (Collins 2012; Paveglio, Brenkert-Smith et al. 2015; Paveglio, Jakes et al. 2009; Petty et al. 2015), which impacts their willingness to cooperate. These differences and their impact on intergroup interactions also fluctuate over time based on demographic and broader social changes (e.g., resource policies, regulations, economic developments), as well as interactions between residents and natural resources agencies across various scales (local, county, state, national) (Langer and McGee 2017; Stidham et al. 2014; Sword-Daniels et al. 2018). The complexities and nature of interactions among various distinct actors (individual, neighborhood, city, county, region), natural resources agencies, government agencies, land tenure regimes, and natural ecosystem variability create a plethora of foci and barriers that directly impact a cohesive, coordinated response to wildfire across ecoregions of scale (Paveglio and Edgeley 2017).

This combined land and social fragmentation necessitates an understanding of how a sense of "community" emerges spatially and temporally across variability in human values, knowledges, skills, perspectives, ownership patterns, and relationships to the land (Slemp et al. 2012), and how this sense of community impacts adaptation to wildfire (Paveglio et al. 2012; Paveglio, Abrams, and Ellison 2016; A. M. S. Smith 2016). Despite this, wildfire mitigation research has primarily conceptualized "community" in terms of discrete units such as fire districts, neighborhoods, or homeowner's associations (McGee 2011; Stidham et al. 2014) or has simply compared mitigation action across states (Jakes et al. 2007; Paveglio et al. 2015; Toman et al. 2014). Policy and science recommendations also continue to be predominately based on biophysical evidence (Eckerberg and Buizer 2017; Paschen and Beilin 2017; Paveglio et al. 2015), entirely ignoring the fragmentation elephant in the room. Even social research has tended to focus on individual groups with management control over particular lands (Dunlop et al. 2014; Dupéy and Smith 2018; McCaffrey 2015). The study of continuity, or consistent collective adoption, of actions like fuel reduction, is nonexistent, with research instead focusing on the generic efforts of particular agencies (Ager et al. 2017; Prato and Paveglio 2018; Spies et al. 2017) or intended efforts on private property (Brenkert-Smith et al. 2013; Dickinson et al. 2015; Paveglio et al. 2009; Toman et al. 2013). Evidence is clear, however, that the capacity of diverse groups to work together while holding incompatible values on what is "natural" and how nature ought to be related to may dramatically influence actual outcomes (Petty et al. 2015; Toman et al. 2014).

The federal government too has only recently "scaled up" its processes for wildfire management across tenure regimes to address mitigation costs and risks at a larger landscape-level (Otero and Nielsen 2017; Spies et al. 2014; Steelman 2016). This includes land-use planning, fuels reduction, evacuation planning, and building codes (Ager et al. 2017; Prato and Paveglio 2018; Tedim, Leone, and Xanthopoulos 2016). Programs such as the Chiefs' Joint Landscape Restoration Partnership, the Collaborative Landscape Restoration Program, and Good Neighbor Authority (USDA 2018a, 2018b) facilitate the US Forest Service's "All Lands, All Hands" collaborative approach that promotes coordination across landownerships, managing agencies, and governments to improve the effectiveness of ecosystem management at the level of ecoregions (Charnley, Kelly, and Wendel

2017). Within this programming, collective action is framed as a necessity for landscape-level mitigation that requires tradeoffs among values, goals, and benefits (Bardsley et al. 2018; Prato et al. 2014; Spies et al. 2017). Notably, however, these programs offer embedded mechanisms and structures that facilitate collaborative planning and decision-making among diverse stakeholders, across land ownerships.

Research and policy that are effective in creating fire-resilient landscapes require an understanding of the level of land and social fragmentation in impacted ecoregions and the potential for an emergent sense of community across diverse land tenure and social dynamics (Field and Jensen 2005; Paveglio et al. 2019; Spies et al. 2014; Steelman 2016). Specifically, researchers would need to aggregate the fire-mitigating actions of distinct groups (e.g., land-use regulations, fuel reduction, suppression agreements), at various scales (individual to ecoregion), across private and public landownership, within a fragmented ecoregion (Abrams et al. 2015; Brenkert-Smith et al. 2013; Canadas, Novais, and Marques 2016; Chas-Amil, Touza, and García-Martínez 2013; Jakes et al. 2011; Labossière and McGee 2017; McLennan and Eburn 2014; Steelman 2016; Williams et al. 2012). Indeed, the present structure of emergent ecoregion-wide human "community" and its aggregate management actions and agreements may be considered that community's "adaptedness" to phenomena such as wildfire (Brenkert-Smith et al. 2017; Paveglio, C. Moseley et al. 2015; Paveglio, Boyd, and Carrol 2017; Steen-Adams, Charnley, and Adams 2017). To grow this adaptedness, researchers, managers, and policy makers ought to always consider the human landscape (Beilin and Reid 2014) and promote cooperation by proposing a variety of actions that appeal to a variety of values on this landscape (Labossière and McGee 2017; Tedim, Leone, and Xanthopoulos 2016; Williams et al. 2012).

Unity and Relationality

Hang around a Lakota person long enough, and you are bound to hear two phrases: *Ówaŋžila uŋk'úŋpi* ("we are united" or "we are together") and *Mitákuye owás'iŋ* ("all my relatives"). These phrases have been a regular part of our prayers and ceremonies for thousands of years. They are sentiments that relate two important values central to the Lakota way of life: unity and relationality. For a pragmatic application of these values, read the final section of this chapter. Here I introduce only what these expressions mean and the values they hold for the Lakota, as my elders have taught them to me.

Ówaŋžila uŋk'úŋpi is an expression used to speak of our unity with one another. It is intended to express solidarity with our relatives, human and more-than-human alike. It is most often used when we come together to defend the rights of Unči Maka (Grandmother Earth); when we show up to protect sacred water, or soil, or mountains, or rocks, or plants, or animals, or humans. The key elements here are showing up and being present to the other in need and to the place being harmed, being united to the land and to the people that gave us life. More than this, being united means, we have a shared purpose, shared visions, shared priorities, and shared destinies. Therefore, if your life is threatened, I put my body and my life on the line to defend you and ensure your well-being, whether you are a human or a buffalo. Inherent in this concept is the understanding that I am part of something much larger than myself; and though my existence is a sacred and necessary life-giving force, it belongs to and serves the collective of all life-forces. Hence, we say, "We are forces of nature, defending herself." The expression is also often used when we welcome back a relative that was taken from us, like Tatanka (buffalo). In this context, it means that we are united with the Buffalo Nation in a Nation-to-Nation relationship and will work to provide them with a suitable home where they are safe and can thrive. In other words, this expression is not one of false or social-media-type solidarity but one where I live out my responsibility to the tribes and nations and individuals with whom I express unity and a common purpose.

Mitákuye owás'iŋ is often loosely translated as "all my relatives" or "we are all related." The phrase has been misappropriated by non-Lakota and given some holistic, pseudospiritual meaning, something to the effect of communicating the idea that all Native Americans are at one with nature and live in harmony with it and with each other. It has also been overused and misunderstood by younger Lakota like me, who use it openly in academic presentations or literature without discussing its significance or understanding the responsibility it places upon them. In reality, this phrase has very specific and powerful meanings within Lakota metaphysics, cosmologies, epistemologies, ontologies, and axiologies. I recall using the phrase around one of my elders, Sandra Black Bear, who was also my Lakota language teacher. She said to be careful using it. She told me that when young people like myself use the phrase freely and without care, the elders shudder and cringe. When I asked why, she said that the phrase does not communicate some superficial idea of interconnectedness with other humans or with nature. Rather, translated in its ancestral spiritual context and within our oral traditions, it communicates the reality that "everything is related to the existence of all my relatives." Therefore, the phrase acts (yes, language is an act) in several ways: (1) it reminds me of my positionality within the cosmos as a small but significant part of it, (2) it calls into reality the fact that my existence and that of all my people, my tribe, are inextricably linked to and contingent upon the existence of everything else in the cosmos, and (3) it places responsibility on me and my tribe to live out the respect and reciprocity that this interconnected reality requires. Acknowledging that everything is existentially related means I am kin to all life-giving forces in the cosmos, and this holds me responsible for enhancing that life. It is not a spiritual edict but one of responsibility and duty.

Something important to note here is that at the heart of the Lakota values of unity and relationality is the antidote to the disease of fragmentation and all of its consequences: humility. For one tribe to engage another with the respect and reciprocity required to build long-term relationships, each tribe must have an implicit understanding that their people do not have it all figured out; if they did, they would not need to know anything else about anyone else. They embody an understanding that they have not uncovered all the mysteries of the universe and have much to learn about the very places they and their ancestors have stewarded for millennia. This is why they listen to, speak with, smell, touch, and taste their homelands, like children continuously exploring with openness. In other words, the foundation of Traditional Ecological Knowledge is humility. Contrary to those who claim to know humility, an irony in itself, my experience with many elders and spiritual leaders has taught me that humility is not what most think it is. The humble do not claim ignorance of things they obviously do not know, like astrophysics. Those who embody this value often understand that the more experience they have had with something, the more they have realized how little they know of it. What is humility?: an elder medicine man who approaches the spirit world with caution, a professor emeritus of astrophysics who is fascinated by dark matter like she has just heard about it for the first time, a president who refuses to leave his people and instead risks his life to fight for them and fulfill his professional duties, a tribal chief who gives his life in order that his people might keep theirs. Indigenous peoples across the globe have developed deep understanding of their ancestral places precisely because they approach with humility. Over the long term, the practice of humility bears the fruit of unity and relationality.

Being Pragmatic about Fragmentation

Values are only helpful if we live by them. I can talk about unity and relationality until I am blue in the face, but if I and others I hope to engage with do not abide by them, then the fruits of my labor will be rotten. The wise can sense when a reconciliatory, collaborative, or coordinated effort is worth pursuing, and when it is not. Those who live only by the values of exploitation and domination often cannot be reasoned with or "enlightened via information" into understanding the importance of coming together as a community, even when it leads to their own suffering and death, as recent pandemic history clearly proves. More on the limitations of collaboration later, but for now, How do we pursue unity and relationality in a fragmented world?

The mistake people make is that they base their willingness to work with others on the delusion of perfect cohesiveness of wants and needs and perfect alignment of values and beliefs. If this is your understanding of community, you should not be surprised when you fail miserably in all your relationships. Community is an emergent reality; it exists because we make it exist and tend to it. All parties must be involved and must hold themselves accountable to their responsibility to uphold the values of unity and relationality despite their differences with others. Hence, to define community based solely on race, ethnicity, gender, profession, locale, or administrative/policy unit is the very essence of a fragmented understanding of the world.

We begin our efforts at unity and relationality by exploring the fragmented social-ecological landscape that is of interest:

1. What are the different stakeholder groups? What are their demographic and institutional characteristics and patterns? (Jakes and Langer 2012; Paveglio, Brenkert-Smith et al. 2015; Paveglio, Jakes et al. 2009)
2. What are their economic interests, social/professional networks, perspectives, skills, resources, and resource- and service-based dependencies

that impact their functioning? (Flint, Luloff, and Theodori 2010; Paveglio, Boyd, and Carroll 2017; Paveglio, Nielsen-Pincus et al. 2017; Theodori 2005; Theodori and Kyle 2013; Wilkinson 1991)

3. What are the different stakeholder "values-at-risk"? (Paveglio et al. 2019)
4. How do stakeholders define landscape sustainability and community well-being? (Jakes, Kruger et al. 2007; Jakes, Nelson et al. 2011; Paveglio et al. 2015; Stasiewicz and Paveglio 2017)
5. What are the land tenure, land rights, and ownership patterns on the landscape?
6. Is there an extant history of relationships or collective action or interactions between stakeholders? (Flint, Luloff, and Finley 2008; Larson et al. 2015; Mainzer and Luloff 2017)
7. What are the potential emergent "communities" that can develop based on the interactions of stakeholder groups? (Balfour and Alter 2016; Wilkinson 1991)
8. What is the structure of communications in the region and between stakeholders?
9. Are there community organizations or collaboratives that may serve as connecting points for diverse stakeholders?
10. What access do various stakeholders have to scientific knowledge, and how receptive are they to that knowledge?
11. What is the place-based knowledge / experience and who holds it; do people have direct experience with the management "issue" at hand?
12. What are the different stakeholder's relationships to the landscape, both historical and current? (Paveglio, Abrams, and Ellison 2016; Paveglio, Brenkert-Smith et al. 2015; Paveglio, Jakes et al. 2009; Paveglio and Kelly 2018)
13. Who are the newcomers, if any, and what are their values, priorities, and awareness of the "issue" (e.g., new residential settlement)? (Champ, Brooks, and Williams 2012; Eriksen and Gill 2010; Larsen et al. 2007; Paveglio et al. 2009; M. D. Smith and Krannich 2000; Ulrich-Schad and Qin 2018)
14. Have there been any shifts in values or relationships between groups or with regard to attitudes toward the "issue" both within generations and between generations? (Eriksen and Simon 2017; Lyon and Parkins 2013; Steen-Adams et al. 2015)

This data harvesting is essential to understanding and building emergent communities that are in constant flux based on the complex interactions among the inhabitants of a given ecoregion (Flint, Luloff, and Theodori 2010; Mainzer and Luloff 2017; Wilkinson 1991). Having this data and understanding the complex interactions between these variables will allow you to make better predictions about how they may help or hinder management goals both now, and, in the future, and will guide the time and resources you inject into these complex social-ecological systems to achieve the best outcome for everyone involved (Paveglio, Boyd, and Carroll 2017; Paveglio, Nielsen-Pincus et al. 2017).

Once we understand the landscape, we can begin the process of solution-oriented "community" emergence. The literature tells us that stakeholder agreement on the parameters of land management is key to transboundary, collective efforts. This requires

1. A shared understanding of the "issue" at hand and the proper scale at which it should be managed. (Ager, Kline, and Fischer 2015; Ager et al. 2017)
2. A sense of trust and willingness to work with other stakeholders across multiple scales.
3. Development of clearly stipulated partnerships that describe in detail how each collaborator will contribute to management goals and outcomes.
4. Institutionalization of these partnerships and expectations so that turnover does not cause upheavals.
5. Incentivization of every step of this process to whatever extent possible. (Every et al. 2016; Fairbrother et al. 2013; Jakes and Sturtevant 2013; Kyle et al. 2010; Sharp et al. 2013; Stidham et al. 2014)

In a socially and geographically fragmented landscape, this process of community emergence is impossible unless stakeholders interact and do so regularly. Cohesion, shared purpose, and trust are foundational to emergent community and will likely not form without the interaction that is necessary for the development of meaningful relationships and for collective action (MacDougall, Gibbs, and Clark 2014; Prior and Eriksen 2013; Stasiewicz and Paveglio 2017). Indeed, with a decrease in interaction in rural communities comes a decrease in civic action in support of the collective (Flora, Flora, and Gasteyer 2016; Putnam 2000; Sarracino 2010). On the other hand, for wildfire mitigation, higher social capital has been demonstrated to lead to greater collaboration on fuel reduction, wildfire planning, and mitigation efforts (Bihari and Ryan 2012; Dickinson et al. 2015; MacDougall, Gibbs, and Clark 2014). The key is to get people to act in ways that benefit a larger set of actors, and this requires the social capital built over time through reciprocity, good will, and a sense of shared purpose (Harrison, Montgomery, and Bliss 2016; Lin 1999). Ultimately, as social capital builds over time, the emergent "community" becomes a network of shared knowledge, where ideas spread across diverse actors on the landscape (Barnes-Mauthe et al. 2015; Jakes et al. 2007; McCaffrey et al. 2011) and spread in contextually meaningful ways to the various actors (Fischer et al. 2016; Jacobs and Cramer 2017).

Recall that we cannot force communities to happen when stakeholder groups or individuals are unwilling to participate. Hence, based on the level, duration, and entrenchment of fragmentation in an ecoregion of interest, you may find that community emergence and collective action are only possible at a small scale (e.g., households, neighborhoods) (Paveglio et al. 2019), or perhaps not at all. Furthermore, since social dynamics constantly change, you may find that relationships that once worked no longer do and that a process shift may need to take place (Smith and Krannich 2000; Ulrich-Schad and Qin 2018). Finally, remember that one-size-fits-all approaches are a fool's errand across the board in fragmented landscapes (Douglas and Wildavsky 1983; Miller 2001).

Note that the solution to land and social fragmentation I propose here is not one that is void of nuance, or that equates diversity and fragmentation, or one that is based on some utopian vision for the world where people are perfectly aligned in every way. On the contrary, a lack of social diversity as with all other forms of diversity causes a community to be less adaptive to change, which is an existential death wish. Diversity indeed is required to achieve broader community goals (Jakes et al. 2007; Jakes and Sturtevant 2013; Wilkinson 1991). Imagine, for example, if a fire-prone ecoregion were filled with one stakeholder group that had no skills, equipment, landscape knowledge, or relationship with land that had anything to do with wildfire mitigation, but they were all perfectly the same. They may be very cohesive, and decision making may be very easy, but their ability to protect themselves from wildfire is virtually nonexistent (Paveglio 2015).

Last, and perhaps most significant, it is important to understand that land and social fragmentation begins and ends with individuals. In other words, you yourself may be the ultimate problem and the fragmenting force in your own work context, home context, and relational contexts. Recall that values, such as unity and relationality, are embodied and lived daily. This means we need to make them habits and develop them as we would any other skill set. Since they are values that focus us on the needs and natures of others, any activity that helps you focus on others and not on yourself may help you in developing these values. In this effort, you may want to attempt some of the following:

1. Dedicating a few hours every week to volunteering your time for a cause that immerses you in the needs of others: a soup kitchen, a domestic violence shelter, an animal shelter, and so on.
2. Dedicating a few hours every week volunteering your time to strengthen democracy: attend local city council meetings and school-board meetings, organize a local neighborhood solidarity group, organize a reading group, protest, vote, and so on.
3. Find someone you disagree with politically, religiously, or in another way and have a conversation with them where you only ask questions that genuinely attempt to understand their position, not change their position; do this as a regular exercise for your social and emotional muscles, at least as much as you go to the gym.
4. Spend at least thirty minutes every day in silence, shutting up your mouth and your mind. This will be virtually impossible for you at first, which is direct evidence of how fragmented your mind has become. Do not fret, however: every religious tradition has a meditative practice, discover yours; or simply download one of the dozens of guided meditation apps.
5. Put these activities in your calendar; hold spots for them the way you do for meals, exercise, and sleep.

If any of the above efforts are "too challenging," just remember that it took you years to learn to speak or walk well.

References

Abrams, J. B., M. Knapp, T. B. Paveglio, A. Ellison, C. Moseley, M. Nielsen-Pincus, and M. S. Carroll. 2015. "Re-envisioning Community-Wildfire Relations in the U.S. West as Adaptive Governance." *Ecology and Society* 20 (3): 34.

Ager, A. A., J. D. Kline, and A. P. Fischer. 2015. "Coupling the Biophysical and Social Dimensions of Wildfire Risk to Improve Wildfire Mitigation Planning: Coupling the Biophysical and Social Dimensions of Wildfire Risk." *Risk Analysis* 35 (8): 1393–1406.

Ager, A. A., C. R. Evers, M. A. Day, H. K. Preisler, A. M. G. Barros, and M. Nielsen-Pincus. 2017. "Network Analysis of Wildfire Transmission and Implications for Risk Governance." *PloS One* 12 (3). https://journals.plos.org/plosone/article?id=10.1371/journal.pone.0172867.

Balfour, B., and T. R. Alter. 2016. "Mapping Community Innovation: Using Social Network Analysis to Map the Interactional Field, Identify Facilitators, and Foster Community Development." *Community Development (Columbus, Ohio)* 47 (4): 431–448.

Bardsley, D. K., E. Moskwa, D. Weber, G. M. Robinson, N. Waschl, and A. M. Bardsley. 2018. "Climate Change, Bushfire Risk, and Environmental Values: Examining a Potential Risk Perception Threshold in Peri-urban South Australia." *Society and Natural Resources* 31 (4): 424–441.

Barnes-Mauthe, M., S. A. Gray, S. Arita, J. Lynham, and P. Leung. 2015. "What Determines Social Capital in a Social–Ecological System? Insights from a Network Perspective." *Environmental Management (New York)* 55 (2): 392–410.

Beilin, R., and K. Reid. 2014. "It's Not a 'Thing' but a 'Place': Reconceptualising 'Assets' in the Context of Fire Risk Landscapes." *International Journal of Wildland Fire* 24 (1): 130–137.

Bihari, M., and R. Ryan. 2012. "Influence of Social Capital on Community Preparedness for Wildfires." *Landscape and Urban Planning* 106 (3): 253–261.

Brenkert-Smith, H. 2010. "Building Bridges to Fight Fire: The Role of Informal Social Interactions in Six Colorado Wildland–Urban Interface Communities." *International Journal of Wildland Fire* 19 (6): 689–697.

Brenkert-Smith, H., K. L. Dickinson, P. A. Champ, and N. Flores. 2013. "Social Amplification of Wildfire Risk: The Role of Social Interactions and Information Sources: Social Amplification of Wildfire Risk." *Risk Analysis* 33 (5): 800–817.

Brenkert-Smith, H., J. R. Meldrum, P. A. Champ, and C. M. Barth. 2017. "Where You Stand Depends on Where You Sit: Qualitative Inquiry into Notions of Fire Adaptation." *Ecology and Society* 22 (3): 7.

Canadas, M. J., A. Novais, and M. Marques. 2016. "Wildfires, Forest Management and Landowners' Collective Action: A Comparative Approach at the Local Level." *Land Use Policy* 56 (November): 179–188.

Champ, J. G., J. J. Brooks, and D. R. Williams. 2012. "Stakeholder Understandings of Wildfire Mitigation: A Case of Shared and Contested Meanings." *Environmental Management* 50 (4): 581–597.

Charnley, S., E. C. Kelly, and K. L. Wendel. 2017. "All Lands Approaches to Fire Management in the Pacific West: A Typology." *Journal of Forestry* 115 (1): 16–25.

Chas-Amil, M. L., J. Touza, and E. García-Martínez. 2013. "Forest Fires in the Wildland–Urban Interface: A Spatial Analysis of Forest Fragmentation and Human Impacts." *Applied Geography* 43 (September): 127–137.

Collins, T. 2012. "A Landscape Typology of Residential Wildfire Risk." In *Wildfire and Community: Facilitating Preparedness and Resilience*, edited by Fantina Tedim and Douglas Paton, 3–65. Springfield, IL: Charles C. Thomas Publisher, LTD.

Dickinson, K., H. Brenkert-Smith, P. Champ, and N. Flores. 2015. "Catching Fire? Social Interactions, Beliefs, and Wildfire Risk Mitigation Behaviors." *Society and Natural Resources* 28 (8): 807–824.

Douglas, M., and A. B. Wildavsky. 1982. *Risk and Culture: an Essay on the Selection of Technical and Environmental Dangers*. Berkeley: University of California Press.

Dunlop, P. D., I. M. McNeill, J. Boylan, D. Morrison, and T. C. Skinner. 2014. Preparing . . . for What? Developing Multi-dimensional Measures of Community Wildfire Preparedness for Researchers, Practitioners and Households. *International Journal of Wildland Fire* 23 (6): 887–896.

Dupéy, L. N., and J. W. Smith. 2018. "An Integrative Review of Empirical Research on Perceptions and Behaviors Related to Prescribed Burning and Wildfire in the United States." *Environmental Management* 61 (6): 1002–1018.

Eckerberg, K., and M. Buizer. 2017. "Promises and Dilemmas in Forest Fire Management Decision-Making: Exploring Conditions for Community Engagement in Australia and Sweden." *Forest Policy and Economics* 80 (July): 133–140.

Eriksen, C., and G. Simon. 2017. "The Affluence–Vulnerability Interface: Intersecting Scales of Risk, Privilege and Disaster." *Environment and Planning A: Economy and Space* 49 (2): 293–313.

Eriksen, Christine, and Nicholas Gill. 2010. "Bushfire and Everyday Life: Examining the Awareness-Action 'Gap' in Changing Rural Landscapes." *Geoforum* 41 (5): 814–825.

Every, D., C. Bearman, R. Matthews, A. Reynolds, P. O'Donohue, and L. Clarkson. 2016. "Contacts versus Connectors: The Role of Community Fire Safe Group Coordinators in Achieving Positive Bushfire Safety Outcomes." *International Journal of Disaster Risk Reduction* 19 (October): 390–398.

Fairbrother, P., M. Tyler, A. Hart, B. Mees, R. Phillips, J. Stratford, and K. Toh. 2013. "Creating 'Community'? Preparing for Bushfire in Rural Victoria." *Rural Sociology* 78 (2): 186–209.

Field, D. R., and D. A. Jensen. 2005. "Humans, Fire, Forests: Expanding the Domain of Wildfire Research." *Society and Natural Resources* 18 (4): 355–362.

Fischer, A. P., K. Vance-Borland, L. Jasny, K. E. Grimm, and S. Charnley. 2016. "A Network Approach to Assessing Social Capacity for Landscape Planning: The Case of Fire-Prone Forests in Oregon, USA." *Landscape and Urban Planning* 147 (March):18–27.

Flint, C. G., A. E. Luloff, and J. C. Finley. 2008. "Where Is 'Community' in Community-Based Forestry?" *Society and Natural Resources* 21 (6): 526–537.

Flint, C. G, A. E. Luloff, and G. L. Theodori. 2010. "Extending the Concept of Community Interaction to Explore Regional Community Fields." *Journal of Rural Social Sciences* 25 (1): 22–36.

Flora, C. B., J. L. Flora, and S. P. Gasteyer. 2016. *Rural Communities: Legacy and Change*. Boulder: Westview.

Harrison, J. L., C. A. Montgomery, and J. C. Bliss. 2016. "Beyond the Monolith: The Role of Bonding, Bridging, and Linking Social Capital in the Cycle of Adaptive Capacity." *Society and Natural Resources* 29 (5): 525–539.

Hilliard, R. C., and C. G. Johnson. 2018. "Sport Fan Attitudes and Willingness to Commit Aggressive Acts." *Journal of Sport Behavior* 41 (3): 305–329.

Jacobs, D. B., and L. A. Cramer. 2017. "Applying Information Network Analysis to Fire-Prone Landscapes: Implications for Community Resilience." *Ecology and Society* 22 (1). https://www.jstor.org/stable/26270104.

Jakes, P. J., and E. R. Langer. 2012. "The Adaptive Capacity of New Zealand Communities to Wildfire." *International Journal of Wildland Fire* 21 (6): 764–772.

Jakes, P., L. Kruger, K. Nelson, and V. Sturtevant. 2007. "Improving Wildfire Preparedness: Lessons from Communities across the U.S." *Human Ecology Review* 14 (2): 188–197.

Jakes, P. J., K. C. Nelson, Sherry A. Enzler, Sam Burns, Antony S. Cheng, Victoria Sturtevant, and Daniel R. Williams et al. 2011. "Community Wildfire Protection Planning: Is the Healthy Forests Restoration Act's Vagueness Genius?" *International Journal of Wildland Fire* 20 (3): 350–363.

Jakes, P. J., and V. Sturtevant. 2013. "Trial by Fire: Community Wildfire Protection Plans Put to the Test." *International Journal of Wildland Fire* 22 (8): 1134–1143.

Kyle, G. T., G. L. Theodori, J. D. Absher, and J. Jun. 2010. "The Influence of Home and Community Attachment on Firewise Behavior." *Society and Natural Resources* 23 (11): 1075–1092.

Labossière, L. M. M., and T. K. McGee. 2017. "Innovative Wildfire Mitigation by Municipal Governments: Two Case Studies in Western Canada." *International Journal of Disaster Risk Reduction* 22 (June): 204–210.

Langer, E. L., and T. K. McGee. 2017. "Wildfire Risk Awareness and Prevention by Predominantly Māori Rural Residents, Karikari Peninsula, Aotearoa New Zealand." *International Journal of Wildland Fire* 26 (9): 820–828.

Larsen, S. C., C. Sorenson, D. McDermott, J. Long, and C. Post. 2007. "Place Perception and Social Interaction on an Exurban Landscape in Central Colorado." *Professional Geographer* 59 (4): 421–433.

Larson, E. C., A. E. Luloff, J. C. Bridger, and M. A. Brennan. 2015. "Community as a Mechanism for Transcending Wellbeing at the Individual, Social, and Ecological Levels." *Community Development* 46 (4): 407–419.

Lin, N. 1999. "Building a Network Theory of Social Capital." *Connections* 22 (1): 28–51.

Lukianoff, Greg, and Jonathan Haidt. 2019. *The Coddling of the American Mind: How Good Intentions and Bad Ideas Are Setting up a Generation for Failure*. New York: Penguin Press.

Lyon, C., and J. R. Parkins. 2013. "Toward a Social Theory of Resilience: Social Systems, Cultural Systems, and Collective Action in Transitioning Forest-Based Communities." *Rural Sociology* 78 (4): 528–549.

MacDougall, C., L. Gibbs, and R. Clark. 2014. "Community-Based Preparedness Programmes and the 2009 Australian Bushfires: Policy Implications Derived from Applying Theory." *Disasters* 38 (2): 249–266.

Mainzer, S., and A. E. Luloff. 2017. "Informing Environmental Problems through Field Analysis: Toward a Community Landscape Theory of Pro-environmental Behavior." *Community Development* 48 (4): 483–498.

McCaffrey, S. 2015. "Community Wildfire Preparedness: A Global State-of-the-Knowledge Summary of Social Science Research." *Current Forestry Reports* 1 (2): 81–90.

McCaffrey, S. M., M. Stidham, E. Toman, and B. Shindler. 2011. "Outreach Programs, Peer Pressure, and Common Sense: What Motivates Homeowners to Mitigate Wildfire Risk?" *Environmental Management* 48 (3): 475–488.

McGee, T. K. 2011. Public Engagement in Neighbourhood Level Wildfire Mitigation and Preparedness: Case Studies from Canada, the US and Australia. *Journal of Environmental Management* 92 (10): 2524–2532.

McLennan, B., and M. Eburn. 2015. "Exposing Hidden-Value Trade-Offs: Sharing Wildfire Management Responsibility between Government and Citizens." *International Journal of Wildland Fire* 24 (2): 162–169.

Miller, S. 2001. "Public Understanding of Science at the Crossroads." *Public Understanding of Science* 10 (1): 115–120.

Moritz, M. A., E. Batllori, R. A. Bradstock, A. M. Gill, J. Handmer, P. F. Hessburg, and J. Leonard et al. 2014. "Learning to Coexist with Wildfire." *Nature* 515 (6): 58–66.

Otero, I., and J. Ø. Nielsen. 2017. "Coexisting with Wildfire? Achievements and Challenges for a Radical Social-Ecological Transformation in Catalonia (Spain)." *Geoforum* 85 (October): 234–246.

Paschen, J., and R. Beilin. 2017. "How a Risk Focus in Emergency Management Can Restrict Community Resilience: A Case Study from Victoria, Australia." *International Journal of Wildland Fire* 26 (1): 1–9.

Paveglio, T. B., J. Abrams, and A. Ellison. 2016. "Developing Fire Adapted Communities: The Importance of Interactions among Elements of Local Context." *Society and Natural Resources* 29 (10): 1246–1261.

Paveglio, T. B., A. D. Boyd, and M. S. Carroll. 2017. "Re-conceptualizing Community in Risk Research." *Journal of Risk Research* 20 (7): 931–951.

Paveglio, T. B., H. Brenkert-Smith, T. Hall, and A. M. S. Smith. 2015. "Understanding Social Impact from Wildfires: Advancing Means for Assessment." *International Journal of Wildland Fire* 24 (2): 212–224.

Paveglio, T. B., M. S. Carroll, P. J. Jakes, and T. Prato. 2012. "Exploring the Social Characteristics of Adaptive Capacity for Wildfire: Insights from Flathead County, Montana." *Human Ecology Review* 19 (2): 110–124.

Paveglio, T. B., M. S. Carroll, A. Stasiewicz, and C. Edgeley. 2019. "Social Fragmentation and Wildfire Management: Exploring the Scale of Adaptive Action." *International Journal of Disaster Risk Reduction* 33 (February): 131–141.

Paveglio, T. B., and C. Edgeley. 2017. "Community Diversity and Hazard Events: Understanding the Evolution of Local Approaches to Wildfire." *Natural Hazards* 87 (2): 1083–1108.

Paveglio, T. B., P. J. Jakes, M. S. Carroll, and D. R. Williams. 2009. "Understanding Social Complexity within the Wildland–Urban Interface: A New Species of Human Habitation?" *Environmental Management* 43 (6): 1085–1095.

Paveglio, T. B., and E. Kelly. 2018. "Influences on the Adoption and Implementation of a Wildfire Mitigation Program in an Idaho City." *Journal of Forestry* 116 (1): 47–54.

Paveglio, T. B., C. Moseley, M. S. Carroll, D. R. Williams, E. J. Davis, and A. P. Fischer. 2015. "Categorizing the Social Context of the Wildland Urban Interface: Adaptive Capacity for Wildfire and Community 'Archetypes.'" *Forest Science* 61 (2): 298–310.

Paveglio, T. B., M. Nielsen-Pincus, J. Abrams, and C. Moseley. 2017. "Advancing Characterization of Social Diversity in the Wildland-Urban Interface: An Indicator Approach for Wildfire Management." *Landscape and Urban Planning* 160 (April): 115–126.

Petty, A. M., C. Isendahl, H. Brenkert-Smith, D. J. Goldstein, J. M. Rhemtulla, S. A. Rahman, and T. C. Kumasi. 2015. "Applying Historical Ecology to Natural Resource Management Institutions: Lessons from Two Case Studies of Landscape Fire Management." *Global Environmental Change* 31 (March): 1–10.

Prato, T., and T. Paveglio. 2018. "Multiobjective Prioritization of Preselected Fuel Treatment Strategies for Public Forestland: A Case Study in Flathead County, Montana." *Forest Science* 64 (1): 41–49.

Prato, T., T. Paveglio, Y. Barnett, R. Silverstein, M. Hardy, R. Keane, R. Loehma, A. Clark, D. Fagre, T. J. Venn, and K. Stockmann. 2014. "Simulating Future Residential Property Losses from Wildfire in Flathead County, Montana." *Advances in Environmental Research* 33:1–40. (University of the Sunshine Coast, Queensland).

Prior, T., and C. Eriksen. 2013. "Wildfire Preparedness, Community Cohesion and Social–Ecological Systems." *Global Environmental Change* 23 (6): 1575–1586.

Putnam, R. D. 2000. *Bowling Alone: The Collapse and Revival of American Community*. New York: Simon and Schuster.

Sarracino, F. 2010. "Social Capital and Subjective Well-Being Trends: Comparing 11 Western European Countries." *Journal of Socioeconomics* 39 (4): 482–517.

Schoennagel, T., J. K. Balch, H. Brenkert-Smith, P. E. Dennison, B. J. Harvey, M. A. Krawchuk, and N. Mietkiewicz et al. 2017. "Adapt to More Wildfire in Western North American Forests as Climate Changes." *Proceedings of the National Academy of Sciences* 114 (18): 4582–4590.

Sharp, E. A., R. Thwaites, A. Curtis, and J. Millar. 2013. "Factors Affecting Community-Agency Trust before, during and after a Wildfire: An Australian Case Study." *Journal of Environmental Management* 130 (November): 10–19.

Slemp, C., M. A. Davenport, E. Seekamp, J. M. Brehm, J. E. Schoonover, and K. W. J. Williard. 2012. "'Growing Too Fast:' Local Stakeholders Speak Out about Growth and Its Consequences for Community Well-Being in the Urban–Rural Interface." *Landscape and Urban Planning* 106 (2): 139–148.

Smith, A. M. S., C. A. Kolden, T. B. Paveglio, M. A. Cochrane, D. M. J. S. Bowman, M. A. Moritz, and A. D. Kliskey et al. 2016. "The Science of Firescapes: Achieving Fire-Resilient Communities." *Bioscience* 66 (2): 130–146.

Smith, M. D., and R. S. Krannich. 2000. "'Culture Clash' Revisited: Newcomer and Longer-Term Residents' Attitudes toward Land Use, Development, and Environmental Issues in Rural Communities in the Rocky Mountain West." *Rural Sociology* 65 (3): 396–421.

Spies, T. A., E. White, A. Ager, J. D. Kline, J. P. Bolte, E. K. Platt, and K. A. Olsen et al. 2017. "Using an Agent-Based Model to Examine Forest Management Outcomes in a Fire-Prone Landscape in Oregon, USA." *Ecology and Society* 22 (1): 25.

Spies, T. A., E. M. White, J. D. Kline, A. P. Fischer, A. Ager, J. Bailey, and J. Bolte et al. 2014. "Examining Fire-Prone Forest Landscapes as Coupled Human and Natural Systems." *Ecology and Society* 19 (3): 9.

Stasiewicz, A. M., and T. B. Paveglio. 2017. "Factors Influencing the Development of Rangeland Fire Protection Associations: Exploring Fire Mitigation Programs for Rural, Resource-Based Communities." *Society and Natural Resources* 30 (5): 627–641.

Steelman, T. 2016. "U.S. Wildfire Governance as Social-Ecological Problem." *Ecology and Society* 21 (4). https://www.jstor.org/stable/26270036.

Steen-Adams, M. M., S. Charnley, and M. D. Adams. 2017. "Historical Perspective on the Influence of Wildfire Policy, Law, and Informal Institutions on Management and Forest Resilience in a Multiownership, Frequent-Fire, Coupled Human and Natural System in Oregon, USA." *Ecology and Society* 22 (3). https://www.jstor.org/stable/26270161.

Steen-Adams, M. M., N. Langston, M. D. O. Adams, and D. J. Mladenoff. 2015. "Historical Framework to Explain Long-Term Coupled Human and Natural System Feedbacks: Application to a Multiple-Ownership Forest Landscape in the Northern Great Lakes Region, USA." *Ecology and Society* 20 (1). https://www.academia.edu/31754652/Historical_framework_to_explain_long_term_coupled_human_and_natural_system_feedbacks_application_to_a_multiple_ownership_forest_landscape_in_the_northern_Great_Lakes_region_USA.

Stidham, M., S. McCaffrey, E. Toman, and B. Shindler. 2014. "Policy Tools to Encourage Community-Level Defensible Space in the United States: A Tale of Six Communities." *Journal of Rural Studies* 35:59–69.

Sword-Daniels, V., C. Eriksen, E. E. Hudson-Doyle, R. Alaniz, C. Adler, T. Schenk, and S. Vallance. 2018. "Embodied Uncertainty: Living with Complexity and Natural Hazards." *Journal of Risk Research* 21 (3): 290–307.

Syphard, A. D., A. B. Van Butsic, J. E. Keeley, J. A. Tracey, and R. N. Fisher. 2016. "Setting Priorities for Private Land Conservation in Fire-Prone Landscapes: Are Fire Risk Reduction and Biodiversity Conservation Competing or Compatible Objectives?" *Ecology and Society* 21 (3): 2.

Tedim, F., V. Leone, and G. Xanthopoulos. 2016. "A Wildfire Risk Management Concept Based on a Social-Ecological Approach in the European Union: Fire Smart Territory." *International Journal of Disaster Risk Reduction* 18 (September): 138–153.

Theodori, G. L. 2005. "Community and Community Development in Resource-Based Areas: Operational Definitions Rooted in an Interactional Perspective." *Society and Natural Resources* 18 (7): 661–669.

Theodori, G. L., and G. T. Kyle. 2013. "Community, Place, and Conservation." In *Place-Based Conservation: Perspectives from the Social Sciences*, W. P. Stewart, D. R. Williams, and L. E. Kruger, 59–70. New York: Springer.

Toman, E., B. Shindler, S. McCaffrey, and J. Bennett. 2014. "Public Acceptance of Wildland Fire and Fuel Management: Panel Responses in Seven Locations." *Environmental Management* 54 (3): 557–570.

Toman, E., M. Stidham, S. McCaffrey, and B. Shindler. 2013. "Social Science at the Wildland-Urban Interface: A Compendium of Research Results to Create Fire-Adapted Communities." General Technical Report NRS-111, 1–75. Newtown Square, PA: US Department of Agriculture, Forest Service, Northern Research Station.

Ulrich-Schad, J. D., and H. Qin. 2018. "Culture Clash? Predictors of Views on Amenity-Led Development and Community Involvement in Rural Recreation Counties." *Rural Sociology* 83 (1): 81–108.

USDA Forest Service. 2018a. "Collaborative Forest Landscape Restoration Program Overview." https://www.fs.usda.gov/restoration/CFLRP/overview.shtml.

USDA Forest Service. 2018b. "Good Neighbor Authority." https://www.fs.fed.us/managing-land/farm-bill/gna.

Wann, D. L., G. Haynes, B. McLean, and P. Pullen. 2003. "Sport Team Identification and Willingness to Consider Anonymous Acts of Hostile Aggression." *Aggressive Behavior* 29 (5): 406–413.

Wilkinson, K. P. 1991. *The Community in Rural America*. New York: Greenwood Press.

Williams, D., P. Jakes, S. Burns, A. Cheng, K. Nelson, V. Sturtevant, R. Brummel, E. Staychock, and S. Souter. 2012. "Community Wildfire Protection Planning: The Importance of Framing, Scale, and Building Sustainable Capacity." *Journal of Forestry* 110 (8): 415–420.

19

Ethnography of the Protectors of the Menominee River

DOLLY POTTS

Introduction

Protectors of the Menominee River is a grassroots organization to help protect the river that bears the Menominee name against the Back Forty Mine project. The group is composed of Menominee members and nonmembers who participate in various activities in opposition to the Back Forty Mine project. I am the Secretary of the group, and there are about twenty members who participate on and off in activities and meetings. We meet in various locations, currently the Culture Center building on the College of Menominee Nation campus. Generally, the meetings are weekly, but some members travel to other locations to speak or to attend meetings of like groups.

Some issues are disruption of sacred burial mounds/sites, mining, oil pipelines, and toxic waste dumping—concerns for Native tribal lands and resources. Native and non-Native people and grassroots groups have begun to stand up in courts to stop companies from removing limited resources and disturbing sacred sites. The recent Dakota Access Pipeline (DAPL) on the Standing Rock reservation protest is an example of the uniting of

https://doi.org/10.5876/9781646425105.c019

Native people against water pollution of their river. The Cannonball River is a resource of their water for their reservation and thousands more along the Missouri. The report will detail the data and connect the Menominee Sustainability Model to show how the components correlate to each of the six individual facets of that model.

Description of Subjects

The subjects of the group, Protectors of the Menominee River, are Native and non-Native; the majority of the members are local Menominee women. Three of our members have ties with the college. The different relationship criteria make for some interesting exchanges, and all of the members have become close, developing outside relationships with each other. Everyone is respectful of each other. I asked permission of the group to do this ethnography. They wanted assurance that I would not use names, so from here on I will refer to them by initials. G.R. is the leader and started the group. He is a traditional Menominee man and speaks the language. T.B. is another Menominee man; he sometimes will be the spokesperson for the group. We begin each meeting with a potluck and each with a prayer. G.R. generally does the prayer and leads the group. Of M.M., D.W., D.M., C.P., C.T., and J.Z., who are Menominee women, M.M. and D.W. will do the prayers when G.R. is gone. D.W. will chair the meeting. Then there is my role; I take minutes and will read the previous minutes at the start of meeting. D.V., M.R., and S.W. are our members from the college. This has been the core group; other members come and go, but organizing activities, rallies, and fundraising has pretty much been accomplished by this main group.

Fieldwork of Interaction

In the description of the subjects, I noted that everyone gets along and is very respectful of each other. There is a respect for diversity, and the recent Standing Rock coverage I believe had a significant role in the interaction of the group. G.R. approached me and asked if I would like to join the group. My being a traditional elder and knowing the other elders he asked for counsel from was probably why he knew I would fit. I accepted the honor. At times, it is work, but for the most part enjoyable. D.W. was part of the Community Builders group prior to the start of this group. We have managed to make our goal unity and family, and not individual glory. Our Motto is "Don't get mad—Organize." Food is always a draw, so each meeting is potluck. Our meetings are at 5:30 p.m., so most of us are hungry after work or school. Our goal is to stop the mine for the sake of the Menominee River and Ancestors.

Group Role and Interaction Using Menominee Sustainability Model

Land and Sovereignty: The Creation story of the Menominee dates back thousands of years, when the Ancestral Bear emerged for the mouth of the Menominee River. The Menominee reluctantly entered into the treaty of 1836 with the United States (Menominee Tribe 2017). Menominee presence has been documented and established in the "60-island" area in what is now Michigan through oral history and documented accounts. D.W and her sister take groups up to the area to tour the mounds and agricultural sites. Some members have been to the area. Trips will begin again this spring.

Natural Environment: Aquila Resources, a Canadian development company, proposes to dig an open-pit mine that will sit only 150 feet from the banks of the Menominee River. Sulfide mines are extremely harmful to freshwater rivers, lakes, and streams and to groundwater. Aquila will not only extract mineral but also process the mineral at the site.

Our group chant is "Water is Life—No Back 40 Mine." The group has formed a relationship with the Menominee River and has vowed to stop the mine from polluting a pristine river.

Institutions: Aquila Resources is seeking the necessary approvals to mine and process gold, zinc, copper, silver, and other minerals at the site. The Michigan Department of Environmental Quality (MDEQ) has approved three of four permits to begin digging. One remains, the wetlands permit, the toughest. Menominee burial mounds, places of worship, village sites, and ancient agricultural beds are in the footprint of the mine. On February 24, 2017, the Menominee filed a petition with MDEQ challenging the permitting of the mine (Menominee Tribe 2017). The Menominee have set up a Task Force to address the issue. J.Z. and I set up coffee and doughnuts on the main street of Keshena, giving out information about the tribe's involvement in stopping the Back Forty Mine.

Technology: Taking a cue from Standing Rock, we found that using social media was an excellent way for the group to relay information and share with other grassroots groups. There are several Facebook pages. Ours is the Protectors of the Menominee River, the group from Marinette is Save the Menominee River—Stop the Back 40, and the tribe's is www.noback40.com. The group also uses text messaging and conference calls. Social media is, for our group, a way to stay on top of any new developments and interaction with other grassroots groups such as the Marinette group, who is right at the mouth of the Menominee River. The drive there is about two hours for us. J.Z. and I also are part of a focus group that consists of town officials, landowners, and concerned citizens around the immediate area.

Economics: It takes money to fight corporations; this was a big concern early on when the mine was first proposed. Officials of Aquila stated that they were not worried that the permits would go through MDEQ, because the groups opposing the mine had no money to fight the permitting. The Menominee Nation stepped up and challenged MDEQ after creation of the Task Force. The Task Force works with our grassroots group, coordinating speaking tours to educate the Wisconsin public about the Back Forty Mine.

M.R., D.M., and I have held food sales to fund our efforts. The group sells T-shirts at several events. At our walk and rallies, people have given our group donations. M.M. is our Treasurer and keeps records for us. The group uses the money to get the word out and fund more fundraising projects. We will begin our tours again and hope to encourage our youth to participate by taking them on tours of the area. Gas, food, and van rental are costs we will need to cover.

Human Perception, Activity, and Behavior: At every meeting we have a potluck and begin each with a prayer but also a thanksgiving for each other. The group's beginnings was with a "Water Walk" from Menominee Reservation to the mine site. The group has done rallies at the mouth of the Menominee River across the bridge from Marinette to Menominee. We have done a Spiritual Gathering, placing a prayer bundle in the Menominee River. We have offered our tobacco, sharing with everyone present—tribal and nontribal—to pray and place in the river. The group is not alone in this fight. The Protectors have many allies, including local citizens, local governments, environmental organizations, and other grassroots groups.

Aquila is offering ten $2,000 scholarships to students of the counties near the site to write an essay entitled "Why Mines Are Beneficial." C.T. has contacted the schools in our area to do a presentation on stopping the Back Forty Mine. The response has been tremendous. It is our hope that with education, the future for our children will not include a sulfide mine.

Conclusion

In conclusion, some startling facts about the Proposed Mine: The open-pit portion of the mine would measure over 750 feet deep and be 2,000 feet wide. That is 7 stories deep and 5.5 football fields end zone to end zone. The open pit of the mine will sit only 150 feet from the banks of the Menominee River. The Michigan Department of Environmental Quality has received over 2,000 comments, 98 percent opposed to the mine. The tailings (waste rock) management facilities on site hinge on a proposed land swap with the state of Michigan and Aquila (Menominee Tribe 2017).

Our group knows there is one permit left, so at times we wonder of our success. I interviewed G.R., the leader of our group. He quoted Margaret Mead, an American cultural anthropologist, saying, "Never doubt that a small group of thoughtful, committed, citizens can change the world. Indeed, it is the only thing that ever has." Coming to know the group of individuals in the last year, I had a Facebook memory with C.T. from when we went on our first Water Walk to protect the Menominee River. I have no doubt this group of individuals and the many that live on the Menominee River will not give in or give up.

Reference

Menominee Tribe. 2017. "Menominee Indian Tribe of Wisconsin." www.noback40.com/.

20

American Indian Decolonization through Minecraft

CHRISTOPHER DENNIS

Through coding with JavaScript, Minecraft players were able to create a virtual reality in-game block representing every cubic meter of the Earth's surface. On March 21, 2020, a YouTube channel, PippenFTS, uploaded a video titled *The Earth in Minecraft, 1:1 scale . . . for the first time* (PippenFTS 2020). The video's call to action was to re-create our world by using Google Maps as the reference of an in-game world. This program is titled BTE in the Minecraft community and is currently compatible with the Minecraft Java Edition, which allows users to explore the planet rendered into 64-bit graphics. Implementing this technology, users now have access to a new medium of Indigenous activism including the revitalization of Indigenous languages, storytelling, and educating about ecological hazards such as dams through virtual exploration of a computer-generated ecosystem based on satellite images, and reconstruction of both contemporary and traditional Indigenous sites.

This discovery implied a realization: one can create an immersive experience for members of my tribe to learn the Cowlitz language. In order to do

https://doi.org/10.5876/9781646425105.c020

this, the programming software known as Unicode, Bitmap2LCD, JavaScript, and WordPad were used. All four programs are free to download and use for MS Windows. We now have the capability to start coding Indigenous-language video games. On October 26, 2016, Marc Zankl wrote a wiki article documenting Chris Lipscombe's successful translation of Minecraft's menu texts in English into a fictional language used in the show *Star Trek* known as Klingon (2016). This accomplishment led me to the understanding that one can make a language program also work for underrecognized American Indian languages such as Lushootseed or Cowlitz. This program would require generating our characters such as "ƛ" into an International Unicode font, since this is what Minecraft uses. This rendering can be done with the Bitmap2LCD programming tool (Bitmap2LCD 2018).

In February 2021, the Louis Riel School Division in Manitoba partnered with the Microsoft Canadian Division using Minecraft Educational Edition to learn about the Anishinaabe people (Aki 2021). This type of partnering could also be done with tribes but without having to work with corporations. Through the "BTE 1.1.2.2." JavaScript modification, one is capable of in-game teleporting to a 64-bit-generated version of Mossyrock Dam, which is currently an ecological threat to endangered salmon and is sitting on the Upper Cowlitz ancestral homeland, to give a lecture on dams and the threat they pose. Furthermore, one could remove the dam in game as a visual aid to assist students in understanding that Indigenous communities can be restored through allowing these blocked river ways to flow and therefore providing local salmon an opportunity to reach their ancestral spawning grounds. I was able to teleport very easily by hitting "/" and typing the coordinates of the Mossyrock Dam following a space after typing the text "tpll"; that is, I typed "/tpll 46.534700, -122.424847" into the chat bar and pressing the enter key. This can also be done with historical sites and at the very minimum give a general reference point.

It's important to bring up the ability to protect the rights of privacy of our ancestors, however. I was taught to keep the locations of our villages secret due to the existence of grave robbers. I am not worried about others learning my native language, because my family, particularly my matriarchs, gave the majority of the Cowlitz language back to the tribe. My teachers are not only these family members but also the linguists who work with our tribe and serve as conversation partners. However, I am also sensitive to the desire to keep one's language protected. A solution to have both language teaching opportunities within Minecraft while keeping teachings within the tribal community would be by setting up a "whitelist" for a server. There is a setting when configuring an online Minecraft server so that only specific users can join the virtual session. As long as the server is created by an Indigenous person who does the work to ensure the players are from the same tribal community through a verification process, there are language and teachings within the game. Additionally, all users could set up a meeting through Google Hangouts or Discord to have users share their screen to ensure that no screen-recording software is being used. The last suggestion I would have to offer as a kind of security measure would be to require the user being recorded so the administrator of the web server could ensure no physical phones or video-recording equipment is being used by any of the users to record the teachings of a tribal group's culture. If a user is caught recording the session against the wishes of the administrator, server administrators could ban that user and prevent them from rejoining for breaking the rules and undermining the security of protecting one's culture.

Ilani Casino's layout was also in my game, which provided me the opportunity to start building my own miniature version of the building. This became possible through the height measurement of one of the front doors and converting it into meters. The door's height served as a guide to figuring out the total height of the building's entryway, which was approximately six meters. I then built the rest of the casino walls in-game and am currently working on the roof. Outside the Minecraft casino walls, I placed twenty-nine signposts, writing down the locations of the former twenty-nine Lower Cowlitz Village sites and the number of Longhouses at each, using two 2013 newspaper articles published in the local Longview, Washington, newspaper from former Spiritual leader Roy Wilson (Wilson 2013). The second was a PDF file of a twenty-three-page documentation of Cowlitz place-names by the late M. Dale Kinkade (1997). More in-game signs were constructed for the words I didn't yet recognize as being part of Lower Coast Salish villages as described by Roy Wilson. Unfortunately, I did not notice that Kinkdade had provided a map of the locations of former Cowlitz villages within this document before taking it upon myself to type out every location description listed after the names of these villages (Kinkade 2004, 259–260). Matching the locations of these numbers on the map with Google Maps gives me approximate locations of where my ancestors and tribal family lived, which can now be plugged into the virtual simulation to give me a first-person view of the local terrain. With these tools, we as Indigenous people can get a sense not of what is or even was but what can be for our future generations. We can design our homes how we want and strive outside the simulation to make our dreams a reality and tell our own stories referencing our history and potential growth as sovereign nations.

Taking into consideration the teachings and styles of storytelling from our ancestors, we could do what many members of the American Indian Movement did in the late twentieth century, namely, pursue new storytelling mediums to portray our sovereignty and use our newly gained popularity as a platform to speak about oppression of our Indigenous brothers and sisters. There are currently identifiable patterns of growth in celebrities who have received millions of dollars as live-stream storytellers on the streaming services Twitch and YouTube, such as username YouTube Dream, to amass over 10 million subscribers in under a year using search engine optimization tools such as Google Trends and planning to create a large audience, accumulating a total of 21.6 million subscribers as of the present date. On April 25, 2020, Dream's World created Dream SMP (a Minecraft server), which grew to have over thirty users all streaming on Twitch, playing, and eventually storytelling. These stories led to celebrity guest invitations such as the musician Lil Nas X, YouTube personality and philanthropist MrBeast, among other millionaires under the age of thirty. American Indians could follow this type of innovative behavior manifesting Indigenous voices projected on a scale required to recruit new activists. Inspiration to make independent works such as those with the themes of *Smoke Signals* (1998) and *Powwow Highway* (1989) come to mind, as these combine the necessity of attention-grabbing humor alongside vital tragedy, demanding acknowledgment of our genocide and that we as American Indians are still here. We could also translate the moral values outlined in the works of Indigenous women authors such as Mourning Dove, Louise Erdrich, and Leslie Marmon Silko into videos, turning the written word into visual and auditory experiences utilizing innovation and cultural traditions simultaneously.

Decolonizing opportunities can be found in surprising places like Minecraft. With a little programming, it'd be possible to get friends together on a server to type out phonetics that would preserve our endangered oral traditions.

Doing so would serve as an extremely useful linguistics tool, since according to Demkah and Bhargava (2019, 170–174) education is most impactful when engaging, and personal. Google Maps may serve as an extremely useful tool partnering with scripts for generating models of our ancient local environment, allowing us to construct basic models based on the measurements of our historical buildings in a game compatible with most computers and gaming consoles. Combining this information alongside extroverted personalities, search engine optimization of data trends, and proper scheduling, we could discover new profound ways to engage in game-changing activism.

References

Aki, M. A. 2021. "Explore Indigenous History and Culture with Manito Ahbee Aki." *Minecraft Education Edition Blog*. February 16. https://education.minecraft.net/en-us/blog/explore-indigenous-history-and-culture-with-manito-ahbee-aki.

Bitmap2LCD. 2018. *Generate Unicode Font*. YouTube video. December 4. https://www.youtube.com/watch?v=SXmDcFOWIDo.

Demkah, M., and D. Bhargava. 2019. "Gamification In Education: A Cognitive Psychology Approach to Cooperative and Fun Learning." In 2019 *Amity International Conference on Artificial Intelligence (AICAI)*, 170–174.

Kinkade, M. D. 1997. "Coast Salish Place Names." *University Of British Columbia Papers In Linguistics* 249–249. https://lingpapers.sites.olt.ubc.ca/Files/2018/03/1997_Kinkade.Pdf.

Kinkade, Marvin Dale. 2004. "Cowlitz Dictionary and Grammatical Sketch." *University of Montana Occasional Papers in Linguistics*, 18. Missoula: Linguistics Laboratory, University of Montana.

PippenFTS. 2020. *The Earth In Minecraft, 1:1 Scale . . . For The First Time*. March 21. YouTube video. https://www.youtube.com/watch?v=8_bW3ab8YAk.

Wilson, R. 2013. "The Spirit of the Cowlitz—Their Villages Part 1." Hometowndebate.Com. https://www.hometowndebate.com/the-spirit-of-the-cowlitz---their-villages-part-1-cms-283.

Zankl, M. 2016. "Klingon.Wiki: Teaching The Galaxy Klingon." Minecraft. https://klingon.wiki/En/Minecraft.x.

21

Expressions of Native Womanhood

A Conversation with Nani Chacon

GEORGINA BADONI

I am already empowered by being a woman.
—*Nani Chacon*

The Native woman's story and contributions have received little recognition in history, and when it is recognized, her words are often misrepresented (Mihesuah 2003). Much of western art history documents the historical narratives of Native American artists and art as despairing to historical atrocities, excluding stories of perseverance, the continuance of traditions, and the role of art in maintaining Indigenous identity (Berlo and Phillips 1998). Native women artists are reclaiming their Native female voice through expressions including ceremonies, songs, poetry, and visualities. This reclamation is demonstrated by Native artist Nani Chacon (Diné and Chicana), as she shared her artistic journey of Native womanhood in stories and conversations discussing representation, art making, and motherhood.

Womanhood from an Indigenous worldview differs from western constructs of womanhood. Native womanhood in most Indigenous societies involves the maturity of the body, followed by coming-of-age ceremonies signifying the transition from childhood to adulthood (Markstrom 2008). During ceremonies, young women learn from a maternal figure the responsibilities

https://doi.org/10.5876/9781646425105.c021

and obligations of womanhood and the importance of this position within their communities (Fox 1999; Markstrom 2008). I expand upon this practice of Native womanhood by seeing it as a continuous process of upholding our family, communities, and acts of expression (Anderson 2000). This expanded thought is needed as modern realities have, in many ways, added to the traditional role of Native women. With the diverse cultures and belief systems of Native women, Native womanhood is a broad concept, and there is not a single definition applicable to all Indigenous women and their experiences.

My work with Nani began in 2016 as she agreed to be a participant in my dissertation, *Visual Expressions of Native Womanhood: Acknowledging the Past, Present, and Future*. During the interview process, I experienced the beauty and strength of Nani's art. However, her stories offered a deeper understanding of Native women artists' lived experiences. As we are both Diné women, Nani Chacon challenged me to look beyond the surface qualities and the elements of art; we must understand the meaning, the process, and the actions demonstrated in the art. Her stories revealed the artistic expressions of Native womanhood by Native artists.

The beginning of our connection, or kinship, was established by *k'é* (family/kinship). In Diné philosophy, k'é determines relationships and values that "connect Navajos to family, clan nonrelatives, and people in general" (Austin 2009, 84). K'é values are respect, kindness, cooperation, friendliness, reciprocal relations, and love (Austin 2009). From this understanding, I am mindful and respectful of building our kinship. I chose to tell Nani's story in a narrative format to honor the oral knowledge often undervalued in westernized academia. Indigenous storytelling positions the listener to make meaning of art through stories (Archibald 2008; Wilson 2008; Chilisa 2012; Anderson 2000).

For the Diné people, introductions are beyond saying your name; we make exchanges by sharing who we are and where we come from. For Nani, this is "I am Diné and Chicana, my mom is Diné and my dad is Chicano. My mom is from Chinle and my dad is from Northern New Mexico. I was born in Gallup, but lived in Chinle. My clans are To'da' Chiini, my grandfather's clan is Kin'ya'anni, on my dad's side Chicano and my grandfather on my dad's side is Chicano. I grew up in Chinle, Albuquerque, and I-40 (interstate 40) because my entire life was going back and forth" (personal communication, January 28, 2017).

At an early age, Nani began noticing that women were well regarded in Diné culture as opposed to western culture. She believes there is a more considerable responsibility as a Diné woman.

> As I got older, I began to appreciate that. I appreciate the freedom in who I was and a strength there when I started to learn of who I was, my clans, and how the clan systems work, the matrilineal aspect. This is when I was a teenager, punk rock girl, learning about feminists. We are already a feminist culture, we don't struggle with this the same way white women do. Because Diné culture is more of a partnership and there is dual role. The struggle for western feminists, this equality with man. And in some way, it gets weighed heavier, like I want to be bigger than the man. Coming from this dual background I didn't see it that way. I'm already empowered by being a woman. (personal communication, January 25, 2017)

In her female figurative paintings and murals, Nani resists negative representations, stereotypes, and roles of Native women in her work by

> making messages, and personally, it's been about satisfying what I have not seen before. When I do traditional this woman putting on a moccasin, putting on her jewelry, but make it in this sexual, sensual kind of manner, within that juxtaposition, I'm creating a dialogue of something we don't talk about. That's the way I resist it. I could have painted that scenario a hundred of different ways; I could of painted her out by monument valley with a sheep, covered up, with her moccasins poking out. That wasn't the focus. The focus was her sensuality. In those ways, I'm resisting those stereotypes. (personal communication, January 28, 2017)

Nani rejects the cliche of Native women. "I try to show something deeper; it is about showing this moment within identity you don't get to see all the time. Our identity is in nuances[.] I try to preserve identity" (personal communication, January 28, 2017). *Against the Storm, She Gathers Her Thoughts*, the mural completed for the Navajo Nation Museum in December of 2012 in Window Rock, Arizona, depicted a Diné woman collecting her unraveled hair and tying it into a Tsiiyéé (hair bun). The woman is placed against a Navajo rug pattern, an underlying presence of first female figures such as First Woman and Spider-Woman from Diné creation stories. The wind blowing suggests the challenges, and the unraveling of her hair implies

> how as Navajo women, we have to be composed and strong. We don't let our hair get wild. And the pattern behind breaking apart. Understanding the piece is about vulnerability, the woman doing her hair also became this symbol of women's beauty. Navigate sexuality, confronting those sensitivities and wanting to show a woman in a weak state. The Navajo Nation scheduled to be painted over the mural, but the museum made an extension. My early work was female-based. It was about rewriting American culture and putting Native women and Chicana women within these roles and making them prevalent. And making the images, I never saw. It was about creating images I wish I had seen growing up that my mom would of seen growing up, that my grandma would of seen growing up. Showing that we are not always out yonder on a horse, and we lived through all these times, and we are here now, and we are very modern. We learned to navigate modern culture, western culture, and we've learned how to tie that in with our traditional culture and still find the beauty in that. (personal communication, January 28, 2017)

The female figurative work Nani painted emerged from the interest in 1920s mid-century portrayals of women; she was in awe of those artists and studied their work. Nani realized that many of the depictions of the women she saw did not relate to her experiences in life. She understood that was an oppressive time for women, but Nani "felt like they really used women in the forefront, like keepers of the home, holding the family unit figure that I could relate to. Except it was wrong. It was this posed, beautiful white woman with a ten-inch waist. It wasn't anything I could relate to" (personal communication, January 28, 2017).

At times, Nani Chacon's print of a Diné woman *Walk in Beauty* received criticism for the piece not being Navajo. Nani explains:

> It was this defiant thing and me embracing being a woman. Are you really saying that's not Navajo? Or you really saying that's not being a woman? The work itself was to talk about both of those. It's a simple action. We are not showy with our sexuality in Navajo culture and respectfully so. But that doesn't mean that, as women, we don't have this inherent sensuality or inherent beauty about us; that is with us all the time, no matter what we are wearing or doing, we can't help it. That's a power, that's nothing we should be ashamed of, that what makes us attractive, that what makes us women, that's our femininity and strength. And I think western culture and western

> feminism reject femininity. I couldn't identify with western feminism because we possess femininity and sensuality all the time. (personal communication, January 28, 2017)

Nani does appreciate the ways Diné culture maintains respect and balance; that is something she tries to navigate in her work but not to the point that her work is inappropriate and that she loses the conversation (personal communication, January 24, 2020).

Nani shared that she gains strength from her role as a mother. The personal changes in her artwork were most significant when Nani turned from graffiti artist to painter due to her pregnancy. "I couldn't be out there on the street with graffiti—pregnant," Nani shared (personal communication, January 24, 2020). Nani believes women artists can merge motherhood and artistic practices; she explained it as a livelihood she needed to maintain herself. Motherhood and artist life are not separate; Nani shared that our children are part of everything we do. She explains that her son understands his mother's art-making and that it is a part of her well-being and livelihood (personal communication, January 24, 2020). She shares how her son has influenced a gallery exhibit arrangement; he has traveled with her, been on scaffolds, sharing the process with his mother. Nani believes, "It has always been very integrated, and I think that's the only way that I could have ever made it work, if he goes along on the journey with me" (personal communication, January 24, 2020).

I questioned whether when creating artwork, Nani intended to begin a dialogue or inspire reflection; she commented:

> I feel like as Native Indigenous women artists, we are the most underrepresented voice in the establishment . . . the art market, art industry is mostly run by white men. Being an Indigenous woman and having a voice within that is extreme counter to that white-male voice. If we did nothing else but stand in a gallery, we are already making a statement alone because we are so underrepresented. I feel anytime Indigenous women can talk about the issues that pertain to Indigenous people, their people, it's important and revolutionary. That's the voice that will aid a revolution; we do have a unique perspective. Unique connection to the many things that are happening. And it should be heard. (personal communication, January 28, 2017)

In closing, Nani Chacon shared the following when I asked about how her artwork reclaims Native women's voice and identity: "It's important to put women of color and especially talk about Indigenous histories in the forefront. It's something we don't see enough of. I am not interested in talking about the past anymore, in the regard of putting an Indian in a headdress on a horse on a mural. I feel like we are only existing in people's minds in that time; we don't exist in that time. A lot of my work talks about who we are now. And where that leads us" (personal communication, January 2017).

Diné woman artist Nani Chacon's artwork reclaims Native identity, strength, and voice through her art for the betterment of family, communities, nations, and, most important, herself. Nani Chacon shares her visual journey, cultural beliefs, and strength as a mother. It is determined that she will continue to create with purpose and persistence and elevate Native women's voices.

References

Anderson, K. 2000. *Recognition of Being: Reconstructing Native Womanhood*. Toronto: Women's Press.

Archibald, J. A. 2008. *Indigenous Storywork: Educating the Heart, Mind, Body, and Spirit*. Vancouver: UBC Press.

Austin, R. D. 2009. *Navajo Courts and Navajo Common Law: A Tradition of Tribal Self-Governance*. Minneapolis: University of Minnesota Press.

Badoni, G. 2017. *Visual Expressions of Native Womanhood: Acknowledging the Past, Present, and Future*.

Berlo, J. C., and R. B. Phillips. 1998. *Native North American Art*. Oxford: Oxford University Press.

Chilisa, B. 2012. *Indigenous Research Methodologies*. Thousand Oaks, CA: SAGE Publications.

Markstrom, C.A. 2008. *Empowerment of North American Indian Girls: Ritual Expressions at Puberty*. Lincoln: University of Nebraska Press.

Mihesuah, D. A. 2003. *Indigenous American Women: Decolonization, Empowerment, Activism*. Lincoln: University of Nebraska Press.

Wilson, S. 2008. *Research Is Ceremony: Indigenous Research Methods*. Black Point, NS: Fernwood Pub.

22

Lessons of Eco-Mindfulness

MICHELLE MONTGOMERY

In my short path in life, I never imagined missing the marked changes of a passing year. The four seasons—winter, spring, summer, and fall. The cycle of the seasons is caused by the Earth's tilt toward the sun. The seasons relate to specific points in Earth's trip around the sun; the summer and winter solstice, the longest and shortest days of the year, occur when the Earth's axis is either closet or farthest from the sun. The summer solstice marks the first day of summer, while the winter solstice is considered the first day of winter. I remember learning in my elementary schooling the seasons by months: spring—March, April, and May; summer—June, July, and August; fall—September, October, and November; and winter—December, January, and February. Each season would bring its own unique beauty. My favorite seasons are the splendor of fall colors and the stillness of winter.

The magnificence of trees will never cease to amaze me; during the fall, an orchestrated mixture of red, purple, orange, and yellow is the result of a chemical process that takes place in trees as the seasons change from summer to winter. The genus *Acer*, commonly known as the maple, has about 111 species,

https://doi.org/10.5876/9781646425105.c022

11 of which occur in North Carolina and 9 of which are considered native to the state: Hedge Maple (*Acer campestre*), Sugar Maple (*Acer floridanum*), Chalk Maple (*Acer leucoderme*), Black Maple (*Acer nigrum*), Japanese Maple (*Acer palmatum*), Silver Maple (*Acer saccharinum*), Red Maple (*Acer rubrum*), Striped Maple (*Acer Pennsylvanicum*), and Mountain Maple (*Acer spicatum*).

The leaves of trees are like little factories that work through the spring and summer to manufacture the necessary food for tree growth. The food-process takes place in the cells of each leaf containing chlorophyll, which gives the leaf its green color. The chlorophyll absorbs from sunlight the energy that is needed to transform carbon dioxide and water into carbohydrates such as sugars and starch. There also other pigments that are yellow and orange, carotene and xanthophyll; however, most of these colors are masked by significant amounts of green coloring. Due to changes in daylight and temperature, in fall, the symphony of changing colors begins. As the leaves stop their food-making process, the chlorophyll breaks down; the green color vanishes and gives the leaves their colorful display. The beautiful orange leaves of the Sugar Maple (*Acer floridanum*) are a result of the development of a red anthocyanin pigment. The fall colors are due to the mixing amount of chlorophyll residue and other pigments in its leaves during this particular season. Because of climate change, it is difficult to determine when or how long each season will begin or end. As a result, the warm fall colors are a fast-paced, elaborate musical composition with an abrupt, short end.

A favorite chore growing up, no matter how old or young, was raking piles of leaves and watching their colors change as they shed as if they were large snowflakes, all while taking in the early-morning scents of the crisp air. My grandfather would remind me that trees are perfect examples of qualities we should all aspire to achieve. Like trees, we are forever changing but growing stronger with each season and always giving without question. I worry our future generations will not experience the joys of the symphony of trees and the spiritual connection to the change of seasons. As North Carolinians, how will we teach the moral qualities of trees if we do not respect their gifts of protection and the knowledge that they share without asking a single question? There is an alarming rate of deforestation as urbanization takes its toll in the form of concrete kingdoms adorned with high-rise castles, massive amounts of new-age carriages under the guidance of zombies, and air traffic filled with autopilot-controlled flying dragons. The heartbreaking reality as

I dwell in my memories of the past, in this new age kingdom, is I do not understand how the key component to improve urban air quality has been disregarded and ignored, the knights as guardians—the trees.

The winter season in North Carolina is often accompanied by sleet storms that transform trees into large, crystalized characters, as if in a winter fairytale. I would often ask my dad if sleet storms were bad for the trees, as the ice seemed too heavy and cold. He reminded me that the winter months are for resting. Trees slow down their cell growth as the temperatures decrease and go through a process similar to hibernation. Dormancy is like hibernation in that everything slows down—metabolism, energy consumption, growth, and so on. The first part of dormancy is when a tree loses their leaves. They do not produce food in the winter, so they shed their leaves and any obligation to produce the necessary food to maintain them. When it is time for trees to lose their leaves, a chemical called abscisic acid is produced in the terminal buds. The terminal bud is where the leaves break off. Abscisic acid suspends growth, preventing the cells from dividing. Impeded growth is another act of dormancy. As the tree's metabolism slows down during dormancy, the cell's growth is impeded to conserve the food she/he has stored. When I imagine an elder's reciprocity of relationships, I am reminded of trees and the seasons. I am also aware of my inherent responsibility as the seasons share the warnings we must heed.

As a forever student and passionate Eco-Critical Race Theorist, I am concerned with the related impacts of extreme changes to the ecosystem processes and how to decolonize the narrative of climate justice through both Scientific Ecological Knowledge (SEK) and Traditional Ecological Knowledge (TEK) (Kimmerer 2012; Montgomery 2022a, 2022b). Climate change is expected to directly affect human health and widen the disparity gap, in particular mental health. This loss of biodiversity in culturally important native plants and animals will increase the risk of a disconnect to place-based knowledges and identities of Indigenous peoples. We, as Indigenous peoples change our knowledge base to adapt to environmental changes, whether it is becoming a visitor to a different land and seascape, or a result of ecological shifts to honor and respect the responsibility of reciprocity to our more-than-human relationships.

The act of decolonizing the climate justice narrative would empower TEK and Indigenous knowledges as being viewed as holistic with a moral value through lived experiences and the underlying foundation of justice. Daniel Wildcat explains this as a synthetic attentiveness: "By synthetic attentiveness, I mean the ability to have all our senses simultaneously attuned to an environment—such that one can scan environments and identify movement and change at an environmental level" (2022, 5). The attentiveness of stories connected to place and identity illustrates the importance of cultural traditions and knowledge of Indigenous communities; yet, as we move forward, there are thousands of multigenerational stories that remain untold (Deloria 2006; Deloria and Wildcat 2021; Wildcat 2009). We must find ways to call one another into a conversation with humility and grace to engage eco-mindfully through synthetic attentiveness.

Reciprocity of Southern Roots

Although I am visitor of the Pacific Northwest, my social and cultural construction of my place-based identity is rooted in the northeastern North Carolina and the New River Valley regions, which are part of the Appalachian territory in Southwest Virginia. My land-based knowledge of diverse bodies of trees and ecosystems has given me a different lens to navigate the two different worldviews of scientific and traditional knowledge. A missing component of SEK is the disconnect from the multigenerational relationship of the synthetic attentiveness of place-based Indigenous identities and knowledges. A multigenerational relationship to the environment would provide a historical recollection of the natural resources and the impacts of industrial capitalism (Menzies 2006).

For generations, a major source of income for my family was provided by sustainable agriculture, in particular, Virginia Bright Leaf tobacco (*Nicotiana rustica*) and Burley tobacco (*Nicotiana tabacum*). My elders passed on the teachings of healthy farm practices that focused on crop rotation, with the main objective being the maintenance of soil fertility. Rotations that included nitrogen-producing legumes such as garden peas (*Pisum sativum L.*) and lima beans (*Phaseolus lunatus*) would provide the subsequent crop with a substantial amount of critical nutrients. Nitrogen from legumes remains in the soil longer than does nitrogen in synthetic fertilizers, leaving less to leach into the groundwater or run off fields and pollute streams. Large plots for rotation purposes were divided into smaller plots that often included a mixed variety of vegetable gardens. By growing a greater diversity of crops, an environmentally sustained method to control pests and weeds is established.

My youthful memories from childhood are filled with being barefoot and memorizing how the soil textures felt between my toes. It seemed appropriate that the fields of biology and plant pathology would allow me a contemporary lens to explore the natural world. I was particularly fascinated by a graduate course in soil microbiology, since there seemed to be a commonality of learning through observation. My attentiveness of placed-based learning gave me an edge in a graduate-level soil microbiology course. A part of growing up in farming communities is you learn generational knowledge of the land, such as the types of soils, which are divided into six main different groups—clay, silt, loam, sand, chalk, and peat. During lab activities, we practiced how to determine the soil texture. Sand, silt, and clay are the variation in sizes of the soil particles. Sand is the largest size and feels gritty. Silt is the moderate size and feels smooth. Clay is the smallest particle and feels sticky. Clay always reminded me of being free from the pressures of the world as a child. When I was a student, instantly my memories traveled to moments in times of stained jeans and T-shirts from drying my hands after molding wet, red clay into round balls. Other memories include observing my grandfather feeling the soil when we would walk around the farm. It was as if he were recording each touch as he pressed the soil with his thumb and forefinger, after which he would reply, "Michelle, you have the best way to remember this place—those bare feet. And it will remember you." In western science, the touch and observation of the soil are known as a ribbon test. This method is used to estimate texture and determine the amount of clay in the soil. I have always been taught that predominate clay soils are not good for planting despite their mineral content. Their thickness and lack of aeration are difficult for the roots of growing plants to penetrate. Throughout the semester, I often wondered if my grandfather would chuckle about this method. There were moments, though, where I enjoyed my graduate education that connected my place-based learning. However, I often felt a familiar feeling of isolation and loneliness navigating my pursuit of higher education as an Indigenous woman.

I had the privilege of attending Hollister Elementary School for grades K–5 in my hometown of Hollister, North Carolina. In elementary school, my great-uncles would often visit me. It was always a treat to see their smiles, knowing that I would have an opportunity to visit my great-great-Uncle Henry's store for an afternoon treat. Unfortunately, in the more advanced grade levels, we were bused to schools outside of our community and I no longer received regular family visits. Nonetheless, being greeted with breath-taking hugs and a kiss on the forehead by my uncles created a strong sense of resilience.

A Memoir of Resilience

Resilience comes with many enlightened transformative questions that nurture your authentic self and intuitive awareness. As an Indigenous woman, I ask myself daily, Have I chosen a path to listen with my heart or fear? During the winter of 2016, I was diagnosed with renal cancer. My diagnosis did not come as a surprise, knowing the "c-word" has been lurking within the shadows of my family and beloved community for four generations. Yet, the evening phone call from my doctor was the furthest thing from my mind. For forty-four years, I had escaped an uninvited companion, which lead me on a quest for a deeper understanding of what it means to be "well lived." On the day I received the inevitable news, my routine was—as it has always been—a morning run to pray among the trees in the Redmond Watershed Preserve, a cup of tea to enjoy, and a dark chocolate treat to begin my workday.

The Redmond Watershed Preserve is 800 acres primarily managed as a nature preserve of second-growth forest that includes Douglas Firs (*Psuedotsugua menziesii*), Western Red Cedars (*Thuga plicata*), Black Cottonwoods (*Populus trichocarpa*), and Big Leaf Maples (*Acer macrophyllum*), to name a few. Personally, the meanings of a second-growth forest are filled with emotional loyalty. Second growth refers to the second generation that grows after an old growth is catastrophically destroyed. Those humble me, so disrespectfully taken. An old-growth forest in this region would refer to Douglas Fir and Western Hemlock forests older than 200 years. I have always been reminded the trees hear and feel our presence without our speaking or being in direct contact with them. The direct connection is through the air we breathe. For this reason, we share a sacred life bond. However, on this morning I was more in tune to my surroundings: listening carefully, my protectors—the trees—were whispering, and now I know they were sharing the much-needed medicine to prepare me for the untold challenges of the stages of grief that come with finding the freedom and fear where courage meets resilience. Robin Kimmerer's view of the natural world speaks volumes of truth: "Action on behalf of life transforms. Because the relationship between self and the world is reciprocal, it is not a question of first getting enlightened or saved and then acting. As we work to heal the earth, the earth heals us" (2013, 340).

I always dreamed of becoming a Willow Oak (*Quercus phellos*), Beech Family (Fagaceae). It is one of the most familiar large trees in North Carolina, with a height up to seventy feet and equal in width. Willow Oak is an excellent large shade tree, a member of the red oak group with lobed leaves. Similar to my grandfather, it gave me unconditional love, shelter, and countless huge embraces; it patiently listened to the details of my life, was the best seat to gaze at the evening fireflies as they danced so eloquently through the twilight of the night, and supplied the devotion to protect those that have always kept me safe through the years—the trees. The Willow Oak is a grandparent as I view all trees.

During each doctor appointment, I discovered unexpected gifts of awareness that cancer presents. I recollected every detail of my grandfather, particularly the smell of curing tobacco as we drove down a long, bumpy dirt road, where I held so much anticipation to hear his voice ask the notorious question, "What did you learn today?" And, in this very moment, I would have given anything to hear his voice in between shuffling consent forms to prepare for a right kidney nephrectomy. In my eyes, like the Willow Oak, my grandfather could calm the brewing storms of life, the rumblings of thunder that caught you off guard, seemingly as if time had stood still. My awareness has become that it takes a very strong individual to sit with yourself, calm your storms, and heal all your issues without trying to bring someone else into a journey they are not prepared to travel. This is the resilience of self-love guided by my ancestors and more-than-human relationships.

My grandfather, James Ossie Baker Sr., son of late Ossie Baker and Carrie Rudd Baker, was born on September 23, 1923, in North Carolina. He served in the United States Navy and received an honorable discharge. During my sophomore year of college, my grandfather was diagnosed with terminal lung cancer. I remember being invited to meet my grandfather and Great-Aunt Earlene for what I believed to be an annual exam at the veterans hospital in Durham, North Carolina. As always, I was eager to see my grandfather.

When I arrived on the fourth floor, his face was with filled sadness. He kept his illness a secret from me, knowing that a university education would not have taken priority. A month later, my grandfather started his journey, leaving me with one last gift. He shared, "I will not be with you physically, but I am here always. You have to be strong." I was by my grandfather's side when he took his last breath, knowing his unconditional love was branded on my soul. It is a humble honor to be gifted life on his birthday. Like the Big Leaf Maples, Black Cotton Woods, Douglas Firs, Western Red Cedars, and the Willow Oaks, grandparents are always sending you their love and medicine to guide you through the storms of life. On the day of my surgery, I remembered how often my Great-Great-Uncle Ellison reminded me, "You are like your grandfather. You should be . . . you were born on his birthday." The resilience of my grandfather's love has guided me to not become consumed with grief and despair from cancer. Instead, I focused on "how do decolonize diversity to increase the inclusion of Indigenous knowledge to protect the natural world." It is a big task, but like my grandfather, I am loyal and do not take light-heartedly the duty to protect family.

Pre and post my renal cancer surgery, Stinging Nettles (*Urtica dioica*) was a major part of my diet. As my elders have taught me, we should ask the medicines of the places where we live and reside as visitors for protection and good health. The Creator's gifts—calm waters of the Shishole Bay Marina, my sailboat *Salish Star*, and nettles tea—gave me the strength to endure the unimaginable. When we ask for strength at our weakest moments in life, our more-than-human relatives revive our spirits to take on the challenges that have yet to come.

In March 2017, a week after surgery, I returned to work at the University of Washington (UW) Tacoma to begin the spring quarter with the intent of continuing the course of being resilient, but most important to change the narratives of climate justice and the impact on Indigenous peoples. As a visitor to the traditional lands of the Indigenous peoples of Pacific Northwest for over nine years, I had an inherent responsibility to Indigenize and decolonize institutional spaces through my acts of resilience to decolonize diversity.

I use the term *decolonized diversity* to recognize the cultural rights of Indigenous communities in accordance with their identities, history of place, and knowledges. With decolonization practices being at the core of my perspective of diversity, I strive to uplift climate justice by honoring TEK and the relational accountability to the natural world. As Daniel Wildcat explains, "In North America many Indigenous traditions tell us that reality is more than just facts and figures collected so that humankind might wisely use resources. Rather, to know 'it'—really—Requires respect for the relationships and relatives that constitute the complex web of life" (Wildcat 2009, 9).

For this reason, I have a strong commitment to utilize the written word and the conduit of voice as a justice tool for empowerment. Decolonized diversity has a special role to play in promoting the equitable inclusivity of knowledges and promoting more humanized understandings of one another. A perspective to guide critical awareness of diverse knowledges is to better understand how systems of oppression distort our sense of self and other, in particular creating otherness.

There are multiple ways to protect the natural world through decolonized diversity. One method is creating safe spaces for bidirectional knowledge sharing—to listen and engage in dialogue. An important criterion of critical reflective dialogue is "unpacking" synergistic perspectives. It is essential to practice engaging people in conversation versus the disengagement of a person's perspective (Montgomery 2022a, 2022b). We have a collective responsibility to provide opportunities to bring our whole selves along with emotional engagement to draw a deeper understanding of climate justice. We must now become the guardians and remember the wisdom of Robin Kimmerer, "As we work to heal the earth, the earth heals us" (2013, 340).

References

Deloria, V. 2006. *The World We Use to Live In: Remembering the Powers of the Medicine Men*. Golden, CO: Fulcrum Publishing.

Deloria, V., and D. Wildcat. 2001. *Power and Place: Indian Education in America*. Golden, CO: Fulcrum Publishing.

Kimmerer, R. W. 2012. "Searching for Synergy: Integrating Traditional and Scientific Ecological Knowledge in Environmental Science Education." *Journal of Environmental Studies and Sciences* 2 (4): 317–323 (New York: Springer-Verlag). https://doi.org.10.1007/s13412-012-0091-y.

Kimmerer, R. W. 2013. *Braiding Sweetgrass*. 1st ed. Minneapolis: Milkweed Editions.

Menzies, C. R. 2006. *Traditional Ecological Knowledge and Natural Resource Management*. Lincoln: University of Nebraska Press.

Montgomery, M. 2022a. "An Indigenous Feminist Lens: Dismantling Settler Colonial Narratives of Place-Based Knowledges in a Climate Justice World." In *The Routledge Handbook of Sustainable Cities and Landscapes in the Pacific Rim*, edited by Yizhao Yang and Anne Taufen, 862–868. Milton Park, UK: Taylor and Francis. https://doi.org/10.4324/9781003033530.

Montgomery, M. 2022b. "Indigenous Moral Epistemologies and Eco-critical Race Theory." In *Re-indigenizing Ecological Consciousness and the Interconnectedness to Indigenous Identities*, edited by Michelle Montgomery, 53–63. Lanham, MD: Rowan and Littlefield.

Wildcat, D. R. 2009. *Red Alert! Saving the Planet with Indigenous Knowledge*. Golden, CO: Fulcrum.

Wildcat, D. 2022. "Traditional Ecological Knowledges: An Antidote to Destruction." In *Re-Indigenizing Ecological Consciousness and the Interconnectedness to Indigenous Identities*, edited by Michelle Montgomery, 5. Lanham, MD: Rowan and Littlefield.

23

Existence as Resistance

BARBARA WOLFIN

A nation is not conquered until the hearts of its women are on the ground. Then it is finished, no matter how brave its warriors or how strong their weapons.

—*Tsistsistas, Cheyenne*

Introduction

The epigraph quote demonstrates how vital Native women are to their Tribal Nation. In order to prevent the survival of a Nation, the enemy focused on the extermination of the carriers of the next generations, the mothers. The perpetuation of mistreatment and genocide waged on Native women in California will be briefly discussed as well as an insight on how California Native women, including Pit River, were targeted by *nillaaduwi's* (wanderer/white man) to ensure the eradication of all Native *iss* (Pit River people) in order to achieve, over time, total ownership of the land. Specific examples of Pit River women's resistance will illustrate the utilization of their in-depth knowledge of their ancestral territories. A focus will be on Lela Rhoades's experience and perspective. The following section will allude to how Pit River women's existence can be understood as an interruption and disruption of profit making of a major corporation, thus making their ongoing existence a revolutionary act. The last section will conclude with how Native men protected girls and women of their Tribal Nation through

https://doi.org/10.5876/9781646425105.c023

retaliation and reobtaining women and girls from their abduction by nillaaduwi's. The strength of a Tribal Nations heartbeat is dependent upon the balanced ancestral relationship between both the men/women and the *iss/dey ' qaade* (Mother Earth).

Before beginning, I want to make clear, the information provided is not a victim narrative; rather, it is a testimony of land-based strength and resistance against the nillaaduwi's invasion.

Genocidal Acts

War was waged upon Native women of California because of their ability to carry and give birth to the next generations of iss. A plethora of policies, committees, and acts were formulated and conducted to eradicate the existence of Native iss in California. Euro-American men, specifically in California, volunteered to rid their community of the "Indian problem" by forming Volunteer Committees. The members of these committees used tax funds to suit, arm, and provide provisions for themselves to "root out Native Americans living nearby and kill them," which often meant "killings [of] Native American women, children and elderly" (Lindsay 2012, 210). An expedition account of a committee took place in Tehama County, and when asked about the expedition by then California governor Weller, a committee member admitted:

> A few weeks since, a party of whites, to recover some stock the Indians had driven off, pursued them into the mountains and surprised a Rancheria [Native village] in which there were a few bucks and a greater number of squaws and children, and I am pained to say that in the heat and excitement of the attack, exasperated with the recollection of the many injuries they had suffered from these Indians, cornered them and then a war of extermination, by shooting down the women and children. And it is since these Indians have commenced the fearful work of burning houses. (Lindsay 2012, 197)

Adding to the questioning of the morality of Volunteer Committee members, committee member Hall was asked by a member of the California State legislature if any women or children were hurt during their pursuits, and Hall openly admitted, "I think all the squaws were killed because they refused to go further. We took one boy into the valley and the infants were put out of their misery and a girl 10 years of age was killed for stubbornness" (194).

In short Native women and children were exterminated because they were scared and unsure of what would happen once the Volunteer Committee took them to their end destination. During this time in California there was no system of justice for Natives, although Natives could be sold into slavery or whipped for something as minuscule as incorrectly being accused of stealing a horse. In startling contrast to the experience of Natives, the only common crime white men could conduct was the selling of alcohol to or buying of alcohol from Natives. According to B. C. Lindsay (2012, 219–220), "Many brutal crimes committed against Native peoples, no matter how gruesome, could not be prosecuted in the region." Here we clearly see how crime is socially constructed by those who wield economic, political, and cultural power over others. The murder and other crimes of humanity against Native people were seen as noncriminal acts where often the mere existence of Native people making claims to their right to survive was seen as an affront to settlers, who often killed with impunity. Women often bore the brunt of this colonial settler violence.

Pit River Women Were Strong

This section provides specific examples of Pit River women's experiences from Lela Rhoades, a Pit River woman, as told to Molly Curtis. It is vital to highlight the experiences of Pit River women as told by a Pit River woman because it decentralizes the troublesome male anthropological narrative while bringing forth and giving the rightful space to the experiences of Pit River women. Furthermore, it is important to document the experiences for our future iss to remember not only what our women went through but to be reminded that we have the strength, love, and capacity to overcome any policy, act, or committee waged against us.

As documented, the first nillaaduwi's arrived in Pit River ancestral territories in 1827–1828 (Garth 1953, 129). According to Lela, the longevity of their stay usually lasted around four days. However, during the gold rush era, the influx and squatting of nillaaduwi's began. Lela remembered when the first family of nillaaduwi's illegally took up space next to her family's village. Her family noticed the nillaaduwi's had cut down trees everywhere they roamed. Lela's grandfather sat down and watched them to see what they were doing with the trees. The nillaaduwi's made logs out of the cut trees to build houses and fences. They fenced off their house to prevent other nillaaduwi's from taking up their squatted area. During the *ee 'waamaq* (fall, when the leaves change), the Ichattawi (Goose Valley area) women traditionally gathered specific roots that grew in certain geospatial locations, which happened to be within the fenced-in portion of the nillaaduwi's squatted area. Lela shared, "The Indian women went into a field to gather their roots. And of course they were inside the fence the white men built. A white man got mad and chased them out with a pitchfork. They thought that was awful mean. They said they didn't understand why he did that, chased them out when they didn't do anything but just dig their own roots. Then the white men set dogs on them. They did that all the time" (Curtis 2013, 13).

The nillaaduwi's foreign ways of agriculture and illegal squatting on land—traditionally used to dig specific roots—forced most Ichattawi women to travel upriver to *At' 'waami* (Big Valley) territories to dig for the specific roots. Lela's great-grandma, grandmother, and great-aunt were among the women who traveled upriver to gather roots. Lela shared a time when the women in her family were digging roots in At 'wammi. "Some soldiers came in and killed some of those old ladies. My great-grandma had been digging roots with her daughters—my grandma, and her sister—when the soldiers came upon them. They shot at all of them and they got my great-grandma in the hip. She fell and she laid there until the soldiers left. They went away; they thought she died. Then she rolled into a ditch, where in the wintertime the water runs. She laid in there all day; she couldn't walk" (Curtis 2013, 13).

Andrea Smith's work "Heteropatriarchy and the Three Pillars of White Supremacy: Rethinking Women of Color Organizing" (2016) states that the three pillars of white supremacy are (a) Slavery/Capitalism, (b) Genocide/Colonialism, and (c) Orientalism/War. The acts displayed by the soldiers stems from the third pillar of white supremacy: the "logic of Orientalism." The logic of Orientalism, as explained by Smith, "marks certain peoples or nations as inferior and as posing a constant threat to the well-being of empire." Native women were perceived as inferior because they would dig in the dirt/ground for roots, a lifeway they had practiced since their creation, like animals, and also because they dug on or adjacent to the illegal squatted area of the nillaaduwi's, therefore making them a constant threat to the nillaaduwi's. Furthermore, this Orientalist mentality supports and perpetuates a second pillar of white supremacy: Colonialism/Genocide. The two of three pillars are demonstrated in Lela's account of Ichattawi women participating in a generational cultural protocol and being executed for it. The soldiers targeted women gathering roots because it was an easy way to kill large numbers of Native women at one time. Another story of Lela's demonstrates the in-depth knowledge the women have of their ancestral territories and how this knowledge ultimately saved their lives:

> The soldiers had caught my grandma and her sister, and they left one man there to watch the girls. My Grandma said, "Let's dig roots and eat. We don't know when we'll get something to eat. We'll be hungry." So they pretended like they were digging. My grandma said, "Sister, now kind of get away from me a little bit, and when you break to run, you run the short way, and I'll take the long way," because she could out run her little sister. She stood there and glanced, and her sister made the break, the little plump one. She broke and she ran! My grandma broke and ran the other way. They ran apart, see. And he chased her. "I just let him come, just so close," she said. He shot at her. She could hear the bullets whiz over her head. She said, "I came to a big ditch, and I jumped almost clear across, but I jumped into the water. The ditch was so deep I couldn't reach the top. I jumped up and grabbed the weeds that grow down, and I swung myself up there. He was still coming! I ran and I never looked back till I got to the edge of the timber. When I looked back I couldn't see anything, no horse no nothing." She had told her sister, "If you escape, and if I escape, we'll meet at that place where that big rock is. If I get there first I'll put a sign there, a rock on it. If you get there first, you just put a rock up and go on, don't wait," because [it was] about twenty-five miles from Big Valley [back] to Pit One, where they lived. "When I got to the rock, I started to put up my sign, and here my sister came running, so I didn't have to. We ran, both together then. We were both saved," she said. (Curtis 2013, 13–14)

If one is not immersed in their homelands, they are not free nor can they be set free, because our knowledge and livelihoods are provided to us from the de ʻ qaade. Lela's grandmother and her sister's knowledge of their territories—knowing which trail was the long one or short one, knowing which rock to meet at and knowing their way back to their territories by running twenty-five miles—contributed to the safety of not only their lives but their iss's lives as well. Once Lela's grandmother and sister made it to their territories, they informed the iss of what happened and the location of the soldiers. Later, the tribal men retaliated against the soldiers and moved camp. Last, this short description of a forced march from Pit River to Owens Valley Paiute-Shoshone provides perspective on how inhumane the soldiers were, no matter what the age, gender, or disability of Native people. "The youngest ones, the nursing one, they had already got rid of all of them. They took them away from their mother or father and slapped them against a tree. The mothers saw it and cried. But they couldn't do anything about it. The soldiers whipped them for crying. They would have fought if it had been just a fistfight, but the soldiers had guns" (Curtis 2013, 23).

When looking at these events, especially from a western linear view, it may seem outdated or "in the past"; however, the events, from a Native perspective, occurred only five generations ago. Given that our timelines are so long and that we embody a generational gaze (McIntosh 2018), this event occurs in our very near past. It continues to have intimacy and deep relevance in our personal and collective lives. Native women, including Pit River, have resisted invasion, kidnapping, and the occupation of the nillaaduwi's since contact. It is crucial to our understanding that every baby born since the contact of nillaaduwi's is a continued act of resistance in itself and attributed to Pit River women's love and determination to keep our iss's existence on dey 'qaade alive. It is a constant reminder that Pit River women were and are strong.

Existence as Interruption

Pit River women's existence is an interruption to the settler-colonial state in pursuit of exploitation of the land for "resources." Currently, within Pit River ancestral territories the protection of Saht-Tit-Lah (Medicine Lake) has been an ongoing battle for over fifteen years. A geothermal corporation has made many attempts to develop geothermal plants adjacent to Saht-Tit-Lah. If the geothermal energy plants were to be constructed, the process of obtaining the energy, below the ground, would compromise the land greatly due to the chemicals used to break the through the layers of earth when drilling (Bertani 2005). Pit River men, women, elders, and children have demonstrated and protested against the attempted exploitation of dey' 'qaade and her "resources." If built, it would be owned by Calpine Corporation, the largest American geothermal energy company. However, because of the continuation, importance, and transference of cultural protocols—such as not compromising the land for profit and not disrupting the home of our animal relatives—the Pit River iss has so far prevented the development of the plants (Pit River Tribe 2019). When women are on the front lines fighting against unjust multi-million-dollar corporations, they simultaneously teach their children and the next generations to recognize the importance of protecting dey 'qaade and our life-worlds. As demonstrated earlier, Pit River women were killed for simply living and being Pit River. Now the Pit River women continue to unapologetically carry, birth, and teach the next generations the importance and transference of cultural protocols, making them revolutionaries in their own right. It is the revolution of everyday practice.

Native Men Protection

Since the creation of iss, Indigenous peoples have had their own governing and justice systems that followed cultural protocols while upholding the original instructions. One of the cultural protocols, for the men, was the protecting and defending of the women, children, elderly, and the land. This cultural protocol is demonstrated through Lindsay's (2012) example of a Tribal Chief (tribe unknown) who utilized traditional Native practices to bring justice to his daughter. "On one occasion, a member of Willard's emigrant company raped the daughter of a local Native leader from an unidentified group. The chief visited the leader of Willard's company at their camp and offered a solution to make matters right between them: if the man who had violated his daughter would come forward, he would exact justice where justice was due. If not, he would slay all of the company. After a time, one of the young men came forward and confessed. After 'the Indians tore out his heart,' they let the rest go in peace" (220).

Lindsay (2012) documents another incident in which a captain of a volunteer company led Native prisoners through a mining camp, and the men took possession of all the "squaws" for personal use, "likely meaning they raped them or forced them into slavery in their camp. Only trouble came of such acts, as Native men became enraged and took up arms to reclaim their wives, mothers, sisters, and daughters from the rapacious miners" (219–220). The two examples given of Native men protecting and defending the women of their Nation are nowhere near the totality of the Native men's attempts. As Native peoples, our existences would not be valid without maintaining the respectful relationship between the men and women as well as the iss and dey 'qaade. Honoring our Native men as protectors of the women, children, elderly, and dey 'qaade is crucial to the understanding of our cultural protocols.

Conclusion

Practicing cultural protocols as a form of resistance, against the status quo of heteropatriarchy and heteropaternalism, brings back the respectful relationship between men/women of a Tribal Nation and the relationship between the iss/dey 'qaade. The two relationships are imperative to maintaining the respectful symbiotic balance. This is a testimony to the love, strength, power, and resiliency of Pit River women and all Indigenous women during the times when war was waged upon them with the end goal of preventing the next generations to be born. However, it is important to give credit where it is due. When we think of Native women as resistors and revolutionaries, we need to also think of those Native men who have contributed to the livelihoods of their Native women. It is because of the cultural protocols that uphold the original instructions of the iss that the generations (from contact) are alive, resisting, and to some extent continuing to maintain the respectful relationships. The strength and love of Pit River women have proven to carry their Nation through policies, committees, acts, or legislation waged against them from the past to the present and into the future.

Glossary

At ' waami: Big Valley

Dey ' qaade: The Mother Earth

ee ' waamaq: Fall, when the leaves change

Ichattawi: Goose Valley

Iss: Pit River people

Nillaaduwi: Wanderer, white man

Saht-Tit-Lah: Medicine Lake

References

Bertani, Ruggero. 2005. "World Geothermal Power Generation in the Period 2001–2005." *Geothermics* 34 (6). Oxford: Elsevier Ltd: 651–90. https://doi.org/10.1016/j.geothermics.2005.09.005.

Curtis, M. 2013. *Lela Rhoades, Pit River Woman*. Berkeley, CA: Heyday.

Garth, T. R. 1953. *Atsugewi Ethnography* 14 (2): 129–212 (Berkeley: University of California Press).

Lindsay, B. C. 2012. *Murder State: California's Native American Genocide, 1846–1873*. Lincoln: University of Nebraska Press.

McIntosh, T. 2018. "Indigenous Rights, Poetry and Decarceration." In *Prison and Human Rights*. Basingstoke, UK: Palgrave.

Pit River Tribe v. Bureau of Land Management. No. 17-15616 (9th Cir. 2019).

Smith, A. 2016. "Heteropatriarchy and the Three Pillars of White Supremacy: Rethinking Women of Color Organizing." *Color of Violence: The INCITE! Anthology*, edited by INCITE! Women of Color against Violence. Durham, NC: Duke University Press, 2016. https://doi.org/10.1515/9780822373445.

24

Nā Māmā, Pāpā, Arohanui, from Mum and Dad, with Love

KELVIN TAPUKE AND SYLVIA TAPUKE

At the entrance of our whare (house): Kia ora and greetings from Aotearoa New Zealand, Welcome to our chapter of the Indigenous International Speaker Series' Nā Māmā, Pāpā, Arohanui—From Mum and Dad, with love. . . . First, we acknowledge our Creator in ensuring that we stay connected, despite long distances, many generations, and the places we have rooted ourselves. If it were not for our shared spiritual connections, we would have never met in person and followed up in this new digital realm. Ciarra, Michelle, and your team—thank you and bless you both for the invitation to host a chapter in your book. Thank you sincerely for granting us space to express ourselves this way.

We feel very honored and appreciative of this opportunity. After much deliberation and discussion, we decided to write love letters for our sons. Our writings are in English, although we will provide these instructions in Te Reo Māori (later) because English is a second language for our sons. This book chapter is the first one we have written as a couple. We thought it would be appropriate to pass messages on to our sons. First, a book chapter provides a way to capture and share our thoughts with our children, which would last

https://doi.org/10.5876/9781646425105.c024

a long time. Second, when they read these letters, we hope they will also read the other chapters and feel the voices and stories of our Indigenous brothers and sisters. Finally, a chapter in an Indigenous book means our messages are not just for our sons, though we will direct our messages to them. Our thoughts are also for their cousins, aunties, uncles, nieces, nephews, and friends. This book is essential and will guide young people as they make their way through changes in our world. Although our sons have some idea of our work, we don't get to share deeply with them. Of course, modernity, technology, and life catch up, and then the next thing you know, you have missed time with each other. Capturing our messages in this way means our sons can reflect and think and, if they wish, use the letters.

We have written this chapter as if we were talking directly to our children. In keeping with Indigenous oral traditions, we will communicate using traditional forms from Aotearoa New Zealand, to express our dreams, visions, and aspirations to our young adult children and many young people like them. We have also written the conversation in English, and although we all speak and write Te Reo Māori, this is how we converse. We hope that we can normalize Te Reo Māori in our household. Based on our family tradition of people entering our home, we have organized our chapter to follow a similar welcome process. First, we call you into the chapter through acknowledgment. We will use a *pao* (call) to acknowledge you; although we usually reserve these for more formal situations, we think this is appropriate. We will have some time to get to know each other (usually, there is a response, but thoughts are also fine!).

We usually guide people through our home and explain the different spaces through messages so that you can feel comfortable yet know the protocols of what we refer to as Te Whare Tapawhā.[1] Kelvin will *kōrero* (talk) about five areas of well-being critical to us as individuals, as families, and even as nations. These well-being areas are known as *taha whenua* (land), *taha wairua* (spiritual), *taha whānau* (social), *taha tinana* (physical), and *taha hinengaro* (mind). His kōrero will include *pūrākau* (family-based stories) and *mātauranga Māori* (Māori knowledge), but they are mainly *tohutohu* (instructional) in nature. After each

1 Te Whare Tapawhā was created by Māori academic Mason Durie in the 1990s. This term means "the four sides of a house." We have added another part, which is *taha whenua* (land), where the lands sits on. We understand that Durie had intended for whenua to be a part of this. The main purpose of Te Whare Tapawhā was to help people in the health sector.

key message, a supporting *waiata* (song or chant) will follow. The songs either support or add to the letter, representing our distinct lineages. Females usually perform the songs, but anyone can sing. You will see in the layout of the chapter that some of the words are on the left-hand side (female voice) and some on the right-hand side (male voice). Upon completion of the speeches, we invite you to engage and meet, and finally, we extend an offering of goodwill in the form of a *whakataukī* (proverbial saying).

Nau mai, haere mai—Welcome and enter. . . .
Welcome into our whare (home):

Haka pōhiri / Welcome chant

A ūtaina A-hi!
A ūtaina A-hi!
Ūtaina mai ngā iwi o te motu
Ki runga te marae e tau nei.
A hiki nuku e! A hiki rangi e!
A hiki rangi e! A hiki nuku e!
Iā! Ha! Ha!
Ka hikitia tana iwi
Ka hapainga tana waka
Aue! Aue! Aue! Ha!
Aue! Aue! Aue! Ha! Hei![2]

Haul together!
Haul together!
Bring all the tribes of the land
Upon our ancestral grounds
Exalt the land, exalt the sky
Exalt the land, exalt the sky
Iā! Ha! Ha!
Lift the people
Lift the boat
Aue! Aue! Aue! Ha!
Aue! Aue! Aue! Ha! Hei!

2 This *haka pōhiri* is used for welcoming people into new spaces. This is one of Pāpā's favourite haka to do. He uses it in different ways when he is presenting.

Waiata whakaeke / Welcome song

Mihi mai rā
Mihi mai rā
Tēnā rā koutou katoa
E te iwi, nui tonu rā,
Tēnā rā koutou katoa.

Welcome
Welcome
Greetings to you all
To the esteemed people
Greeting to you all

Mihi ki ngā taiohi / Acknowledgments to our youth

Whakarongo
Whakarongo!
Ki te reo Māori e karanga nei
Whakarongo!
Ki ngā akoranga Rangatira
Na Te Atua i tuku iho kia tātou e
Pupuritia
Kōrerotia
Mo ake tonu . . .
. . . Tēnā kia purea te hauora e
He kupu tukuiho mo tēnei reanga
He kupu tukuiho mo tēnei reanga
Whakarongo[3]

Listen
Listen to the Māori language, which is saying
Listen! Listen to the noble teachings
It was the Lord almighty who bequeathed it to us
Retain it, speak it for all time

---

3 This *waiata* was penned by the great Ngāti Porou composers Tuini Ngawai and Ngoi Pewhairangi. These composers had very strong influence over your nanny Muriwai and Pāpā.

Ritually purified by the life-giving winds
Let these words be a commandment to this generation
Listen!

To our children,

We thank you both for choosing us as parents. We acknowledge our ancestors for our meeting so we could bring you into this world. It hasn't been an easy job, and you don't receive any books on caring for your kids. Yes, your aunties, uncles, grandmothers, and grandfathers can pass down some of their teachings to us. Some of those teachings we carry and will share with you in this book. But today, we also faced different challenges from their time. We had to figure out those things by ourselves and with the help of our whānau, who also faced the same issues as us, including changing technologies, new ways of communicating and getting around places, and so on.

A long time ago, your ancestors lived off the land and the sea. They knew how to be one with nature and how to read the stars, the moon, and the sun. They had special knowledge about the creation of the world, the mountains, the plants and trees, and how people came to be. One story is about how our people were born out of the mountains and mist in Aotearoa New Zealand. From your koro [grandfather] Lemuelu's line, people were born out of worms of the sea and carved their way onto the land. From your koro Jim's side, his people came from the land of ice and fire. From your koro Tori's side, the people were born out of the majestic mountain, Taranaki. You have many stories of origins from all over the world. We haven't touched on your nanny's side either! We also have stories, songs, carvings, and prayers about how some of your ancestors traveled across the oceans using the knowledge handed down to them from their ancestors to find their home in the land of Aotearoa New Zealand.

After some time, they lived on the land and learned about the rivers, the birds, and the insects and memorizing special karakia (prayers), waiata (songs), and toi (art) about the world. Your ancestors also saw and recorded large events like earthquakes, eruptions, tsunamis, and floods. They could hand down knowledge about which areas were safe to live in and which were not. They could also tell you which fish or plant was poisonous and which were safe to eat. They also developed traditions around gathering, and harvesting kai, often shared across tribes. They also had a language for everything they saw, felt, and heard. Your ancestors had received warnings about new people arriving on the land and that it would change the world they had known.

Some of the visions came to our prophets, and they went around sharing that information.

When your ancestors first made contact with the people from Great Britain, it was first around accidental discovery. Soon after, they started trading, and some of our people went to the new churches to learn how to read and write. Our people became leaders through the churches and changed who had power in the tribes. Many land scouts came looking for new land to bring over; the settlers searched for new homes because they were struggling in their homeland. Many of these people lived peacefully with many of the tribes. However, officials from the same lands decided to set up a type of contract, the Tiriti o Waitangi, to allow the visitors to settle and govern throughout Aotearoa New Zealand. Not everyone signed this treaty. Soon our people could see that the settlers were not abiding by the treaty. They fought wars to take our people off their lands. Sometimes our relations even helped the settlers to fight against our people.

We can share this part of our history with you when you return home. Many laws were passed and accepted by some people to rule the land. These rules helped to get rid of our language, beliefs, and medical practices, divided up our lands, and ensured we learned new languages and religions. By the 1930s, many of our lands were lost to the law. With the loss of land, we also lost our values, knowledge, language, and identity.

Back in the days of World War II, your nannies and koros moved from their homes to the cities. They supported the Motherland in Great Britain and their war efforts. Remember that waiata, Rua Kenana?? "*They told his people not to go to war, let the white man fight the white man's war.*" Yip, that's one of many wars your koros fought. Your nannies and koros also shifted to find work in the cities. Some of them worked in the factories, and others found jobs wherever they could to feed the whānau back home. For your ancestors to survive a new way of living, they had to learn the English language, the English way of doing things, and the English Gods they brought with them. Of course, this happened way before this war. They were taught that being Māori was useless and had no place in our country. So that meant that over time our people began to believe it. Many of our whānau stopped speaking Te Reo and going to the marae.

In the '70s, our whānau started mixing with other Māori people to talk about the issues facing our people—lots of unemployment, poor school grades, homelessness, addiction to alcohol, and loss of identity. These people decided to try and get Te Reo Māori back into our communities. The teachers in our whānau have been involved in trying to bring our language back to life.

We tried to shift our tribal knowledge back into the schools. Your nannies and koros worked hard to hold onto our knowledge. Like many of your cousins, aunties, and uncles, you have taken part in significant tribal events that have been set up to bring our Māori ways back to life. Our Māori worldview is impressive. It all happens in front of your eyes; if you belong to that area, you will see and feel what our old people could see. Your face must be seen on the marae, but more important, be seen with your whānau, wherever they may be. We are proud of you both and hope that should you have children, you both chase those goals too.

Now we refer to this beautiful waiata, a favourite of Māmā, "Whakarongo." Nanny Muriwai was taught by the composer Ngoi Pewhairangi. The teachings of your ancestors have been handed down in different ways to us. Some of the teachings are strong, some we have forgotten, and others we must go back to school or learn from other people. We know that you are both enjoying your jobs as tradies. Maybe one day, you may decide to teach, do further study, or return home to work the land. Whatever you choose, we ask that you remember and carry on the teachings of your ancestors and, most important, karakia (prayer). We love you and pray you are continually protected, healthy and blessed.

We will explain afterward why we laid the paper out this way. For now, enjoy our love letters to you.

Waiata Tautoko / Supporting Song

Kua rongo ake au . . .
E tuku whakamoemiti kau ana
Ngā manu, ngā rākau, te moana
Ngā mea katoa, kī ō rātau
Kaihanga, ko tēnei he rā hou

I have learned that . . .
Each day
Birds, wind, sea and all nature
Speak with the music of praise
For their Creator saying thanks
for a new day.

(Williams 2019)

Whenua—Land: *E kore au e ngaro, he kākano i ruia mai i a Rangiātea*[4]

I will never be lost, for I am of the seed scattered across the Pacific from my ancient home in Hawaiki[5]

You might have heard a saying "ko au te whenua, ko te whenua ko au." These words mean "I am the land, and the land is me." In other words, you and the land (that you were born of) are deeply connected. It also does not mean you have the same status as the land. If you look at our language, it is special because *whenua* means both the land and the placenta where the baby is born. We say this because the land is also our ancient mother; her name is Papatūānuku. This means that the earth will always care for you and nurture you if you care for her. This also means that just as you should respect your mother, you should also appreciate Papatūānuku. You will notice that we added a *whakataukī* just preceding. We use these as triggers or reminders with many lessons within them. You might have heard the words from the earlier whakataukī when listening to Koro Hohepa's *waiata* (song), "He kākano ahau . . ." This whakataukī (proverb) always reminds you that we come from *Hawaiki nui* (the great Hawaiki), *Hawaiki roa* (the great long Hawaiki), and *Hawaiki pāmaomao* (distant Hawaiki). Although we are no longer connected to our physical Hawaiki, it is always written in our hearts, minds, and DNA. Back in your *nans'* (grandmothers') and *koros'* (grandfathers') time, they were taken, or they had to make a choice to leave our whenua (lands), our whānau (families), our *ūkaipō* (our bosom) homes to earn a living and move to other lands. Your ancestors moved for a number of reasons. They got married; they needed food; there were fights over land and relationships. Nothing different from today. The laws and policies of the day such as the Hunn Report (Biggs 1961) wanted to make sure that our people would mold and fit to the systems and culture of their motherland in England, because that's what the rules and the laws were based on. We have been lucky to still have ancestral land. Look after it! The obligations are to be respected. Stand tall and proud.

---

4 Rangiātea is our ancestral home of our *tīpuna* (ancestors).

5 Hawaiki is the spiritual home of our ancestors.

Kōrero / Speech

Waiata
Taku tūranga ake,[6]
Taku tūranga ake nei
Noho mai e ki rō wānanga
Ka uia e ahau
Kei hea taku mātāpunatanga? . . .

I stand,
I stand in this place
and I ponder
Where do I belong? . . .
(Jones 1987)[7]

Te Taha Wairua / The Spiritual Dimension: *Ka mua. Ka muri.* Walk backward into the future.

Te taha wairua refers to the spiritual part of a person, land, or anything else. You hear about how we go on about *karakia*, and it's been taught to you. You notice how we would recite karakia at night before you sleep or when we eat, or when we're traveling to new places, we karakia. You'll notice in all the different schools, marae, and whānau events we always start and end with karakia (prayer). We do this because it's an important part of us. Karakia is the way to connect to Io, to God, to Buddha, Yahweh, and so on. It is also the way to connect to your *tīpuna* (ancestors). You will also notice that Pāpā and I have different types of karakia because we have different beliefs, and that is fine. It means we are always trying to work things through and figure things out. Sometimes, we can do it; other times, we will go our own way. The most important thing to remember is that there is a higher source: there is a Creator. Between us we have given you everything we have or want to give you—at the end of the day, only you will know your own belief system. The earlier whakataukī also reminds you that your ancestors have gone

6 Where is my real place of standing?
7 Part of this waiata was written by nanny Muriwai. It is about youth wondering about their identity. This question was typical of youth she taught at school.

through this journey many times over. They have found a way to connect to the Creator. They have also found a way to name their Creator. To develop your spiritual path ahead, listen to your *puku* (gut) and your puku will connect to your *hinengaro* (mind). Did you know that your gut is connected to the brain through neurotransmitters? The neurotransmitters pass messages and controls feelings, emotions, and thoughts (Robertson 2020). When you are doing daily business and you need support, you can listen to your puku, then karakia. You can do this anytime, anywhere, and in any way—as long as you observe respect for the *mauri* (life force), *mana* (integrity), and *tapu* (restrictions) of where you are, and whom you are with.

Waiata Tautoko

Fa'afetai i le atua
lena tatou tupu ai
ina ua na alofa fua
ia te tatou uma nei
Ia pepese, ia pepese
Aleluia Fa'afetai
Ia pepese, ia pepese
Aleluia, Fa'afetai

Whakatauākī

Our mountains give us sustenance and life.
Likewise, we give our mountains sustenance and life.
Ko rātou tō matou okiokinga.
Ko rātou tō matou okiokinga.
(Te Kōtahitanga o Te Ātiawa wānanga–Taranaki 2022)

Te Taha Whānau

Whānau refers to family and extended family, and it is also about you, your brother, cousins, aunties, uncles, nieces, nephews, nannies, and koro. This relationship extends to the sky, clouds, rain, wind, oceans, mountains, rivers, trees, geysers, and volcanoes. They are part of your extended family. You are not a lone island, but you belong to all these entities, and they belong to you—in other words, you must care for or respect each other. To feel connected to your whānau, you must acknowledge them and have regard for them, even if you don't get along. If you can and desire, make time to be present with them. If you can connect, share your dreams, aspirations, sorrows, and celebrations. As you walk through challenging times together, find ways to settle, be at peace, and be still. Finally, your whānau will grow when loved ones from other whānau enter and share space. Be kind, be loving, be tolerant and guide them into being a part of our whānau and be humble as you learn to work in theirs.

Waiata tautoko

E ngā iwi o te motu nei
He raukura rā tēnei
E titia nei e Te Atiawa
I te iti i te rahi te katoa
E ngā iwi o te motu nei
Noho ia ra te whenua nei
Manaakitia rā ngā iwi
I te iti i te rahi te katoa
Kua tū kua tū a Te Whiti
No runga i āna mahi pai
No runga i āna mahi tika
I tōnā ngākau pai

Karakia

Waerea ki a Ranginui e tū nei.
Waerea ki a Papatuanuku e takoto nei.
Waerea ngā tapuwae ā-nuku.
Waerea ngā tapuwae ā-rangi.
Wahia ki tōna tauranga e.
Hai!

(Wilson 2019)

Clear the heavens above.
Clear the earth below.
Clear the pathway below and above.
Till the end.

Te Taha Tinana: Tama tū, tama ora; tama moe, tama mate.

An active person will remain healthy, while a lazy person will become sick.

Taha tinana refers to anything physical—your body, land, resources, shelter, and vehicles. The important thing to remember is that the tinana helps you earn a living, take you places, and enjoy new experiences; in most cases, you are in control. The tinana is critical for you and your whānau to change or to move. The tinana requires you to treat it with care and respect and keep it moving—so maintain the ethic of working hard, and do not be lazy. Care and respect look like being clean, exercising, feeding your body well, drinking lots of water, and keeping healthy. The tinana reflects what is on the inside. If your emotions and feelings are not well, your body will show that. It can also show in your trees, waters, and environment if they are not well. Many diseases and unhealthy habits are not suitable for our tinana. Unfortunately, a poor tinana can look like diabetes, drug and alcohol abuse, obesity, and many other conditions. Do not be afraid to use our traditional knowledge to maintain and care for your tinana. Goodness for your body can also come from other people and nations facing similar issues with their tinana. Connect with them, and share the remarkable things that are happening.

Te Taha Hinengaro: He iti taku iti, he iti kopara, pioi ana te tihi o te Kahikatea.

Even the small bellbird can sway the mighty Kahikatea.

The hinengaro refers to your mind, the area of yourself that guards many hidden rooms, so many that you may not even open them in your life. The mind is great because it holds a thought. A single idea can make or break you, as this whakataukī from Torere reminds you. For instance, it can transport you to the past, future, and today. The mind is also vital for sharing and connecting with others who also hold their thoughts. The reason is very important because sometimes it can override a person's heart, even if it goes against what the person feels in their puku. Allow your mind to wander and be still so it can connect to your puku. Keep checking that it is your puku talking, not your ego and that you are true to your connection. This isn't easy, and you will need karakia to help get you into that space. Finally, in the words of Apirana Ngata:

E tipu e rea, Ko tō ringa ki nga rākau a te pākehā, Hei ora mō te tinana, Ko tō ngākau ki ngā tāonga a ō tipuna Māori, Hei tikitiki mō tō māhuna. [Grow and branch forth tender youth, Take on and use the tools of the pakeha, For the sustenance of your well-being, Your heart to the treasures of your ancestors, To wear as an adornment/plume for your head.] (qtd. in Te Ao Maori News 2017)

Kōrero: Dad's sayings

Have vision.
Be strong in your thinking. Know your limitations.
Together lead/support the whānau, hapū, iwi.
Walk and interact with your lands, oceans,
rivers, mountains, and stars in a Māori way.
Surround yourself with like-minded people.
Learn from wise elders. Tell stories.
Make mistakes. Learn from them.
Teach the whanau younger generations.
Speak our language. Don't leave it just for formal occasions.
Honor your language(s).
Quickly get to the point.
Don't suffer fools.

Waiata tautoko

Ka mea a Tawera e
Me kawe rawa ia ki te wai
Kia wetewete kia tō kiri e
Ki te wetewete ngā Kahukura I te ati
Ara pea koe rā
Kei runga o Arikirau
Ki tū māi koe rā
Ki te tuku whakaparara
Ki te hopu ika I te ati e
Kai hoki te ingoa . . .

Hokia ki ō maunga kia purea ai koe e ngā hau a Tāwhirimātea.

Return to your mountains so that you can be cleansed by the winds of Tāwhirimātea.

The five areas that represent all of yourself include your wairua (spiritual self), whānau (social self), tinana (physical self), hinengaro (intellectual self), and whenua (environmental self). We spoke briefly on each of these things, and there will be teachers and *tohu* all around to guide you and provide direction. The messages we have shared were in the form of Te Whare Tapawhā. I know we have spoken about this a couple of times. I remember Te Rangimarie when you came home excited because one of your teachers, Matua Dan, had talked about Te Whare Tapawhā. This concept was created by one of our great Māori doctors in the country, Professor Mason Durie. He is a great thinker who can take difficult thoughts around knowledge, science, and education and make them easier for everyone to understand. That's why we used Te Whare Tapawhā in this chapter. Te Whare means "house," and *tapawhā* means "four sides." Each of the topics relates to each side of the house and applies to the four sides of a person. You both help to build or put power into houses, and you have also worked on many ancestral homes. Hopefully, when you are working, the buildings you work in may jog your memory about these messages. We will also look at the fifth side of the human, and yes, tapawhā relates to four, but we think it's important to include the fifth element, which is the whenua, the land. He noticed that the world was too focused on just treating the physical part of the person and not looking at them as a whole. This whare is not just about being a shelter, but also, in the words of Tamā Leiite Setefano, "make the most of your opportunities wisely" [family motto, Glen Innes, Auckland]. As you both know, as tradies, each part of the house cannot stand by itself; it requires each other. As you go out into the world building physical and wiring them up, do not forget to build up your whare around yourselves. Take in the messages in the waiata, the *reo*, our tohu, and your puku. Finally, as you go about life and hopefully build and create lives with others, remember your whare is connected to your maunga. As the whakataukī (proverb) says, return home when you need rest, solace, and need to be still or healed.

These messages are also for the youth going through many changes fast. We dedicate our chapter to you, Te Rangimarie and Kotuku, and including your cousins Manawanui and Hinemairangi, your aunties, uncles, nephews, nieces, and friends . . . Nā Pāpā, Māmā, Arohanui.

References

Biggs, B. 1961. "Maori Affairs and the Hunn Report." *Journal of the Polynesian Society* 70 (3): 361–364. http://www.jstor.org/stable/20703918.

Houia, W. 1999. *Whakapiki I te Reo Course*. Hamilton, New Zealand: Waikato University.

Jones, M. 1987. *Taku turanga ake* Personal communication. Tairāwhiti, New Zealand.

Robertson, R. 2020. "The Gut-Brain Connection: How It Works and the Role of Nutrition." Healthline. August 20. https://www.healthline.com/nutrition/gut-brain-connection.

Te Ao Maori News. 2017. "120 Years since Admission of Tā Apirana Ngata." March 23. https://www.teaomaori.news/120-years-admission-ta-apirana-ngata.

Te Kōtahitanga o Te Ātiawa wānanga–Taranaki. 2022. *Mounga Wānanga*. YouTube series. Episode 4. https://teatiawa.iwi.nz/wananga/mounga-wananga-episode-four/.

Wilson, C. 2020. *Tūpuna Wisdom: Karakia. Part 1*. Hamilton, New Zealand: Intrugen Limited.

Wilson, C. 2020. *Tūpuna Wisdom: Karakia. Part 1*. Hamilton, New Zealand: Intrugen Limited.

Williams, Haare. 2019. *Haare Williams: Words of a Kaumatua*. Edited by W. Ihimaera. 1st ed. Auckland: Auckland University Press.

Index

Locators followed by *f* indicate a figure; locators followed by *n* indicate an endnote.

About the Authors

Dr. Georgina Badoni is an enrolled member of the Diné Nation, Assistant Professor of Native American Studies, and faculty of Borderlands and Ethnic Studies at New Mexico State University. She holds a PhD in Native American Studies from the University of Arizona. Her teaching and scholarly activities focus on Native American visual culture, Native American education, and Native American women's studies. Dr. Badoni formally worked for Seattle Public School as a Native Education Consulting teacher for the Native Education Program. Before shifting to higher education, she taught K–12 in Arizona and Washington States for twelve years. Dr. Badoni is collaborating with southern New Mexico schools to meet Culturally Linguistically Responsive education. She serves as an Equity Council member for charter and public schools in southern New Mexico.

Laural Ballew, Ses Yehomia / tsi kuts bat soot is an enrolled member of the Swinomish tribe. She currently resides on the Lummi reservation with her husband, Timothy Ballew Sr. Together they have two sons, Timothy II and Raymond, two grandsons, Hunter and Tandy. She received an AAS degree from Northwest Indian College, a Bachelor's degree from Western Washington University, and a Master's degree in Public Administration, from the Evergreen State College. She is presently part of the International cohort studying for a doctorate in Indigenous Development and Advancement from Te Whare Wānanga o Awanuiārangi, in New Zealand. Her proposed dissertation examines Indigenous knowledge at tribal colleges and the importance of traditional knowledge as a factor for success that depends on the inclusion of Indigenous leadership and governance integrated into the curriculum. Her research develops a model recommendation of a concept to prepare future tribal leaders with the development of curriculum in a baccalaureate degree program of study, Tribal Governance and Business Management at Northwest Indian College, based in sovereignty and cultural values. She is presently the first ever Executive Director of American Indian / Alaska Native and First Nations Relations and Tribal Liaison to the President for Western Washington University.

Mary Banner is of the Ponca Tribe of Indians and an enrolled tribal member of Mille Lacs Band of Ojibwe. Mary is the daughter of Sharon Banner and sister to Ambrose Banner, and cares for four rescued dogs, who all hold a piece of her heart. Mary holds a Bachelor's in Native Environmental Science and a Certificate in Geographic Information Systems (GIS) from Northwest Indian College. Participating in internships with NASA and the Salish Sea Research Center, Mary's work focuses on the impacts Enbridge Line 3 pipeline had on Manoomin (wild rice) waterways, the impacts of environmental change on Arctic and boreal terrestrial freshwater ecosystems, and the implications of these changes for social and ecological systems. Besides school and internships, Mary enjoys being on the road, outside, camping, and adventuring with her dogs.

Dr. Denise Bill is a member of the Muckleshoot Indian Tribe. Denise comes from the villages of Burns Creek, Stuck, Herring House, Crossing Over Place, and Katilbc Denise's Great-Grandmother was Annie Jack, a fluent Lushootseed speaker, and Iola Bill-Lobehan, also a fluent Lushootseed speaker. Denise's father is the late Dr. Willard Bill Sr., a longtime Native Educator, and mother is MaryAnn Bill. Denise is Mother to Elise and Andrew, and Grandmother to Lily. Denise is the Executive Director of Adult and Higher Education. Denise has spent part of her career in K–12 Educational Systems, both public and Native Schools and the other half of her career in Adult and Higher Education for the Muckleshoot Indian Tribe. Denise has a Doctoral Degree from the University of Washington. Her dissertation is titled *Native American Educational Leadership in the Pacific Northwest*.

Elise Bill-Gerrish is a Muckleshoot woman residing in the Southern Puget Sound. Elise comes from the villages of Burns Creek, Stuck, Herring House, Crossing Over Place, and Katilbc. She works as a Muckleshoot Language Teacher to revitalize the Southern Lushootseed Language, the language of her ancestors. Her proudest achievement is being a mother to her daughter, Lily Hope, who is often by her side while Elise teaches their language and working with traditional plants. Elise graduated from Antioch University Seattle in 2014 with a BA in Leadership and Organizational Studies. Her research during that time inspired a lifelong passion for social justice by advocating for holistic healing in all of its forms. She believes that it is essential to address historical trauma in Native communities in order to move forward in a "good way." Elise is actively earning her Master's in Education at the University of Washington Tacoma, with an Indigenous Education focus.

Dr. Paulette Blanchard (Absentee Shawnee Citizen and Kickapoo descendant) holds a Doctorate of Geography from the University of Kansas, Master of Arts in Geography from the University of Oklahoma, and a Bachelor of Arts in Indigenous and American Indian Studies from Haskell Indian Nations University. Dr. Blanchard was a Diversity, Equity, and Inclusion Fellow for University Corporation for Atmospheric Research for 2018–2020. She holds a CoPI on NSF CoPe Rising Voices Changing Coast's grant #2103843 that directly engages Indigenous and non-Indigenous scientists with Indigenous coastal communities to address climate change impacts and variabilities across four regions: Hawaii, Alaska, Louisiana, and Puerto Rico. Her work addresses the challenges and opportunities that Indigenous peoples face in relation to climate change and climate justice. Her work also addresses Indigenous science and science education, Indigenous-led environmental movements, and activism. She incorporates Indigenous Feminist methodologies and philosophies into her geographic framework. Her work includes social, climate, and environmental justice for Indigenous peoples and other marginalized populations.

Dr. Georgina Campelia is an assistant professor in the Department of Bioethics and Humanities at the University of Washington School of Medicine and a clinical ethics consultant for UW Medicine Ethics Consultation Service. In scholarship, teaching, and practice, Dr. Campelia translates ethical theories to clinical practice, mediating or facilitating resolution of conflicts in values. Publications concentrate on critical theory and counteracting race-based and gender-based oppression in healthcare, as well as expanding the applications of relationality, empathy, epistemology, and feminist ethics to clinical ethics.

Christopher Dennis is an enrolled member of the Cowlitz Indian Tribe and has his Master of Science in Psychology from Arizona State University. He is driven to give back to his tribe and local Coast Salish communities by writing research articles in the field of mental health about issues Indigenous people face.

Jessica Dennis. As a Diné (Navajo) woman growing up with no running water or electricity on the reservation in the Southwest, Jessica Dennis has a wealth of experience that prepared her to work with students in limited-access areas. She is an environmental scientist with an extensive background in research and overwhelming passion for education. Currently, Dennis teaches Biology and Physical Science at Washington High School in Parkland, Washington. Some of her aspirations in K–12 education include increasing representation for BIPOC communities, encouraging youth/young women to seek careers in STEM, and increasing education access for English as Second Language (ESL) learners. She continuously seeks out creative and safe solutions for meeting students where they are—those who are experiencing homelessness, have high Adverse Childhood Experiences scores, or come from a domestic violence household. Dennis's hope is that by teaching in STEM—combined with community reinforcement—we can protect and restore the environment, preserve ecosystems, have clean water, and lower negative environmental impacts. She believes these goals are not only obtainable but that we can advance even beyond these measures through honest efforts in community outreach, advocacy, and preserving Indigenous knowledge through language restoration. As an enrolled member of the Navajo Nation, Jessica is currently working on developing educational curriculum in partnership with local Washington Tribes.

Joshua Dennis is Diné from northern New Mexico and has been with the Indigenous Speaker Series since 2020. Josh currently works at the Washington Utilities and Transportation Commission doing regulatory analyst work in energy conservation. He has a Bachelor of Science in Mathematics with a minor in American Indian Studies from the University of Washington, Tacoma, and is currently working on his Master of Environmental Studies at the Evergreen State College, focusing on Diné water rights, tribal sovereignty, climate justice, and the Rights of Nature. As he continues his education, he is dedicated to helping his Indigenous relatives. He hopes to return to his homelands between the Four Sacred Mountains (Diné Bikéyah) to raise sheep and fight for Indigenous peoples' sovereignty through strengthening relationships with the land/water, animal, and plant relatives. Joshua currently resides in the South Puget Sound with his spouse, their two cats, and their dog. When he's not working, Josh enjoys music, cooking with friends and family, reading, woodworking, hiking, camping, and being on the Land.

Dr. Emma Elliott (Cowichan Tribes) is an assistant professor in the Department of Learning Sciences and Human Development in the College of Education at the University of Washington. She holds both a PhD in Educational Psychology and a Master of Social Work in Children, Youth, and Families. The interdisciplinary intersections of her research include culture, learning, and human development; land-based and Indigenous methodologies; and trauma, prevention, and recovery among Indigenous children and youth. By employing a strengths-based approach to healing,

Dr. Elliott rigorously engages youth, families, and communities in the development of integrated educational and behavioral health interventions to address social issues. Her research centers ethical frameworks generated by Indigenous and land-based knowledges and practices to create process-centered approaches that illuminate Indigenous pathways toward collective livelihood. Dr. Elliott is currently partnering with members of the Cowichan Tribes to design programming to strengthen the physical, mental, intellectual, and cultural health of the community.

Dr. Ryan E. Emanuel is an associate professor of hydrology in the Nicholas School of the Environment at Duke University. He studies the movement and status of water in the environment, and he is also interested in historical and cultural aspects of water and watery places. Emanuel's work pays special attention to Indigenous peoples' enduring relationships with rivers, wetlands, and other waterscapes in southeastern North America. He partners with tribal nations and Indigenous communities to identify and address threats to culturally important waters that stem from pollution, climate change, and unsustainable development. Emanuel holds a PhD in Environmental Sciences from the University of Virginia and is an enrolled member of the Lumbee Tribe.

Joseph Gazing Wolf has dedicated his life's work to the empowerment of Indigenous and Black communities globally, with a particular focus on the economically and socially underprivileged. His primary avenue for this has been through education. This has thus far included the mentorship of Black and Indigenous youth in STEM fields, the study and sharing of Traditional Ecological Knowledge within Tribal networks and beyond, and the study of variables that predict the persistence of Black and Indigenous students in the academy. Joseph believes that for communities to be empowered by their own ancestral knowledge as well as scientific knowledge, their basic needs must be met first. Thus, Joseph has dedicated much of his community work to food security, environmental justice, health and safety, and sustainable livelihoods. His work is framed by a vision of universal dignity for all, human and more-than-human. Joseph is a doctoral student in the School of Life Sciences at Arizona State University. He is also a Senior Global Futures Scientist in the Julie Ann Wrigley Global Future Laboratory, a Doctoral Research Fellow in the Global Institute of Sustainability and Innovation, and a Graduate Research Fellow with the National Science Foundation.

Dr. Troy Goodnough serves as sustainability director at the University of Minnesota Morris. Troy was the first sustainability coordinator hired in the University of Minnesota in 2006. Troy works with students, faculty, and staff to develop and implement sustainability initiatives. His work includes creating new educational programs, outreach initiatives, and renewable energy projects. Morris produces the most electricity per student in the United States. Troy provides leadership with the Upper Midwest Association for Campus Sustainability, Minnesota Climate Adaptation Partnership, West Central Clean Energy Resource Team, Morris Model, and other sustainability-focused groups. During his tenure as director, Morris has earned multiple Association for the Advancement of Sustainability in Higher Education (AASHE) STARS Gold ratings; the Second Nature Climate Leadership Award; and recognition by Sierra Club, Princeton Review, Minnesota Environmental Initiative, and other organizations. Troy is interested in Aikido, learning new things, good process, and philosophy.

Dr. Dawn Hardison-Stevens acknowledges we are our Ancestor's future, noting her grandmothers and grandfathers carried stories from their respective Ancestral lands of the Omushkego Cree, Ojibway, Cowlitz, and Steilacoom peoples. An Assistant Professor of Native American Education with the University of Washington in Tacoma, her education fields since 1987 center on the commitment of inclusive and collective leadership and views that prepare learners to live, learn, and strive to better understand their connections to self, family, community, culture, history, land, and worldviews. She understands individual life journeys create one's own unique story. Dawn's ideals guide and lift other's visions and dreams toward their own defined success, noting there should be a love of commitment professionally. Her passion is to elevate Indigenous representation, cultivating Native people's inspirations through intergenerational knowledge applications.

Dr. Lesley Iaukea is a Native Hawaiian from the island of Maui, Hawai'i. She holds a Bachelor's degree in Geography that focused on climate change dynamics in Southeast Asia and a Master's degree from the Center for Pacific Islands Studies that focused on cyclones in the Southern hemisphere and cultural resiliency for the Island Nation of Tokelau. Her second Master's degree is from the Department of American Studies and focused on a culture-based curriculum that she created as a crewmember for the voyaging canoe *Hōkūle'a* in the Worldwide Voyage. She holds a PhD from the Department of American Studies for which she used an interdisciplinary approach in understanding an eleventh-century navigational platform on the island of Kaho'olawe and explained the traditional knowledge that is found in the elements of reference (stars, moon phases, wind patterns, and pathway of the sun) through geospatial science, thus combining two worldviews / two sciences. The fieldwork was then written into a culture-based curriculum and pedagogy for classrooms K–16, where her work is used in schools across Hawai'i and Oceania in understanding climate change, sustainability, and cultural resilience. She also has a graduate certificate in Historic Preservation that focused on traditional landscapes. Over the past decade, Dr. Iaukea has been an active member of the Rising Voices

Center for Indigenous and Earth Sciences and a climate change consultant in Oceania focusing on pathways of resilience through management plans for countries that are forced to migrate secondary to Sea Level Rise.

Dr. Brandi Kamermans is a Postdoc and Molecular Researcher at Northwest Indian College on the Lummi main campus at the Salish Sea Research Center (SSRC), where she monitors harmful algal bloom species in Bellingham and Lummi Bays using molecular techniques. As a biogeochemist, Brandi became an expert in a variety of different imaging and spectroscopy tools. Her most recent publication uses Raman and Scanning Electron Microscopy at the Pennsylvania State University Material Characterization Laboratory to characterize both elemental sulfur and organics produced by *Sulfuricurvum kujiense*, in an effort to distinguish chemical- versus microbial-induced mineral production.

Dr. Clement Loo is an Assistant Professor of Environmental Studies and the Student Success Coordinator for Equity, Diversity, and Intercultural Programs at the University of Minnesota Morris. He is also an Educator and a member of the Faculty Leadership Council of the Institute on the Environment, as well as a member of the Board of Trustees of the Southwest Regional Sustainability Development Partnerships at the University of Minnesota. Finally, he serves on the Advisory Council and the Diversity, Equity, and Inclusion Committee of the Association for the Advancement of Sustainability in Higher Education. His scholarship and teaching focus on food justice and the integration of equity and sustainability. In his free time Clement enjoys playing disc golf, hiking, and exploring the small rural towns in the Upper Midwest.

Dr. Michelle Montgomery (enrolled Haliwa Saponi / descendant Eastern Band Cherokee) is an Associate Professor and Chair, Division of Social and Historical Studies in the School of Interdisciplinary Arts and Sciences at the University of Washington, Tacoma. She is also the Assistant Director for the Office of Undergraduate Education, the Indigenous Curriculum and Community Advisor for the School of Education, Interim Director for Undergraduate Program in the Department of Bioethics and Humanities School of Medicine, and Co-coordinator / External Indigenous Advisor for the University of Minnesota Morris's Sustainability Leadership Program. Dr. Montgomery's heart work focuses on Indigenizing and decolonizing the climate justice narrative through the Indigenous Speaker Series, environmental ethics connected to Indigenous peoples' identities, and eco-critical race theory to eliminate racial and environmental oppression.

Dr. Melissa B. Peacock is a phytoplankton ecologist and the Director of the Salish Sea Research Center at Northwest Indian College in Bellingham, Washington. The research center promotes the development of students as Indigenous scholars, providing opportunities for students to engage in culturally relevant and community-based research. Dr. Peacock's research focuses on freshwater and marine biotoxins, their transfer into the marine food web through shellfish, and how monitoring harmful algae can be used for management and mitigation strategies. Her work is on projects that are community-identified, focus on food and data sovereignty, and involve a network of partners from different backgrounds.

Dolly Potts is an enrolled Prairie Band Potawatomi from Kansas. She has lived on the Menominee Reservation for seventeen years. In 2020, Dolly earned a Bachelor of Arts degree in First Nation Studies from the University of Wisconsin Green. In 2018, she earned an Associate's degree from College of Menominee Nation (CMN). She returned to the Sustainable Development Institute (SDI) at CMN as a Community Elder, sharing traditional approaches to learning. Dolly's greatest interest in SDI is bringing Traditional teaching into the Sustainability and Diversity aspects of sharing Indigenous culture. She hopes that these teachings become a part of the SDI in the future.

Dr. Timothy San Pedro is an associate professor of Critical Studies in Education: Race, Justice and Equity, an affiliate faculty member of American Indian Studies, and cofounder and faculty advisory of the Indigenous Community of Graduate and Professional Students at the Ohio State University. He is Filipino American and grew up on the Flathead Indian Reservation in western Montana. His scholarship focuses on the intricate link between motivation, engagement, and identity construction and curricula and pedagogical practices that recenter content and conversations upon Indigenous histories, knowledges, and literacies. His latest work focuses on the intergenerational lessons learned in the homes of five Native American mothers—specifically, the ways they teach their children Indigenous knowledges and sovereignty rights as they relate to everyday resurgence efforts. He is an inaugural Gates Millennium Scholar, a Cultivating New Voices Among Scholars of Color Fellow, a Ford Fellow, a Concha Delgado Gaitan Council of Anthropology in Education Presidential Fellow, and a Spencer Fellow.

Kelvin Tapuke and Sylvia Tapuke both live in Aotearoa, New Zealand. They share the love of education, learning, curiosity, research, science, Indigenous development, and karaoke. They have two adult children and look forward to many more journeys with their *whānau* and friends.

Barbara Wolfin is a citizen of the Pit River Nation enrolled in the Illmawi Band. Barbara is currently a third-grade teacher at Burney Elementary School located within the ancestral territories of the Pit River Nation. She earned her Master's at the University of Auckland, New Zealand, and wrote a thesis focused on cultural revitalization and familial relationship to ancestral territories. She currently serves on the Pit River Education Committee, Shasta County Office of Education American Indian Advisory Committee, and California Teachers Association.

Thayne Yazzie is an enrolled member of the Diné / Navajo Nation. He was born and raised on the Navajo reservation and has been a K–12 educator for Indigenous communities in both Washington and Arizona States, particularly on the Lummi and Diné / Navajo Reservation. Over the past four years, Thayne has been the STEM Education Outreach Coordinator for the Salish Sea Research Center at Northwest Indian College (Lummi, Bellingham, Washington), and during this time he has been developing place-based STEM / STEAM education materials. Throughout his educational outreach, Thayne shares his perspective on the concepts of Indigenous knowledge. He notes that it is important to remember that his interpretation of Indigenous knowledge does not reflect the beliefs or knowledge systems of all Indigenous people. Additionally, Indigenous knowledge can vary greatly within a "tribe," a specific place, and / or community. Therefore, Thayne encourages all educators to seek out Indigenous perspectives from all walks of life, including various people, communities, and various experiences.

www.ingramcontent.com/pod-product-compliance
Lightning Source LLC
Chambersburg PA
CBHW051530020426
42333CB00016B/1865
9781646425099